W9-BYF-973

SANDY BOTTOM

Robert Downes

Sandy Bottom

Published by
The Wandering Press
Traverse City, Michigan

Copyright © 2020 by Robert Downes
All rights reserved. No part of this book may be reproduced or
transmitted in any form by any means, electronic or mechanical,
including photocopying, recording, or by any information storage
and retrieval system, without written permission from the author,
except for the inclusion of brief quotations in a review.

Library of Congress Control Number: Pending

ISBN 978-0-9904670-2-1

ebook edition published by The Wandering Press in 2020

www.robertdownes.com

Covers by Robert Downes

The Wandering

PRESS

For Allan Nahajewski

Cheers!

Robert Downes

Other books by Robert Downes

Planet Backpacker
Biking Northern Michigan
I Promised You Adventure
Windigo Moon
Bicycle Hobo

There's a Dude Down There

Gladys Mahill made the kind of discovery you'd expect from a woman named Gladys.

"Hurry up, Earl!" she cried. "Can't this thing go any faster?"

"It's an electric motor, dear," her husband said wearily from the rear of the whaler, one hand on the throttle of the troller. "Its top speed is two miles per hour."

"A turtle could outrun this thing. Come on, come on, come on!"

"I'm pushing it to the limit."

"Well push it *past* the limit gol'darnit!"

Earl glared at the back of his wife's head. He'd wanted the Brute Master motor with the electric start and the emergency siren, but Gladys had reminded him that they were on a budget, like *that* ever mattered when *she* wanted something.

"You wanted something cheaper, remember? That's why we got this toy motor that wouldn't budge a cat off a couch. If I had my..." Earl's voice buzzed from the back of the boat like a jar full of mosquitoes.

"Oh, quit your whining and push it Earl! I'm dying here!"

Slowly, the whaler inched toward the dock on Little Platte Lake. Located two miles from Lake Michigan at the northern end of Michigan's lower peninsula, the lake measures a mile across but is only about three feet deep for its entire 800 acres. Thus, it's a wildlife lake with few of the jet skis and speedboats that plague the waterways of the Midwest. One dunk off a jet ski in Little Platte Lake can result in a neck-breaking collision with the muck and mire at its bottom. Only fishing boats and pontoons disturb its surface, along with a smattering of loons.

High overhead a pair of eagles circled in a cloudless sky, gazing down on a disturbance in the water below that was scattering fish in all directions. Further out, a loon dipped beneath the surface of the lake in alarm, bobbing up 100 yards to the west. And from the shelter of the immense swamp to the east, a black bear peered cautiously from a screen of cattails and gave a mystified glance at a bobcat across the way that was gazing in the same direction. Something was up and the critters all knew it.

But Gladys and Earl were oblivious and she writhed in agony as brace of sunfish splashed at the bottom of their boat in a pool of water.

Six feet from the dock, she tumbled out of the boat, banged into a half-submerged log, and ran for the outhouse with her jeans soaked up to her thighs. "Goddammit!" she cried, duck-waddling the 100 feet to salvation.

"Why don't you just pee in the water?" Earl called after her.

"That's just the kind of crazy thing a man would say, isn't it?" she called back, slamming the outhouse door for emphasis.

Gladys ripped down her panties and assumed the Awkward Pose she'd learned in yoga class; no woman would dream of placing her hiney on the sticky seat of a mosquito-infested outhouse in northern Michigan. A stream that would do a horse proud echoed from the chamber below as Gladys exuded a groan of pleasure, the pain of a beer-swollen bladder leaving her body. Three cans of PBR in the middle of an 800-acre lake, and tall boys at that. What was she thinking? She must have been crazy. "Ohhh... gotta' pee, pee, pee!"

Gladys fingered the tissue on the roll next to her and sniffed. As she suspected, it was the cheap, single-ply tissue the State supplied in an attempt to save money, but you had to use three times as much of the stuff to get the job done, so go figure. Remember the days when people used to use corn cobs in the outhouse before the invention of toilet paper? Well, not really, but that's what her grandmother had told her. Back when most folks lived on farms before paper was available they used old chewed-up corn cobs with plenty of scrubbing power for the back end. Bonus: you could rinse them out for reuse. What a tickler that must have been! Grandma said that when she was a girl, sometimes she'd dip the cobs in turpentine as a prank when the minister came calling. A howler, that one, literally.

Thinking of her grandmother brought back memories of the time Granny's false teeth popped out of her head when they hit that speed bump on the family trip down to Chicago in the church van and how she got spittin' mad at Earl for driving too fast over the bump. Lord, what a ruckus that had been.

Hoisting her panties, she peered into the depths of the outhouse. The idiots around here were always throwing beer cans, bottles and diapers into the outhouses, even though there were prominent signs saying not to, since the trash clogged up the cleaning hoses. There was a sign right there on the wall above the potty:

"PLEASE," it read, "DO NOT discard bottles, cans, plastic bags, any diapers or similar items in toilet. Such materials clog pumps used for cleaning vaults."

Yet did people listen? Did they even bother to read? In Gladys's estimation, America was full to the gills with callous oafs and thoughtless jerks who thought nothing of pitching their whisky bottles and soda cans down yonder in any porta-potty or rustic outhouse they happened upon. There should be a special place in hell for people like that - a place where they'd be up to their necks in it. If she were governor, boy, she'd have the outhouse litterbugs sentenced to cleaning the State's honey pits by hand, that's for sure.

It stank in there, but she couldn't resist peering below to check for forbidden trash. To her surprise, the pit was mostly empty; the pumpers must have just been there. But obviously, the cleaning hose had failed to remove some forbidden trash. Dimly, she caught the sheen of aluminum cans reflected in the pale light filtering through the roof of translucent plastic, and also the glint of glass in the tissued billows far below.

But something about that glass... hmm. It looked like a pair of glasses, maybe. Flailing at a cloud of skeeters, she pulled her phone from the back pocket of her jeans and switched on the flashlight.

It looked like a dummy at first, possibly a department store mannikin, but the eyes were wide open and the face was, as they say, strangely familiar.

What the hell was the guy doing down there? she wondered. Didn't he know he was parked in the underside of an out-house?

"Hey dude," she called down, "You doin' okay down there?"

No answer.

Gladys squinted into the darkness below. Overhead, the light through the outhouse roof brightened as a cloud cleared the sun. That face... could it be?

"Earl, I think you better come see this," she called out the door.

"Yeah, no thanks," her husband called back, hunched over the boat where the motor bracket was refusing to budge.

"I'm not kidding, honey bun. Come give this a look!"

"What now?" Earl muttered irritably. He'd had a bad day, losing another hat to the winds gusting over the lake. The hat had cost him thirty bucks at Disney World and was the third one that the lake had swallowed in as many months.

"Hat eater! Gol'dern lake is a gol'dern hat eater," he groused, jerking at the motor. As if that wasn't enough, now his gol'derned wife wanted to have him stick his gol'derned nose in a gol'derned toilet? "I mean, come on."

Back in the outhouse, Gladys suddenly noticed that the floor was sticky, very sticky, a dark puddle thickened at the soles of her shoes. It was like syrup, but no, more like... Her eyes flared - could it be? "Oh my G..." That's when she let out a high-pitched scream. She stuck her head out the door and bawled.

"Swear to God, Earl! There's a dude down there and he's not looking too good!"

The next morning, a headline in the local daily said it all:

Big Bucks Enviro Found Dead in Benzie Crapper

Controversy over the story raged for weeks, not because the body of filthy rich eco-warrior Timothy Bottom was found dumped in a Benzie County outhouse, but because some copy editor's mania for bourbon mixed with over-caffeinated energy drinks finally got the best of him and no one thought to yell stop the presses. Printers, what do they know? The *Eagle* fired the guy that morning but that didn't stop 141 letters to the editor from pouring in over the next few weeks, deploring the idiomatic depravity of the headline.

But who will proof the proofer? I wondered as I ran through a copy of the *Eagle*, pinched from the cubical next door. The byline was that of police beat reporter, A. Tucker Jakeway.

I knew the guy. Jakeway prided himself as a hotshot investigative reporter and one time when we were deep in our cups at some bar, he claimed that the A in his name stood for "Ace," though I thought it more likely that he was named Albert or Arnie.

Whatever, he'd managed to dig up some dirt in time for the morning paper, so respect, right? It seems that Bottom had gone missing after a midnight jaunt of smelt-dipping on the river running through the big swamp that bordered the lake. Bottom had apparently been strapping the mini fish with tiny aluminum tags for some arcane purpose, possibly to inspect them for signs of mercury poisoning, stream migration, or some such thing. Lord knows, he wasn't about to eat the critters: smelt are skinny fish about 6-8 inches long that swim in schools by the thousands. They're freshwater cousins to the sardine, aka, "the shrimp of the Great Lakes," that are devoured bones and all, and Bottom was known to be an iron-pants vegan.

But if the smelt knew anything about Bottom's death, they were keeping it to themselves. When volunteers from the

Lake Township fire department hosed down his corpse they'd found wounds carved two inches deep on his body, with a gruesome bit of attention paid to Bottom's neck.

"Our belief is that Mr. Bottom was attacked by an animal, of what sort, we cannot say," the medical examiner was quoted in Jakeway's article. "We've ruled out any chance of a smelt attack."

Ha, ha. I folded the paper and tossed it back on my neighbor's desk. What else could it be? A panther, maybe. A mountain lion, puma, cougar, catamount, Mr. Jynx, the alleged jaguar of the jackpine forests, which everyone swears is prowling the woods of the great Up North, especially in the Sleeping Bear National Lakeshore, which sidles up next to the lake where Bottom's body was found.

There had been sightings of cougars crossing the highway at the park thirty miles west of Traverse City, along with a photo or two. I personally knew three people who'd seen a cougar padding out that way. That, and heavily-wooded Benzie County had plenty of bears, though none had ever been known to carve up a fisherman the way Bottom had been served.

I had good reason to hate the guy, but that doesn't mean I was happy that he was dead. Only my closest friends knew of the bad blood between me and Timothy Bottom, and they'd probably forgotten all about it by now. As for Bottom, he probably never even knew I existed. The eagle does not speak to the fly, as the saying goes, and to a rich guy like him I would have been nothing more than a bug.

But like I said, I wasn't happy to hear that he was dead. I didn't need any more bad karma than I already had.

Timothy Bottom was mythic in Traverse City; everyone knew him as the firebrand president of the Wildlife Warriors, who were under constant suspicion of vandalizing new development projects, yet never seemed to get caught. His detractors called them the "Wacko Warriors," but never to anyone's face in the group, who were reputed to be a shady bunch of arsonists and knee-cappers.

Bottom was the guy who got a snowmobile trail shut down in the Pere Marquette Forest because the racket was disturbing the sleep of hibernating bears and raccoons. He had managed to cordon off miles of Lake Michigan's beaches on behalf of the piping plover, assuming that the wee birds might prefer to lay their eggs where bikini-clad honeys liked to sprawl like seals in the sand. Defender of the brown trout against irksome dams, founder of a turkey buzzard hatchery, creator of a snapping turtle preserve, willing to chain himself to a beaver dam to prevent its destruction, Timothy Bottom was the good guy of conservation in northern Michigan. He was the guy in the ten-gallon white hat, forever riding to the rescue of the lowly toad, indigenous plant, field mouse or turtle. He was practically a Jain, a religion he had much admired on a youthful swing through India, in which even a bug's life is considered sacred. Bottom literally wouldn't hurt a fly. Yet now this. Karma said he was the wrong guy to get killed by a cougar or a bear. Dead wrong.

But more than that, Bottom was the trustafarian heir to the Better Baby Bottom baby powder fortune, which was HQ'd at a mammoth factory in Shipshewana, Ohio, next to America's biggest talc mine. He rolled in an $200,000 Tesla Roadster, recharged with an array of solar and wind-powered batteries, or he didn't roll at all. Mostly, you'd see him pedaling around town on a recumbent bike. Rumor had it that he spent most of his fortune benefiting wildlife causes from here to Tasmania.

But he was also an operator. Being a trustafarian, he was on easy terms with the high-toned crowd: the heirs of big pharma, chemical plants, pickle jar factories and auto parts fortunes who owned six-bedroom "cottages" out in Leelanau County and Old Mission Peninsula. Folks like the Jenson-Sniggers of Northport Point who were deep into baby food, and Tom Booner, the dotcom millionaire who made his money tricking people out of theirs online. Bottom would get them to pony up for land conservancy crusades and wildlife causes, steering clear of the more wackadoo stuff he was into, like the shenanigans of the Wildlife Warriors. Rumor had it that once he almost convinced Betsy DeVos of the Amway fortune to take a ride on his 60-foot sailboat, the Deep Green, in search of zebra mussels on the isles of Lake Michigan. Almost.

What else? He was what the ladies consider a classy guy, the kind of guy who ate his french fries with a fork and his gluten-free pizza too. He drank only locally-sourced organic wine along with juices squeezed by hand from farm-to-table cherries and carrots. Kept a bamboo straw tucked in his belt like a sword, ready for any emergency that involved drinking a smoothie. Used organic, cruelty-free product in his wavy chestnut-brown hair and kept it neatly combed. Had perfect teeth, white as pearls. Strong jaw, big smile, never forgot a name. Big tipper, and on the board of a dozen charities. In short, unbeatable.

As far as his sartorial habits, Bottom wore nothing but Patagucci, along with hemp shoes and a hemp belt, though mostly his duds were ten years old and tattered at the edges. "There's no point in adding to the world's carbon emissions by buying new clothes," he'd say.

The threadbare clothes helped him fit in with the lower classes, the kind of guys who trucked around in tattered Detroit Tigers baseball caps, camo jackets and a knife in their boots. They would have been shocked to learn that Bottom's raggedy old Gortex jacket retailed for $600.

Yet despite his fancy clothes, teak yacht, Tesla Roadster and hobbit-inspired earth-berm castle out on Old Mission Peninsula, Bottom managed to remain a rebel, and not just the kind who wore white shoes after Labor Day. Who could forget the time he ran for Congress as a write-in candidate for the Wildlife Warriors Party? Word had it that he'd spent a cool $2.8 million of his own money on the campaign, for which he garnered only 217 votes. He famously groused that his supporters were too stoned to make it to the polls on election day during the Midterms, but the truth is, he screwed up and told them the wrong day for the election. That didn't help with his constituency when he decided to run for the U.S. Senate.

Like usual, Bottom was the talk of the town, even in death.

I checked my phone for the tenth time today; maybe I hadn't heard it ring, even though it was in my shirt pocket. Well, what do you know? Still no calls, still no clients. Same as yesterday and the day before that and so on. I'd been wearing my lucky Ganesh t-shirt for three days now, but the elephant-headed god of good luck, also known as the "remover of obstacles," must be sleeping on the job because the rent was due and my checking account had about .83 cents in it. That and my shirt stank... Talk about obstacles. Being broke seemed to be a permanent obstacle that no Hindu god could manage to budge.

The bird call of my ring tone warbled, sending a jolt up my spine. I let the phone ring twice and answered it slow and laconic, like my secretary was out of the office and I was being a nice guy, filling in.

"Nathaniel Bumpo, private investigations," I said in a low purr. "May I help you?"

But it was just another nuisance call, "... press one to qualify for an extension of your auto warranty..."

I snicked off the phone and chucked it on the table. I hadn't owned a car in more than three years, nor did I qualify for Medicare, desire any life insurance or wish to remortgage a home I didn't own, among the other come-ons I received each day.

What I really needed was a client, any client.

"Maybe I should get a dartboard," I said to myself, contemplating the blank wall to my left. I was starting to go nuts sitting in the office all day, waiting for the phone to ring and browsing the unholy trinity of Facebook, Twitter and Instagram. When I had decided to launch my own detective agency I hadn't considered the part where I'd have to go fishing for clients. So far, my marketing efforts had involved pinning my business card on the bulletin boards of supermarkets around town and posting on a Facebook page that got zero "likes" on the average. I didn't know what else to do; private dicks in the detective novels never seemed to have this problem - their clients just showed up. They even had good-looking secretaries to handle the phone, secretaries who were delirious for the likes of Sam Spade or Mike Hammer.

But not me.

But such is the carefree life of a fresh-faced detective, right? I turned down the volume on my police scanner and switched on the radio. Every show with a morning host had the phone lines on fire with callers.

Switch

"Y'ask me, Bottom was under attack by a cougar or a bear and fought it all the way to the outhouse door," one caller opined. "He hid down there and bled out."

Switch

"But if someone stuck him in the outhouse they woulda' dumped him head-first, right?"

Switch

"The guy was a communist loon. What do you..."

Switch

"Well, I seen him around town and he was awful skinny," another caller said. "He was skinny enough to shimmy down a stove pipe. That come from him being a vegan. He coulda' crawled through a toilet seat if he was a mind to."

Switch

The college station, WNMC, had a caller with a metaphysical slant: "There are vortices in northern Michigan which connect to spiritual places around the world, possibly even to other dimensions," she said in a voice that was a trifle spooky and curiously familiar, "possibly even to aliens."

Hmm... White walkers, more likely.

I gave it some thought. Everyone knew that Timothy Bottom was halfway to being Tarzan of the Apes when it came to the animal kingdom. Confronted by a cougar or a crazed bear, he would most likely have reasoned with the beast. And a cougar wouldn't think to open an outhouse door and toss a chap into the dumps, now would he? No, he would have dragged Bottom into the brush and made a meal of him.

My own theory was taking shape, but why should I care? This was a job for an FBI profiler, not a private dick like me.

My cases ran more along the line of catching embezzlers, photographing someone's spouse in the arms of another, and tracking down deadbeat dads. At least, that's what I planned on doing. Unfortunately, I'd had just one case in the past two months, and that had been a stroke of pure luck.

Switch

I switched to a new station. Some guy on the line had a whole new angle.

"It had to be bigfoot," the caller claimed, his voice drenched in smoky resignation. "Only a bigfoot could rip a guy up like that and think to stuff him in a crapper."

"And why do you suppose he'd do that?" the talk show host asked.

"For the fun of it, Maybe bigfoots have a warped sense of humor. Maybe they don't like fishermen trespassing in their swamp."

"You don't seriously believe there's a sasquatch with a warped sense of humor running around here, do you?"

"Is there an echo on the line? I seriously do," the guy with the smoky voice said. "People say there aren't any cougars around here either, but it's true. I seen one m'self."

"A cougar?"

"A yeti. An anonymous snowman. A bigfoot."

"Seriously?"

"Big sucker. I's up in my tree stand, bowhunting out by the Cedar Swamp last fall and one walked right up under me."

"Is that right?"

"That's right. Seven feet tall, I'd say."

"And what did you do?"

"I just kept on watching, glad I's up a tree."

"Then what?"

"Thing took a dump and scrubbed its hiney."

"What?"

"Lavatory stuff, personal hygiene, you know, takin' care of bidness. Caught sight of me and gave me the evil eye. Then it was gone, off like a cat in the bushes."

"So you saw a bigfoot, you're up in a tree stand with a compound bow, and you didn't take a shot?"

The guy on the other end of the line took a long pause, like he was dragging on a cigarette, and came back on the air all breathy with that smoky voice. "I'm a deer hunter, see? I ain't no murderer. 'Specially not with some bigfoot feller I don't even know."

Later on there was speculation that Bottom's death was the work of the Headless Lumberjack. Back in 1852 when hordes of hearty men were busy chopping down every tree in northern Michigan, a lumberjack named O'Grady got his head popped off in an accident involving a tow chain and a team of six horses. Legend has it that O'Grady has been combing the woods at night with a broad axe ever since, looking for a new head. Fortunately, most folks don't go wandering around the woods at night, but Timothy Bottom did.

"But if it was the Headless Lumberjack, he would have taken Bottom's head," a caller pointed out.

Ah, the intellectual nuance of the native Michigander. I switched off the radio and gazed out the window to the street below. The bigfoot angle sucked, even if a tribe of them were wandering around hereabouts. The Cedar Swamp was 20 miles east of where Bottom's body had been found, meaning a bigfoot would have had to hotfoot it across miles of farm country, risking lots of eyes on him. And as for the Headless Lumberjack? I wasn't buying it.

Timothy Bottom was dead, but downtown Traverse City kept right on jiggling with its parade of cone-lickers and tourists in pastel shorts and shirts, scurrying like an army of leaf-cutter ants between gourmet food shops, chic boutiques and t-shirt stores. A line of Pokémon Go players and selfie-stick wavers wove their smart phones down the sidewalk like a stream of guppies. Down below in a narrow through-way alley to the river, a couple of heavily tattoo'ed kids with half-shaved heads were banging out "Radioactive" by Imagine Dragons on their guitars for the sixth time this morning. One of the guys had ear spacers big enough to lasso a robin.

"I'm starting to hate that song," I said to no one. But it wasn't the song so much as the realization that a couple of doofus street musicians were ringing up more dough than me, a professional private eye, or at least, a wanna-be.

My office is a cubicle with a chipboard table and two plastic lawn chairs in one of those shared office spaces that got their start in the '90s. The suite is a big open space divided into twelve cubicles, but only four are occupied. My neighbors include a wedding videographer, a woman who organizes dressage events for wealthy equestrians across the country, and a guy who runs a website devoted to stamp collecting. My own eight-by-eight feet of space runs me two hundred bucks a month, but I have a window on Front Street and the view from the second floor is worth $2,000 at least. I have my dad's old blue steel .44 in a holster nailed to the underside of the table. Not that I intend to shoot anyone, but it feeds the atmosphere. With a strongbox chained to the legs of the table, a laptop, police scanner and a $30 phone from the drug store, I have everything a private dick could ask for, including a nameplate.

Nathaniel Dredd Bumpo, LC, CSP, PI

When you've got a nameplate, the world is your oyster.

Traverse City, Michigan has a breezy sort of energy, quite literally, owing to its placement at the base of Grand Traverse Bay at the northern end of Lake Michigan. The bay was named more 300 years ago by French voyageurs who, along with the native Ottawa and Ojibwa, made "le grande traverse" in their canoes across its wide mouth on their way down Michigan's west coast.

Splitting the bay is the 18-mile-long finger of the Old Mission Peninsula, known for its cherry farms, vineyards and the mansions of wealthy refugees from Chicago, Detroit and California. Thirty miles to the west are the towering sand dunes of the Sleeping Bear National Lakeshore, which rise 300 feet from the ice-blue waters of Lake Michigan. The dunes are the crown of a beach tiara that stretches the entire length of western Michigan in either direction.

There are no freeways to Traverse City; you have to drive 30 miles from the nearest expressway down some awkward secondary roads to reach town. Those roads are treacherous in the winter owing to the frequent storms coming off Lake Michigan, bringing snow, ice and plow trucks dumping tons of salt. The salt attracts deer to the roadside, along with the threat of one leaping through your windshield on a spring evening.

Otherwise, the small city established by lumber barons in the 1850s is an urban island in the middle of forests and farmlands which stretch up to 150 miles. The combination of dunes, beaches, woodlands, wineries and beach towns packed with art galleries and restaurants along Lake Michigan's "Gold Coast" make Traverse City an irresistible destination for millions of tourists each year.

Although Traverse City seems a bit sketchy as a place to launch a detective agency, I was willing to give it a shot. After all, at the age of 32, I have nothing to lose, since my worldly possessions amount to just about that: nothing. By the time I set up shop, Traverse City had become America's go-to paradise for fat-cats from Lincoln Park, Grosse Pointe and Bloomfield Hills, and their investigative needs were all mine. I was one fat check away from buying a wooden office chair upholstered in black leather from the antique store around the corner, and my buns were warm in anticipation.

The place has some quirks, though.

For instance, Traverse City supposedly has more millionaire Millennials per capita than any other town in America, though I don't personally happen to know any of them. The town is also the toast of a hundred Top Ten lists across the country. Best place to retire. Best place to gorge on fudge. Best place to avoid getting murdered by street thugs. Best town for cherry gummy bears. Best beer-guzzling depot for bearded Millennial dudes in baseball caps thickening in the gut and heading for premature middle age. Best place most likely to be on a Top Ten list. There are five beaches of golden sand within the city limits, miles of bike paths spreading out in every direction, and it's Michael Moore's adopted city, boasting his annual film festival to boot. You can hear live music in half a dozen bars every night of the week, and double that on the weekend. The city's population is just over 15,000, but on a summer weekend, you'll find more than 100,000 tourists milling through downtown and along the bay. That's when the town turns into Up North Land, a theme park with non-stop tourists, festivals and parties. What's not to like?

Let me tell you.

There used to be a joke about a sign on the outskirts of town that read: "Entering Traverse City - Set Your Watch Back 150 Years," but the shadow of that old town can barely be glimpsed these days, buried under the steamroller of hyper-development.

Dark forces have been at work in Traverse City since before the town was even christened. In 1847 Captain Horace Boardman sailed from Chicago to the river that now bears his name and established a lumber mill. At that time, only a small camp of Indians existed on the beach in the middle of a spectacular pine wilderness. The white pines here were three feet thick and there were millions of them. Four years later, timber capitalist Perry Hannah and his partners bought the mill and thousands of acres with plans to chop down every tree in northern Michigan. Before you could say Headless Lumberjack the entire region was pulverized into an eroded desert of pine stumps. The timber was used to rebuild Chicago, which went up in smoke in 1871 after Mrs. O'Leary's cow kicked a lantern over in its shed. Half of Michigan's lower peninsula burned down, too, as the result of flaming cinders blowing across the lake.

SANDY BOTTOM

After the timber ran out the town flourished as America's Cherry Capital, owing to ideal orchard conditions created by its temperate bays. For 100 years or so, Traverse City poked along as an obscure small town known for its charm, cherries and fudge. Tourists, including the likes of Ernest Hemingway, began showing up on steamers in the 1890s and the town became one of the most popular destinations in the Midwest.

But then came scores of Top 10 lists and a plague of developers. The transformation began with a host of reporters and travel writers attending a national Governors Conference in 1990. They liked what they saw and wrote about it. The glad tidings accelerated with the advent of the Traverse City Film Festival in 2005, piling on more kudos. Wealthy pros from the national press, film and television industries were delighted to find a small town nirvana where 100 feet of Lake Michigan shoreline and a five-bedroom home went for under $1 million and an in-town condo could be had for the laughably low sum of $350k.

The locals had cheered every new claim, no matter how small: "Best Place to Find Cherry Licorice," "Best Place to Walk a Labradoodle," stuff like that. Gradually, those kudos punctured the national consciousness in the travel pages of the *LA Times, The Wall Street Journal, The New York Times* and such. Then, *Good Morning America* announced that the nearby Sleeping Bear National Lakeshore was the "Most Beautiful Place in the Country," in large part because the locals had nothing better to do than call in their votes.

Traverse City had been knocking the likes of Boulder, Durango, Woodstock, Burlington, San Diego, Taos, Madison and Sedona off Top Ten lists ever since Prince partied like it was 1999. It was like pricking Godzilla's ass with a bamboo spear; inevitably, the monster awoke, belching a lava flow of low-rise condos that began gobbling up every square foot of space in town, towing a cascade of chain stores, brewpubs and restaurant franchises along with them. Property values took off like a Saturn 5 booster, with single-bedroom condos starting at $600,000. The end result meant that today, "affordable housing" in town floats up to around $300,000, far more than any low-paid wait-person or cashier can afford. People moan that their kids can no longer afford to live in the town where they were raised. But who can complain when you can sell a house for ten times what you paid for it in the '80s?

So this is a tale of two cities, because for every Audi, Lincoln Navigator or Cadillac Escalade purring down Front Street there are three dozen exhaust-coughing, rusty-bottomed, debt-ridden mini vans and low-lying sedans rumbling down the backroads outside of town, where masses of the working poor live in trailer parks and rotting shacks out in the woods. You don't have to look far to find angry young men scowling beneath the bills of their baseball caps, gunning their old trucks on the outskirts of town with a noise like cardboard ripping, itching for another road rage confrontation. And for every well-coiffed Millennial sipping $12 cocktails at the gourmet restaurants downtown there are dozens of the same generation living from paycheck-to-paycheck, working three jobs and dressed in hand-me-downs from Goodwill, whose idea of a big night out is the Friday fish fry at the local bar.

It reminds me of the painting by Goya of "Saturn Eating His Children," but what do I care? I'm a member of the permanent underclass and likely to stay there. Other than the lease for my office, my only problem is paying the $400 rent for my room in a boarding house on Eighth Street just west of downtown. It's one of those two-story mansions from the lumber era and by some miracle the owner hasn't raised the rent since the '90s. I have a single room there, but there's a commons area and I have kitchen privileges, a shared bathroom, and a shelf that's all mine in the fridge. It's practically a commune: there's a poster of Kurt Cobain giving the finger that's taped to the wall over the sink with a cartoon balloon reading, "Do Your Dishes, Or Get Out," along with a sign-up sheet for cleaning the bathroom.

For me, that's livin' large.

All of my housemates are single moms with kids that range

from toddlers-to-teens. A couple of them are strippers trying to make ends meet in what is optimistically called the "service economy" by think-tank wonks making six figures and living in Georgetown.

Normally, this would be a perilous situation for an incredibly handsome single guy like me, but everyone knows that I'm seriously broke, including the landlord. I'm not what you would call chick-bait. The girls all treat me like I'm their big brother, or maybe little brother, or maybe just one of the girls, depending. Some of their kids call me Uncle Dredd.

But enough about me.

There was a knock at the door.

"Excuse me. Can you tell me where I can find Alison Beckons? I hear she likes to party."

I looked up to find my part-time boss Smokey Williams standing in the doorway, the full moons of his hyperthyroid eyes gazing down at me with the look of an entomologist examining a new bug.

"At your service," I waved him in.

"Hope so. What up?"

"Just gassin' and grinnin', same as yesterday and the day before that."

"Ah, no gigs yet then, I suppose," he nodded as if it was a foregone conclusion.

"Sadly, no, but thanks for the encouragement."

"You should stick with the repo biz. It's ugly, but it pays the bills."

"Thankfully, my bills are on the lean side."

"Yeah, like your refrigerator," Smokey said with a dry chuckle. "A mouse would starve on what you've got in there."

"Mmm. But that's what keeps me lean and mean."

"Like a wolf."

"Yeah."

"Or a really skinny chicken."

I shrugged. "Think of all the money I'm saving on food. Being broke has its benefits."

"The Natty Dredd diet plan. You could sell that."

"Mmm."

Smokey Williams was Traverse City's most notorious repo man. Today he was wearing a camel-colored mechanic's jumpsuit over a black Marilyn Manson t-shirt from the '90s. Although it was 82 degrees out, his head was crowned with a blaze-orange knit ski hat of the sort that retails for $3.99 at a discount store. For footwear he wore his grandfather's well-oiled hunting boots from the 1950s.

Smokey has an intense, scholarly look about him by dint of a pair of large, black-rimmed glasses and a pile of shiny dark hair that would do an Italian film star proud. It straggled from under his cap in a tangled ponytail midway down his back. A remarkable number of woodsy types in these parts sport ponytails, and though Smokey isn't all that woodsy, it helps him to blend in. Like when skulking down some lonely two-track out yonder in search of a vehicle to repossess.

"You up for some coffee? I mean if I'm not disturbing your reverie."

"I've got a backlog of reverie these days," I said. "Let's go."

Down the stairs and around the bend was Brew, a long, narrow cavern of a place where beer on tap shares a counter with caffeine for a buck a cup. Brew serves as Rick's Cafe Americain for anyone hoping to trade secrets and dig dirt in the Cherry Capital. The place is a magnet for Millennials, screen zombies, and what passes for TC's intelligentsia.

Williams and I got our coffee and walked down a dark row of tables lit by the glow of laptops and smart phones, their owners hunched over the screens like monks poring over ancient texts in a monastery.

"So, what do you know, *jefé*?" Smokey began.

"I know that if six turned out to be nine, I'd feel fine," I said. "I know that if all the hippies cut off all their hair I wouldn't care. I know..."

"Yeah, yeah," he waved. "Did you hear about Bottom? It's enough to make you swear off smelt-dipping, eh?'"

"Yeah, sure. Dead, got kilt."

"So they say, but how?"

"It was either a cougar or a bigfoot. It's all over the radio."

"Or some guy with a grudge, maybe."

"Could be."

Smokey gave me a sidelong look. "Are you a suspect?"

I almost spit out my coffee. "What? Give me a break. Why should I be?"

"Well, you know..."

I made a face and an uneasy silence settled in between us. My grudge against Timothy Bottom was no secret, but I'd gotten over it, kind of, anyway. Our history, if you could call it that, was like a bad auto accident that had left me badly maimed: I didn't want to keep remembering it, and I sure didn't want to be a suspect in Bottom's murder.

"I'd put my money on a bear," he said at last.

"You're just saying that to change the subject."

"Well yeah, but..."

I lightened up. "It would have been a bear with a curious sense of humor."

"It happens. I've seen some funny ones out driving around. Bears are funny critters, unpredictable, smart."

"A bear might be smart enough to dump a guy in an out-house, but I doubt he'd waste his time. That, and Bottom had the kind of enemies that walked on two feet instead of four," I said.

"So what do you think?"

"I figure it had to be some guy working with an animal, and that would mean a dog was involved. A man instead of a woman because it had to be someone strong enough to drag Bottom to the outhouse and dispose of him in the shittiest way possible."

"Hmm."

"Someone got the jump on Bottom and had his rottweiler or pit bull finish him off," I went on. "It had to be some-one who hated Bottom, either that or someone he trusted, but shouldn't have."

"What about the cougar idea?"

"No way. To the critters around here Bottom was Saint Francis, and from what I hear, they could sense that he was on their side. Bottom claimed he could talk to animals, like Dr. Doolittle."

"Yeah? What do you think they say?"

"Oh they talk about food, sex, hiding out - that sort of thing, I suppose."

"Oh really? And what about you? Do you talk to animals? I mean with all of that shaman stuff you got into."

I felt a twinge. In a drunken moment a few weeks back, I'd shared my experience as a part-time shaman with Smokey and now I regretted it. Of course, he'd blabbed it all over town and it led to some awkward conversations with friends. But it wasn't something I wanted to talk about. At. All.

"I missed that part of the curriculum," I said, waving a hand in dismissal. "But enough about me. What's up with you?"

"Oh, like the saying goes, same-same, but different," Smokey said.

By that I knew he was talking about his music, a tragic sideline. Smokey was all business as a repo man, as cool and calculating as a bounty hunter when he was on the prowl for an overdue BMW or the missed payments on a motor home. But he had a screw loose when it came to his part-time gig as a singer-songwriter. He had what I called musicians disease.

"How did your thing go at the book store?" I asked without thinking. Sandy had played a gig at the store's coffee bar.

He gave a feeble shrug and I felt a pang of regret. It wasn't something you should ask Traverse City's most unsuccessful musician.

"It bombed," he said, gazing into his cup as if he might find his fortune there. "I had two people show up and managed to clear the room in under seven minutes."

"No need to sugar-coat it."

"I could have used your support," he said, shooting me a look like a betrayed wife. "Didn't you hear about my show? A little clapping would have helped."

SANDY BOTTOM

"Yeah, sorry, I was on a stake-out that night."

"Staking out tacos down at the Bell, I suppose."

I had nothing to say to that, especially since it was true.

"People, what do they know?" he went on, "I've decided to work on my branding for awhile."

"Branding?"

Smokey cleared his throat. "Yeah, I'm working on my social network. You get a few hundred thousand followers on YouTube, Twitter, that sort of thing, and you're gold. It's the only way to make it. I've already got twelve followers. That's how the Biebs did it."

"Justin Bieber got his start by roping in millions of t'weenage girls."

"I could do that." His face loomed emphatic and earnest in the darkness of the coffeehouse and it seemed cruel to pop his balloon, but that's what friends are for.

"It pains me to point out that you're fifteen years past being bait for thirteen-year-olds," I said. "Have you thought of trying tattoos?"

"Tattoos?"

"All of the musicians have them. Full-length arm tattoos. You can't make it without them these days. If you want to go big, you have to mess with your face too."

Smokey mulled it over. "I can do that," he said, lighting up. "Maybe a little body art would help my network. How's that working for you?" He nodded at my own well-illustrated arms, covered with Mayan symbols, vines, flowers, birds and butterflies.

"It seemed like a good idea when I got inked, but now, not so much," I said, examining the border on my wrists where the ink stopped. "To tell the truth, I don't think the tats are helping business. If I ever manage to land a client I'll probably wear a long-sleeved shirt to the consult."

"At least you didn't put any of that shit on your face."

"Thankfully." I wasn't about to tell Smokey that the tattooist in San Marcos got hospitalized with a case of hepatitis on the day I'd planned to have my face tattooed, and I sure wasn't going to tell him what I was going to have written across my forehead in blue ink.

Smokey had been diagnosed with musicians disease in high school, though the shrink called it bipolar disorder. Doctors, what do they know? I happen to know that musicians disease is a grave mental disorder that strikes teenage rockers who never grow out of their dreams of glory. I'm sure you know the type, he was one of those kids who were seized with visions of rock stardom and never escaped the impossible dream. Most victims end up burning out on the bar band circuit before finding Jesus and playing in church on Sunday, but not Smoke - he was in for the long haul.

I felt his pain, having been there myself. Back in high school we'd been in a reggae-punk band together as dual guitarists, but he'd gone off on a hardcore metal tangent with all of that screaming and yelling shit and we had parted ways. We tried putting something together a couple of times after that, but it went nowhere; we were like syrup and gravy, just a mess.

Unfortunately, the small musical success that Smokey *had* achieved had come from his ability to yell and grunt lamebrain lyrics about death, hell and the impending apocalypse in The Reptile Problem, his post-high school death-metal band. It didn't help that a brief infatuation with smoking meth in college had addled his brains.

Smokey had scored some early success as a metal vocalist, first playing basement parties for dysfunctional teens of the ADD sort and then at a roadhouse bar catering to young rednecks far out in the country called the Ol' 66. The Reptile Problem earned a small following with original tunes like "Bad Struttin' Woman," "I Am Snot Worthy," and the anthemic, "Suck It Satan." The faithful would sway back and forth in the red darkness of the bar like zombies on quualudes, giving the devil horns salute, yelling "hells yeah!" and going full pogo when the power chords kicked in loud enough to blow the fiber panels down from the ceiling. It was that rush of adulation that got Smokey addicted, leading to a full blown case of MD. It never occurred to him that the reason the crowd was so jazzed was because of the band's smoking hot drummer, Suzee Bukowski, who bashed away at her double floor toms wearing a bikini top - a very teeny string bikini - over bobbling breasts the size of cantaloupes.

And now here he was, 32 years old and still holding on to a dream from high school.

Smokey also believed that music was cyclical, like fashion, and was preparing to catch the folk wave when it came back around, "just like the Great Folk Scare of 1961." So he was working on tunes like "Gospel Plow," "No More Auction Block" and "Hang Down Your Head Tom Dooley" that crashed on take-off.

Imagine "Leaving on the Jet Plane" by Peter, Paul and Mary sung in the mode of Cannibal Corpse or Morbid Angel and you get the picture. Smokey wasn't going full Filth Eater with his shouts and grunts, but close enough so that his singing was intensely irritating. He called it "urban hillbilly," trying to channel the faux-Appalachian sound of the early-'60s folkies, but with an update. His demented yelling was punctuated at odd moments by a weird falsetto that sounded like the night terrors of a tropical bird. Maybe it was the brain damage from the meth, but Smokey thought his singing was a cross between that of Post Malone and Ed Sheeran, "for the sweet stuff." His detractors said he sounded like an alley cat having its tail yanked out by the roots.

We'd had this talk more times than I could remember.

"Music isn't cyclical - it's like a virus that keeps evolving into something new," I said. "You don't hear ragtime coming back anytime soon, do you? Or banging on logs with a stick."

"Banging on logs?"

"Primitive stuff, where it all began."

"Drum circles, smart guy," he replied. "Drum circles are totally cyclical back to the Stone Age."

He had me there.

On the bright side, Smokey had taken to mining some old

hits from the '60s until the great folk revival came back around. Songs like Donovan's "Mellow Yellow," performed in a leaden style along the lines of, say, Frankenstein or Crime Dog McGruff. The songs from the '60s actually went over pretty good, since anyone who cared to listen tended to fall off their seat laughing, but that wasn't the reaction Smokey hoped for.

But Smokey's spoken-word cover of Simon and Garfunkel's "I Am A Rock" done with an element of danger in a low metal growl had a certain gravitas that was getting some polite applause. It was a glimmer of hope that kept him going.

All said, Smokey had more faith in his music than the Hindenburg had hydrogen, even though the results had much the same outcome. He'd been asked to quit performing at the farm market because he was driving customers away from buying carrots and tomatoes. He'd been excused from every open mic in town, a near-impossible feat. Nursing homes still welcomed him, but only because the residents couldn't hear him sing or could turn off their hearing aids.

Smokey had also pressed 500 CDs of his debut album, *American Rawbones*, at his own expense, giving most of them away to guys whose cars he'd repossessed.

But give the man credit, he wasn't a quitter.

Smokey munched on a bagel and sipped at his coffee, asking my opinion on various designs for his forthcoming tattoos.

"Well it's not just that, Smokey, you need to work on your music, too."

"Oh? How so?"

"It wouldn't hurt to put a little hip-hop into it. Get a looper; that's where it's at these days."

"Yeah, hip-hop, looping," he said with disgust, fingers twining around his pony tail. "People singing jibber-jabber and playing over background tracks. That ain't music to me."

"Everyone else is doing it," I pointed out.

"Yeah, too bad. People, what do they know? Spare songs of the dispossessed and the downtrodden, that's what I'm aiming for."

"That's already been done. They call it rap."

"Don't push me Bumpo."

"Can a flea push an elephant?"

"If it bites hard enough."

A somber look settled over Smokey's face. "Besides, I've seen the videos on Vevo. I can't compete with that."

"With what, rap?"

"Hip-hop."

"So what next?"

"I'm onto something that no one's thought of, and I mean no one," he confided.

"Really."

"Garage sales."

"No way..."

"Way." He crossed his arms and nodded. "I'm going to play at garage sales. No one's ever tried it, as far as I know."

"Maybe because it smells like desperation."

He shrugged. "I've got to keep my name out there until something breaks. I've got three gigs lined up. People who cruise garage sales love to hear music while they shop."

"Sure, it makes them light-hearted and eager to spend. So what's it pay?"

"I've got a tip jar for starters, and I'm selling my CDs. But once the word gets around, I'll be charging."

"That square business?"

"What?"

"It's a saying."

"Well, yeah, it's square business. Can't go anywhere but up with this thing."

I couldn't imagine how Smokey had talked three homeowners into letting him perform at their rummage sales, unless he'd promised to buy some unsaleable item like an old exercise bike to sweeten the deal.

"Garage sales, hmm. I guess I wouldn't mind hearing some music while poking around in someone's junk," I said, trying to sound encouraging. "You know, in Mexico, musicians play on the buses."

"Is that so?"

"Yup, and all the way down through Central America too. They play some tunes on the bus and pass a Styrofoam cup around for pesos."

"How's that work out?"

I shrugged. "I've seen people digging for change. It's better than cutting sugar cane or pearl-diving for dishes in a restaurant sink."

"I suppose," he mused. "Do you think I could do that?"

"Do you parlez-vous espanol?"

"I could learn."

"Could be a new career path for you then."

"Hmm... You miss it?" he asked. "I mean, south of the border."

I considered. The first thing I thought of was lying in my hammock in Guatemala at night, swaying by the shores of Lake Atitlan and swatting bugs from my face, but that wasn't what Smokey was getting at.

"Yeah, sometimes," I replied. "The chicas, mostly."

I had met some amazing backpackers from all over the world: Europe, Australia, Israel and South America, anxious to share their most intimate secrets with a lonely gringo bartender by the flower-strewn shores of Lake Atitlan in Guatemala.

"You got a girlfriend or two down there? Waiting for you, I suppose."

I shrugged. "Mostly, it was sitting on the dock in San Marcos holding hands with some pretty girl passing through, followed by a warm hug and a promise to be friends on Facebook. But that was a long time ago."

Smokey leaned across the table and snapped his fingers. "Dredd, that was four months ago."

Was it only four months? Back from three years of tending bar in San Marcos, Guatemala?

"It seems like a lifetime," I said.

"And now you're back in town and already a pillar of the community."

"So true."

"This town would be nothing without us."

"Just another place to pile dirt."

"Amen to that."

"We're legends in our own minds." I raised my empty coffee cup. "Here's to the underclass."

"To us," he replied, "the two Musketeers."

We got down to business and the job that kept Williams solvent while he worked on his music. Me too, for that matter. He was the owner of the Track-U-Down repo outfit that combed half the state for vehicles piloted by owners who'd skipped out on their loans. He had a garage and a car lot off 14th Street south of town and I was a part-time associate, helping to track down deadbeats.

I'd been working for him for the past two months, running down loan-skippers on Facebook under the guise of Alison Beckons, a ditzy blonde with big boobs who "likes to party." (Sample line: "Don't I know you from high school?") Alison also claimed to like alpha male types, which was pure sucker bait; it's amazing how many deadbeats think they're the alpha wolf leader of the pack. Alison would arrange a date with some doofus at a bar out in the sticks and Smokey would nab his vehicle while he was inside looking for a clone of Marilyn Monroe who "likes to party."

I also spent my time placing "wrong number" calls and posing as a radio host with happy news about a big prize if Joe Blow-it-All could only provide an address. Once I had the address, we'd swoop in with Smokey's monster tow truck and either sweet-talk the dude into giving up his keys or haul his vehicle away in the dead of night.

Smokey had saved my bacon when I got home from Guatemala with a dream of starting my own private investigation firm. Business had been slow - in fact, nonexistent - and that's when Smokey came along with an offer I couldn't resist, cash under the table.

It turns out I had a knack for tracking down deadbeats. In return, I get 15 percent of the repo. Money-wise, it was almost enough to pay the bills. Plus, Smokey let me use his repo'ed vehicles until they got sent to auction. Having wheels now and then was a nice perk for a low-flyer like me who couldn't afford a moped, much less a car. Mostly I got around on a bike I bought at a garage sale for 20 bucks.

We'd known each other since the age of 16. Smokey had been a big kid in high school and a better roadie than a musician, at least when it came to hoisting amplifiers and speaker cabinets. Back then, he had intervened in an ass-kicking at a high school dance during one of our band's ill-starred performances. I'd tried crowd-surfing with a bunch of drunken jocks in the audience and it hadn't gone over well. Smokey had waded into the fray and laid on his fists. In the spirit of the Japanese ninjas I owed him my life, or at least an intervention in a bar fight.

Not that he'd need my help. Smokey is six-foot-four and keeps a snub nose .38 with parabellum rounds tucked in his pants just west of his belt buckle; they're the kind of rounds that flower in a lethal dance after they pierce the clothing layer of whoever gets in the way of their trajectory.

I could tell he was packing today. He squirmed around in his seat and shifted his gat free of his substantial gut.

"Why do you carry a snubbie?" I asked. "I thought those weren't accurate at a distance."

"They're not," he said dryly, "and a .38 isn't particularly lethal as guns go. But statistically, most gun fights take place within seven feet of whoever's doing the shooting. If someone draws down on me, it's badda-boom, badda-bang."

"You're gonna' blow your nuts off with that thing stuck in your pants if you don't watch out."

"How do you know I didn't already?"

"You're still singing baritone instead of tenor."

"Well if I do, I'll borrow a couple of yours."

We talked biz until my third cup of coffee ran cold. Then we spoke of many things, fools and kings and torsion springs. We trash-talked the Pistons, the president, the jerk-offs in the loyal opposition. Guy talk. Williams was reading a new

Dylan biography while I was hacking my way through the more obscure works of Mickey Spillane, learning the ropes of private investigation one page at a time. Spillane's protagonist, private eye Mike Hammer, beats bad guys to death on a whim and always manages to get away with it. At times he's more of a criminal than the bad guys, but his heart is in the right place.

"It's dopey stuff, but I'm picking up some tips on how to talk like a tough guy," I said. "Cracking wise, sneering, stuff like that. There was a lot of sneering going on in pulp fiction back in the day."

"I don't know why you bother with that trash," Smokey said.

"It's part of my continuing education," I sneered. "I'm going the old-school route."

"And you think folk music is stupid. Physician, heal thyself."

At the table next to us a sallow guy in a gray hoodie and chunky black glasses was combing his scraggly beard with his fingers, live-streaming the 6 O'Clock News on his laptop. News anchor Jodi Brown, a chesty college grad with a brown bowl cut and a glued-on smile was doing a live interview with Gladys Mahill. Jodi was the talk of the town because it appeared as if she had no neck, but I think it was simply because she always wore a huge necklace of silver and gold baubles the size of Christmas ornaments, which seemed to be the latest thing for female newscasters.

As for Gladys Mahill, this was the first time I'd seen the woman who'd discovered Timothy Bottom's body. She had short, wiry, stark-red dyed hair that ran black at the roots, along with oversized glasses in square frames that gave her the look of a pensive owl.

"What did you think when you opened that outhouse door?" Jodi asked, still smiling.

"Well, I had to pee real bad, so I wasn't thinking about much more than that," Gladys said, her owlish face growing thoughtful. "But I did think of one thing. They've got that single-ply toilet tissue in all of the outhouses around here, which doesn't go over real good with those of us in the Two Tissue Movement. There's a few of us around here, you know."

"What's that? The Two Tissue Movement?"

"Yes, it started back in the early '00s as a way to save the environment by using less toilet paper. You just wrap two squares of tissue paper around a finger and wipe the back end after you do your business and then kind of flick it off. You know what I mean? It saves on a crazy amount of toilet paper that gets flushed into our drinking water otherwise."

Straight out of Michigan State University's broadcast journalism program, Jodi gaped at Gladys like a walleye that's just had it tail squeezed right up to the gills.

"I mean, give a girl a break," Gladys rambled on. "Single-ply? With that kind of business going on? I don't want to get all scatological on you, but you've got to have two-ply tissue unless you want to get a stink finger."

"Stink finger?" Jodi breathed in a daze.

Gladys sighed in recollection. "I mean, I'm just glad I didn't have to do a number two."

Death by 'Natural Causes'

Of all the cheap cubicle joints in the world....

There's nothing like a blonde in a tight silk dress, especially sapphire, a dress that hints at a night of murmurs and moans as soon as it can be shed. She was wearing a low-cut cocktail dress on a Monday afternoon, the kind of gauzy wisp that women wear when they dress to kill. Her cascade of golden hair rolled and flowed halfway down her back, expensive hair of the sort that's pampered with exotic conditioners and weekly salon appointments. She slid her bronzed legs from the seat of a Tesla Roadster and touched cinnabar heels to the pavement of Front Street. I'm no expert, but I guessed they were the same kind of heels that women went on about in *Vogue* or *Sex and the City*.

SANDY BOTTOM

Gazing out my window on the street below, a sick feeling twisted my guts with a hard-knuckle pipe wrench. I knew where she was headed, and she wasn't alone. There were footsteps on the stairs, and then her.

"Hello Sandy."

"Hello Dredd," she said. "Been a long time."

Sandy was much the same as I remembered her from three years ago. Her creamy complexion was a bit leathered from too much sun, but still the angel of my dreams, any man's dreams. Timothy Bottom's widow.

I'd been waiting for this moment for three long years. But now I had nothing for her but a look, trying hard not to show that I was caving inside like sheets of shelf ice tumbling into a bottomless sea. Like Samson pulling down the temple. Like a dog begging for a lamb chop. Like... oh stuff it, I told myself. I summoned up my inner Phillip Marlowe, the hardest of the hard-boiled dicks, or damn close to it. What would the knight of L.A.'s back alleys and mean streets do?

Sandy wasn't alone. Her momma stood in the door, smiling and nodding from beneath the kerchief tied around her head. She was an amiable sort, a caricature of a Russian doll-within-in-a-doll with a nose like a potato that had spent too much time in the root cellar. She had Freda Kahlo's mustache and a skirt of whiskers around her chin. That, and she was broad in the beam, I'd say nearly a yard across the bottom in a skirt festooned with red chili peppers and green palm trees. She stood in the doorway, fidgeting in a cable-knit brown sweater. But like I said, amiable, even sweet - a sweet old lady from the Old Country, Sandy's mom.

I forced a grimace into a smile like that of a skeleton and said hello.

"Goot!" she replied, nodding rapidly. "Goot!"

Sandy, by contrast, was a blond goddess with eyes the same color as the blue found in the heart of a glacier, and with the same touch of ice. They were Slavic, foxy eyes, as narrow and twinkling as those of a frost witch, gleaming like pools of blue opals that looked so deep that you could slide right into them and drown. Her eyes were framed by long, silken lashes that could pierce your heart with a flutter.

Nature had blessed Sandy with the face of an angel, open and innocent with cherry blossom lips, those deep blue eyes, and gleaming cheekbones; a face that plucked the heartstrings of any man who crossed her path. By some magical conjuring of bone structure, skin and complexion her face was simply adorable in a girl-next-door sort of way - compelling, sweet, hypnotic. Face of an angel, heart of a devil... for me, at least.

Not that Sandy was perfect. Her forehead was a little on the high side and she had jug ears, the tips of which peeked out of her blond locks like those of a mermaid or an elf. And she was just the tiniest bit cross-eyed, like that French model in the Victoria's Secret catalog. But it was the chemistry of those imperfections that made her all the more spellbinding. Her imperfections made her easier to remember, and harder to forget.

The rest of her wasn't bad either. Men couldn't take their eyes off her, nor could women. Sandy had an elven, athletic look to her, light but solidly built and as curvy as Tomb Raider Lara Croft. Perfect breasts, of course, riding high atop a lean rib cage that tapered down to a twenty-inch waist, slim hips, and legs that had been polished to perfection by endless hours at Yen Yoga and various gyms around town. She ran the Bayshore Marathon and the Cherry Festival 15k each summer in her pink running shoes, crushing it. Arms? Check. I'd seen her do 30 full-body pushups. And as far as I knew, no one could beat Sandy when it came to planking. A sturdy girl, that Sandy.

And though Sandy claimed to have been raised as a simple country girl from Siberia, she could muster a cut-you-dead air of sophistication with the speed of a cobra if she so desired. Even when she was aiming for trashy, Sandy always managed to look classy. She just couldn't help herself.

But now she gave a weak smile when I was too gobsmacked to get past saying hello, all hint of the cobra packed away.

"Now Momma, you wait outside while I talk to Mr. Bumpo," she said, hustling the munchkin out the door to a folding chair out in the hall where there were well-thumbed copies of *Scandinavian Traveler* and *Gut Health* magazine on an end table.

Sandy eased into the plastic chair across from me and we contemplated one-another, me with my elbows spread wide on the table, hands forward like an Egyptian god or else a dude anticipating a mixed martial arts round at any second.

"Been a long time," she said again.

"Not long enough," I said, deciding to play offense. "What's up with the dress?"

"What?"

"It's kind of clingy, isn't it?"

"Clingy?"

"You know, seductive. As I remember, that bridge got burned some time ago."

"Don't be mean to me, Dredd. I just wanted to look nice for you," she said, crossing her legs so the hem hiked up. "It's just a dress."

"Yeah, but so is a kimono."

For a moment Sandy looked flustered.

"This is difficult for you, Dredd, I know. It's difficult for me, too." She pulled a pack of organic cigarettes from her purse and fired one up. That took me a few degrees colder.

"Seriously? You can't smoke in here Sandy," I said, trying not to sound as disturbed as I felt.

"Of course I can," she exhaled. "In Russia we smoke wherever we like."

"We're not in Putinville and I can't afford to get kicked out of here. Besides, if you smoke long enough your face will get all wrinkled and puckered up, and you wouldn't want that now, would you? So give."

Her eyes widened, nostrils flaring in irritation as she pushed back in her chair, studying my face.

"Oh Dredd, why are you so harsh? Let's not be cruel. We're still friends, aren't we?" She exhaled a long plume and waved her cigarette in a slow circle. "Where do you want this?"

"Are we friends, Sandy? Maybe I missed something."

I reached out and took her cigarette, our fingers touching for the briefest instant, sending an electrical charge straight down to my toes. I leaned over to the philodendron on the windowsill that Mom had given me as a office-warming gift and stubbed it out in the flower pot.

Sandy's voice lilted behind my back. "When was the last time I saw you, Dredd, Leland?"

Leland. Yeah, Fishtown, who could forget? I'd spent the summer on the dock there, banging out tunes on my Fender for tips and kicks while I was going to trade school to learn how to cut hair. Fishtown is a big tourist destination on Lake Michigan, 35 miles to the northwest of Traverse City, with a rustic dock lined with shops selling t-shirts, hats, exotic cheeses, foodie stuff and smoked fish. That, and a couple of fishing boats still operate out of its harbor.

"You know the last time Sandy, unless I was less than nothing to you." I was trying to channel Bogart's scene with Ingrid Bergman in *Casablanca* where he reams her for standing him up at the train station in Paris. But it came across a bit too petulant and kind of bitchy. Kind of like Bogey in that scene, come to think of it.

She ignored it. "So what happened to your dreads? I kind of liked that look."

"They were perfect for the beach, but bad for business." I'd left a pile of dreadlocks tangled in a tree branch in Guatemala before returning to northern Michigan. Somewhere, 2,000 miles to the south, it had become nesting material for songbirds. Now, of course, I had the standard Matt Damon American male haircut to fit in with my new gig, even though it was a bit raggedy here and there, since I'd cut it myself in a mirror.

"Too bad," she mused, "they made you look cute. Now, not so much."

"Cute's not so good in my current profession. I'm trying for ugly now."

"Yes, your new profession. Very interesting. I read about you. You are big success already, front page news."

"That's right. Huge." I left off mentioning that I hadn't had a case in weeks.

"You have tattoos now," she said, scanning my arms.

"You noticed."

"Is too much," she clucked. "You look like Rooshian gangster."

I shrugged. It didn't matter what Sandy thought of me now, or at least I pretended that it didn't. "It's what you do in Guatemala," I said. "You get tattoos."

"But your whole arms?"

"And more," I said.

"What's on your chest?"

"Stick around and I'll show you sometime."

Sandy gave a staged yawn. "They are very tribal. Is kind of sexy, I suppose."

I steepled my fingers and gazed at her, my elbows on the table, wondering where this was going.

Sandy's attention wandered in the way that afflicts all beautiful women, like they're on stage preparing for a soliloquy.

"You know, I never asked you, what's with the name?" she asked, fingering the nameplate on my desk. "Nathaniel Dredd Bumpo; you made that up, right?"

"Not really, the Bumpos are scions of Massachusetts," I replied. "My great-great-great grandfather was on the Mayflower."

"Signs? What is this signs?"

"Scions, it means a distinguished family, big shots, people who ate high on the hog."

"Liar," she gave a knowing smile. "Your ancestors were peasants and slaves, just like mine. We called them serfs in Russia. This name of yours is crazy. Were you raised by Mohicans or Rastas?"

"My parents liked reggae and they had a sense of humor."

But Natty Dredd? That's cruel," she said. "I know my reggae."

I shrugged. "Have you ever heard that song, 'A Boy Named Sue' by Johnny Cash? My dad gave me this name so I'd have to be tough and take care of myself, not take shit from bullies, that sort of thing."

"So why didn't he name you Mary or Priscilla?" she wondered, her blue eyes wandering to the window.

"Dad had a sense of humor, I didn't say he was crazy."

"Your parents were hippies."

"Whatever."

Like most of us living in Traverse City, I was a transplant from somewhere else, a refugee. It was rare to meet a native; most residents seemed to hail from suburban Detroit, Flint, Lansing and other towns to the south.

I didn't care to mention that the first four years of my life were spent in a Volkswagen camper van, roaming New Mexico while my folks dabbled in the turquoise trade. After that it was Jamaica, Peru and New Orleans before we moved to Traverse City so I could attend high school. Dad had been a commodities trader in Chicago who decided to hit the hippie trail after he scored enough pork belly futures to last a lifetime. Thus, we never went hungry or lacked for excursions to Disney World, even if we did live like a band of gypsies.

Nor did I care to mention that the name I'd been born with was John Smith. I'd grown tired of being called Captain and being quizzed about Pocahontas in high school. With my mom and dad's blessing, I had changed my name as soon as I reached the age of majority. I had seen the Daniel Day-Lewis film, *Last of the Mohicans,* when I was 16 at a time when my high school band was deep into reggae and punk. A dude named Natty Bumpo the Deerslayer was the hero in that flick, and I thought the name was a lot cooler than John Smith. The reggae moniker mash-up spoke to me. Natty Dredd Bumpo was a good fit for my plan to become a world-famous rock & reggae star, and it was at a time of my life when I wanted to invent myself.

I grew up and the name stuck around. Today most people just call me Dredd.

SANDY BOTTOM

Sandy gave me the sort of look that's used to appraise road-kill. "I think this is a strange name. You should change it."

"Look who's talking, Sandy Bottom. What kind of name is that?"

She gave a sigh. "Tim was progressive in all things but marriage. He insisted that I take his name, expecting that we'd have children."

"You could change it now that he's gone."

"Yes, but there is the inheritance, you know? Better I should remain a Bottom for now."

"I get it."

"Dredd, sweetie, we had our time together, but there's a lot I don't know about you."

"Maybe that's a good thing."

"Like the initials," she pointed to the nameplate on my desk, LC, CSP, PI. "What's up with that?"

"Licensed Cosmetologist, Crystal Skull Practitioner, Private Investigator."

"Crystal Skull? This is new..."

"It's deep. Forget it."

A long pause. "You know, Dredd, I always wanted to explain what happened with us. But you didn't leave me an address and you weren't on Facebook or that Tweeter thing. I didn't know where you'd gone until I read about you in the paper."

"You don't have to explain anything to me, Sandy. I've got my big boy pants on and figured it out a long time ago. It was like Bogie waiting for Ilsa on the train in Paris with the krauts closing in and her not showing up for a good reason. You hooked up with Timothy Bottom and I got hit by a speeding train. What else is there to say?"

"But..."

"Let's skip Memory Lane and try a new road, okay? Why are you here, Sandy?"

"It's Timothy," she said, "I want you to find out how Timothy died."

"Me?"

"Yeah, you."

Timothy Bottom, the man who'd taken Sandy away from me. Or, more correctly, the man she'd chosen to be her personal Santa Claus. That snapped me out of it; suddenly Sandy was just another good-looking gold-digger instead of the love goddess who'd ripped my heart out and tossed it on a flaming grill.

She looked up, eyes locked on mine and I could see the she-wolf lurking there, hungry, ready to bite.

"Sorry to hear about Tim," I said, shaking off the vision with a shiver.

"He was a force of nature, literally," she replied.

"Good man."

"Yes, very good, to the animals and trees, anyway."

"So I heard."

"Tell me, Dredd," she said, her blue eyes still fixed on mine. "Do you know what it's like to be married to a fanatic? I thought Tim loved me, but he cared more about salamanders and snakes. He had so much money, but he made me shop at Goodwill. We ate tofu instead of steak, no meat, ever. He was a pure vegan and wouldn't let me have eggs or even milk. He made his own wine and granola; both were shit. I don't even want to tell you what Christmas was like."

"No, tell me."

"Do you know what he got me last Christmas?" Her eyes went to the ceiling and welled up at the thought of it.

"An ostrich."

"No, he named a product after me. Sandy's Baby Bum Creme, with all of the profits going to some wildlife fund, like, for endangered goats in Albania."

"Poor little rich girl."

"Laugh if you like, Dredd, but it wasn't what I expected. It wasn't what I deserved."

I had some thoughts on the matter, but kept them to myself.

"You don't look like you're hurting," I said. "I saw the car outside."

"Timothy had some money," she said, "under our mattress,

literally. Canadian money, can you believe it? Today it's worth two-thirds of what he packed away five years ago. The rest of his fortune is locked up in accounts behind a wall of lawyers. I'll get nothing unless you help me."

"How so?

"Timothy made me sign a prenup and I found his will," she said. "All of his money will go to wildlife charities unless I can prove that he died of natural causes."

I couldn't help smiling, albeit with a trace of bitter.

"So you're screwed," I said. "Timothy Bottom was murdered."

"That's where you're wrong, Dredd," she said, leaning in close over the table. A cloud of perfume wafted up from her breasts, which rose from the cleft in her dress like the honeyed hills of a Hawaiian sunset. I swallowed hard and kept my eyes steady on hers.

"My attorney says it's all in how you interpret 'natural causes'," she said. "If I can prove that an animal or something 'natural' killed Tim, it will be from natural causes, don't you see? In a way, it's the sort of death he would have wanted."

"Carved up by a cougar?"

Sandy eased back in her chair and tugged the hem of her dress.

"Well, no, not that, but natural causes, he would have understood that. He told me once that he thought Steve Irwin had a fitting death. Can you imagine?"

I thought of Irwin, the reality TV star and wild animal wrestler who died with a stingray's tail through his heart. "No, not really," I said.

"He was a fanatic on that level."

I eased back in my seat. It was my turn to probe.

"So why don't you just call it good and move on?" I began. "You've got a car worth two hundred thousand dollars and a mattress full of Canadian green. With that and your looks you shouldn't have any trouble landing another sucker."

"It's big money on the table, Dredd, and I'm done being a slave to another man."

"Or them to you."

Sandy gave me gimlet smile, her blue eyes glittering. "You men always think it's all about you, don't you? You see a beautiful woman and you think there's no price? Let me tell you a secret, Dredd. There is a price. There's always a price."

"I've been to school on that one," I replied.

Sandy leaned in close again until her face was inches from mine and it was all I could do to keep from kissing her. She didn't need perfume - the scent of her body alone was intoxicating, overwhelming. "You always knew who I was, Dredd. You just didn't want to see."

For a moment Sandy looked more like a dragon than the fairy princess that had been gliding through my dreams for the past three years. But she was right; I'd been a sap all along and knew it. My thoughts drifted to how Sandy must have seen me back in our glory days of sun and sand; just another skirt-chasing beach boy to toy with until a man with prospects came along. A man with money, like Timothy Bottom.

"So, what are we talking about?" I asked, pulling away. "How much?"

"Sixty million dollars," she said, "plus change in the way of the house, Tim's island, all the furniture, his guitars, even the car out front. I'll lose it all unless you help me."

"You mean to tell me that Timothy left you nothing? Nothing at all?"

"He left me what you'd call chump change, chicken feed," she frowned.

"But you were the love of his life, the one he cared about above all others."

"You'd think so, but Timothy was married to the animals and the things of the wild. Do you know we only made love twice in the whole time we were together? Once on our wedding night because it was required and once on the night before he died."

That got me going. "Why the night before he died?"

Sandy shrugged. "He said it was a special occasion and that big things were going to happen. I thought it meant we were going to make a baby, you know?"

I nodded. "And I thought he worshipped you." Like I did.

"No," she sighed. "He was a nature worshipper, like his German ancestors. They worshipped trees, you know. I was just what you'd call a trophy wife, something to dangle before his rich friends so they'd think about donating to his causes. He left me very little, a pittance, barely enough to cover my spa visits."

Jeezus, I could almost hear a sad violin playing "Heartbreak Hotel" off-key in the distance. I let it all soak in. Timothy Bottom was celibate? With a woman that most men would chew their arm off to take to bed? You were one strange duck, Bottom, I thought, or perhaps a cold fish.

"That's all very interesting," I said, "But why me? The State Police and the FBI are working the case. There's nothing I could find that they haven't discovered already."

Sandy gave me a dreamy stare, drilling me with those big blue eyes of hers. "Word gets around, Dredd. I read about your big case in the paper and heard that you had certain powers, things you learned while you were gone."

"But we've got a history, babe."

"That's more your problem than mine."

"Do you know how many detectives there are in town?"

"Three-point-five," she answered.

"Well get one of them to do your dirty work. I don't want the job."

A smile rose on Sandy's face, recalling the sunny blonde I'd met on the dock in Fishtown three years ago. The woman from my days of cold champagne and roses in cellophane.

"Oh, yes you do, Dredd," she said, taking my hand. She placed it in the hollow between her breasts in a tight grip. I could feel her heart beating, slow and strong. I could feel the moisture of her body, her sweat. "I know you do. A woman can always tell."

"You're still the puppet-master, aren't you Sandy?" I said,

losing my breath. But her hand felt good, the electric, animal warmth of it flowing like a current, and I couldn't pull away. I was gasping for breath, panting, my knees skewed sideways. "The answer is still no," I squeaked.

Then Sandy's big blue eyes drank me in until it felt I would drown in their depths, trying to resist but loving every second of it as her face floated close to mine. I made to kiss her, but it was my ear she wanted, not my mouth.

"You give up too easily, Dredd," she whispered.

With that she stood up and turned for the door.

"We haven't talked money," I said, my voice croaking and breathless. My heart took on the throb of a bass drum. "I get $500 per day, plus expenses."

Sandy wheeled around on her heels with the grace of a ballerina. "Your Facebook page says it's $300."

"For you I'll make an exception," I said. "Take it or leave it."

"Do you think you can solve this?"

"You bet your momma's push-up bra I can."

Sandy's eyes went wide, a supernova of blue.

"What is this? A push-up bra for Momma?"

"Forget it. It's a non-sequitur."

"To this I am not understanding. Non-sector?"

"It's because you're Russian. It just means snappy patter."

"What is this 'snappy patter'?"

"It's a detective thing. Something you learn in school."

"So, you went to detective school?"

I shifted in my chair, feeling suddenly very warm as my face began to flush. School for me had been reading a series of pulp fiction detective novels.

"Yeah, sure. Sort of."

"Just bring me the animal that killed Tim," she said, cold as a gin and tonic. She got up and strolled out the door, leaving a scent of jasmine and a breeze wafting up from the sea.

Effing women...

I sat there for several minutes letting things settle, and not just what had stirred in my lap. What would Marlowe do?

He'd reach in the third drawer down and pull out a bottle of old skull-popper.

But I didn't have a drawer, just a strongbox chained to the particle-board table that served as my desk. I filched the key and opened the box, pulling the Crystal Skull Don Pedro from his cave of solitude. I set him on the table and looked into his shallow eyes for how long I don't know. The skull was a lump of white alabaster with a crooked grin that had yet to speak to me. I always thought it was bullshit, but what do I know? Shaman Don Juan del Pedro said it would take awhile before the skull started providing answers; you just had to have faith and keep up with the meditation. That's the sort of thing I needed now. Sandy had given me a bad case of monkey-mind, making my thoughts all scrambled and confused, and I was hot to be somewhere else. Like Jupiter, Venus, Neptune, someplace only the shamans knew, just to get her out of my head.

I popped a Sativa gummy bear and let the buzz settle in, waiting for a message.

But time went by and the Crystal Skull Don Pedro had nothing for me, not a word, so I decided to try Marlowe's remedy. I placed the skull in my fanny pack and headed downstairs for the U&I Lounge. A Jack & Coke, make it a double, that would do it, with some Guatemalan ganga later on to put things in perspective. Heading down the alley to the back door, I was too buzzed to notice the shadow at my heels. But I heard him well enough; even saw his reflection looming like a bigfoot in the dark glass of the U's entryway as he hit me from behind.

"Stay away from Sandy, mudderfugger." At least, that's what I think he said. Truthfully, I couldn't remember.

But something about that voice sounded familiar.

Kisses Sweeter than Wine

The Crystal Skull Don Pedro was finally speaking to me.

"A blood puddle, get it? It's like a mud puddle, only it's

blood," he said, a disembodied voice squawking in my ear like a parrot. *"You're in a pool of blood the size of Walden Pond. Get up!"*

And that's where I woke up in a puddle of blood with a crowd of gawkers hovering over me, voices indistinct, the shadows of their faces blocking out the sky.

I went under again and woke to ministrations of an angel in the ER at Munson Medical Center. She had the face of a bulldog, but the sweetest smile.

"Hi there," she said.

"Hey."

"How are you feeling?"

"Like ten pounds of shit in a five pound bag."

"Do you know what day it is?"

"Seldom."

"Can you tell me your name?"

"Eleanor Rigby."

"Got health insurance?"

"Nada."

"Not even Obamacare?"

"Working on it."

She gave a knowing grunt and somewhere, I suspected, a little box was being checked: indigent.

Angel nurse sighed. "I guess you're okay then," she said, "but you've had a concussion and you're going to lie still for awhile, got it?"

"What hit me?"

She shrugged. "A manhole cover, maybe?"

I'd seen a fractured skull before at a bar fight in Mexico City. The guy's head swelled up like a beach ball in a matter of minutes. The medics drilled a hole in his head on the spot to relieve the pressure. Fortunately, I got beaned on the thickest part of my skull, the parasagittal posterior parietal area, I believe they call it.

A strange feeling washed over me. I'd been beaned in the head, just like Philip Marlowe in the Raymond Chandler novels. Marlowe was always getting blackjacked, sapped with a leather pouch full of ball-bearings. It happened to every detective in the pulps. The nurse said they'd found a metal baton next to me, the kind that snaps out a steel rod with the flick of a wrist. So it was true, I was finally becoming a real dick, like Marlowe, like Mike Hammer, like...

"Mr. Bumpo, are you still with me?"

It was Nurse Angel, gazing down with a look of concern in her eyes.

I nodded.

"Well you just rest now, but don't fall asleep, okay? We'll have someone in later to give you a sponge bath."

"You?"

"If you're lucky," she smiled.

"I'd like that. Nice and warm, okay?"

"You just be a good boy and settle in," she said, giving my chest a motherly pat. "Watch some TV. Judge Judy is on. Do you like Judge Judy?"

"Yeah, sure. I could use a vacation. But hold off on the Judge Judy for a bit."

But that afternoon, I slipped off the gurney and out the sliding doors, shuffling down Seventh Street with my head wrapped like a mummy. No insurance meant goodbye Joe, me gotta' go...

Besides, I had work to do and 500 bucks a day to rake in. For that kind of money I could afford a little headache.

You might imagine that Sandy Bottom is some sort of Britney Spears cheerleader type with not a lot of smarts going on upstairs. Not true. She was a mail order bride straight out of Mother Russia and an operator with the best of them. Smart like a fox, relentless as a shark.

Sandy could be crude and she had a freaky energy of the sort you find in certain aggressive blondes who've been getting their way since junior high school. If you were in a Stone Age tribe fighting another tribe with only rocks for weapons, you'd want Sandy in your corner, cheerfully bashing some guy's head in. And like I said, she was pretty easy on the eyes, providing they didn't pop out of your skull when you saw her.

Back in the Cold War of the 1950s, America's propaganda machine cooked up the myth that Russian women were be-whiskered ogres with breasts like sweet potatoes, noses like turnips and butts like a barn door. In fact, Russian women are some of the most beautiful in the world owing to a melting pot of different races and cultures that's been brewing on the steppes for two thousand years. Various Asiatic hordes out of Mongolia and China had found love (rape, actually) in the arms of Scandinavian Vikings, Baltic peasants, the Poles, and the Greco-Roman culture of old Constantinople. Add in the ministrations of Napoleon's troops, the Cossacks, Georgians, Ukrainians, Nazis and what-have-you and the women of Russia coalesced in a fox-eyed Slavic beauty that is unmatched the world over.

With eyes like blue opals and an unearthly beauty, 17-year-old Sonya Rostova had been snapped up by northern Michigan oilman Derek Smith in the early '00s while he was shopping for a bride in Moscow. Smith hailed from Kalkaska, a small town 25 miles east of Traverse City, and as it happened, Kalkaska sat atop a lake of oil nestled in a vast geological formation called the Niagran Reef. By a stroke of fate, in the 1870s Smith's pioneering ancestors had purchased 1,500 acres of second-growth pine forest that lay smack dab over an oil bonanza.

Yet although he was awash in oil money, Smith suffered from a terminal dweebness that was grating beyond the endurance of the average American woman, not to mention the smoking-hot Playboy bunny types that he thought he deserved. He was conventionally handsome in a bland sort of way: tall, brown hair, brown shoes, with a neat haircut and clothes like what you'd find at J.C. Penneys. But Smith had the personality of a flatworm and his conversation tended to be about golf and   fracking. He was rich, but a bore, and people had been known to fall asleep standing up while talking to him. Hence a series of trips to sex tourism destinations in Penang, Thailand and Sousa in the Dominican Republic, then on to Moscow where he had arranged a meeting with Sandy's mother via a match-making site on the internet.

There was no question of any sex tourism involving Sonya Rostova, for she was held to be as rare as a Fabergé egg, with much the same price for her betrothal.

It's said that after the sham of a courtship and the expense of a wedding you can purchase a drop-dead Russian beauty for $10,000-$15,000. But Sonya - soon to be renamed Sandy - was something special, and her dowry came to $45,000, plus presents, lots of them. At the time Smith had plenty of dough and was happy to spread it around like toppings on an extra large, deluxe pizza, if only to prove that he was the kind of mega-millionaire that young Sonya deserved. He showered her with jewelry and clothing from the pricey boutiques along Tverskaya Street in Moscow. People commented that she looked like Julia Roberts in *Pretty Woman*, walking out of those stores with six or eight shopping bags strapped to her arms. The hand-crafted paper bags alone cost more than most Muscovites made in a week.

Little did anyone suspect, Sandy took to shopping as a drug to dull the pain of being traded like a horse.

"Momma had been a match-maker in Siberia, so when we moved to Moscow she was thrilled with the opportunity to use her skills," Sandy told me much later. "She said I was a princess bride, but I felt like a piece of meat on some man's plate."

As payback, Derek Smith reaped the whirlwind.

He should have been wised up when a horde of Sandy's relatives came out of the woodwork in Moscow, even though she was a transplant from Siberia. All of her brothers, sisters, uncles, aunts, nieces and nephews hit Smith up for loans with Sandy's approval. Anxious to please his fiancé, he started doling out "micro-grants" to her dubious relatives, hoping he could claim them as charitable tax write-offs to the deserving poor of a second-world nation. Then came Sandy's friends, pleading for help launching a business, paying for college overseas, or an operation for their pet cat.

Being a sex tourism veteran, Smith knew he was getting fleeced, but he was willing to pay any price for his new bride. He took to thinking of himself as Sandy's own personal Santa Claus, hoping to eject from Moscow as soon as a ring was on her finger.

Symbiosis is the mutual benefit of two parasites and that's the fairy tale that Sandy and Derek's marriage was based on. It was love at first gush for Derek and a means to an end for Sandy. "I had to hold my nose, but that's the price you pay for a Green Card," she told me back in the day. "We both got what we wanted, but for me there was no love. It was a transaction, you know? A business deal, only."

Indeed, after a wedding attended by more than 300 in a pavilion in Moscow's Gorky Park, Sandy arrived as a 18-year-old bride in northern Michigan, but as it happened, that was just when Kalkaska's oil boom began drying up.

Back then, Kalkaska was a dismal place with most of its stores empty and shuttered on the main drag, which even today is a four-lane highway that invites motorists to pass through town as quickly as possible. All of the oil money that gushed from its soil didn't do a lick of good at a time when small towns all over America were getting kicked in the teeth by big box stores, shopping malls and traitorous residents who took their dollars elsewhere. At best Kalkaska was a stopover of fast food joints for motorists passing through to Traverse City.

But for Sandy it was a giant step up from the squalor of Siberia and the dingy apartment in Moscow that she and her mother shared with a family of five. Smith had a three-story home out in the middle of a pine forest, done up like a faux-English castle that was widely held to be as tacky as a naugahyde tuxedo, but to Sandy it was a royal residence, and she had become an American princess. Then she got a driver's license and a Jaguar S convertible for Christmas. She quickly discovered the mall in Traverse City along with the online shopping possibilities on her new computer and it was off to the races.

As it turned out, Sandy had expensive tastes as well as a talent for walking all over Derek and his pleas to rein in her spending. Within a year, Smith had arranged for Sandy's mother to join them in the United States. A year after that, they built a rambling log mansion on pricey Torch Lake, "so Momma could have more room," selling their Kalkaska Kastle at a huge loss.

All of the above had cost Smith enough cash to fill one of the ore freighters that plied the Great Lakes. Then, bad luck hit him like a series of body blows in a ghetto gym. For starters, the wells on his property ran dry about the time Sandy's mom flew in from Moscow.

Fortunately, the Grand Traverse Band of Ottawa and Chippewa Indians had established a couple of casinos in the area and Smith saw a clear way forward to get back on the gravy train. He rolled the dice, then rolled it again and again, losing everything, including Sandy. Quicker than you can say snake eyes, Sandy had moved out and filed for divorce.

She felt bad about Derek Smith, but not really. Does anyone feel bad about stepping on the rungs of a ladder? Does anyone feel bad when an elevator goes down, instead of up? For Sandy, it was strictly transactional. Smith had gotten what he wanted, for a time at least, and so had she, paying her pound of flesh in the process.

"Men always think there is no price," she was fond of saying, "but there is always a price."

Smith found an easy way out of his problems. He cranked his hot tub up to 125 degrees, drank a bottle of bourbon, and sank into the water up to his chin. Within minutes, he was unconscious as a result of overheating the blood to his brain via his carotid arteries. He slipped under and, presto, no more worries. His housekeeper found him the next morning, as white as a poached fish.

Sandy was free of suspicion; she and her mother were off in Palm Springs at the time, enjoying a spa-and-shopping trip on a credit card that Derek had forgotten. With no proof of suicide, the medical examiner ruled that Derek Smith died of natural causes.

The next two years were the carefree days of a party girl around town. Sonya Rostova had changed her name to Sandy even before she left Moscow and she kept the name Smith after her divorce because she liked alliteration; it gave her a made-in-America authenticity that would be helpful in her quest for citizenship. She joined a gym and kept her figure on par with that of a Vegas showgirl. She danced like a burning flame in what passed for the town's discos. She got proficient in Vinyasa yoga and raced her Jag on the stock car circuit at the M-113 Raceway. She also moved into an apartment on Boardman Lake at the southern end of Traverse City. For the single set, it was like an earthquake had hit town.

Dream girl Sandy Smith, that's who she was when we met in Fishtown, the tourist boardwalk in the village of Leland, nestled on the shore of Lake Michigan.

I was banging out tunes on my Fender down on the boardwalk back then, hoping to collect a few Lincolns before the local busybodies chased me away. I'd gotten through most of my 20s by selling weed to tourists and working as a barista in a coffee bar, but it was playing guitar on the dock that I loved most.

It was a warm day, Indian summer, and the salmon were doing their best to leap over the dam at the start of the dock. Out of the corner of my eye I saw Sandy walking my way, past the cheese hut and the hat shop. I'd seen her before, who hadn't? She drew near, dressed in blue short shorts and a white halter top emblazoned with the logo of a Mexican beer.

I took my shot and launched into "Careless Whisper" by George Michael. I sang it low and warm, looking straight ahead, a musician enraptured by his art. It's a song about a guy getting it on with his best friend's girl and feeling so bad about it that even his feet feel guilty. As a result, he's got no rhythm and ain't ever gonna' dance again. Bummer! Women love it because it has that torn-between-two-lovers vibe that makes their toes curl.

Sandy studied me with the same sort of expression you'd find on a tourist examining a large turtle. More to the point, she stuck around, and by the last bars of the song I was convinced that I had become Orpheus, the god of song who had bewitched a lovely siren. Her pink lips opened and she moistened them with a lick of her tongue. I put everything I had into the last verse, going full-Sinatra, with not too much *crescendo*, nor too much *descrescendo*, just right. The song landed on a dime.

Sandy held up a palm and patted it with the other in an imitation of clapping. "Very nice," she said. "Can you help me?"

"Yes." Yes, I said, wondering, what would this golden goddess say? What would she ask of Orpheus, the master of song?

"I've got to take a dump," she said, squirming. "Do you know if there's a bathroom here?"

Ugh, the sky fell at that moment, but I recovered in a split second as if I was born to help beautiful women find a place to purge their bowels.

"It's over there," I gave her the hitchhiker's thumb to the public restroom by the boat launch. "The door's around the corner."

I figured that was it, but ten minutes later Sandy was back, looking much recovered. "Play some more," she said.

"What's your pleasure?"

"Do you know that song about the margaritas?"

"Sure do." I hated that song, but it was a frequent request. No street musician could get away from it, least of all a guy strumming his six-string for dollar bills on the dock.

To my surprise, Sandy sang along for a bit and her voice was not bad, sweet, actually, with a sultry Russian accent. She licked her lips and I could see she had an orange tongue, like she'd been sucking on a gumdrop or an orange soda. Then it struck me that she was just like any other goofy broad; she just happened to look like a Russian supermodel with a little more meat on her bones. I took my shot where lesser men feared to tread.

"Wow, I'm really thirsty. Do you want to get a drink?"

She did.

Thanks to the benevolence of the gods of tourism I'd made $56 passing the hat that day - a huge haul for a street musician - and we spent it all on margaritas on the patio at The Cove, a restaurant nestled against the river and its dam. Soon enough I learned that Sandy was a party girl, but a lonely one.

"Men are afraid of me," she said, chewing on a lime.

"Yeah? Why's that?" Not that I needed to ask. Sandy was so beautiful that she gave men the willies, got them all tongue-tied and squirming. She was clearly the kind of woman who was destined to hang on the arm of an ugly rock star of boundless means.

"This I don't know, but I haven't been on a date in nearly a year," she said sadly.

Suddenly I felt very warm, afraid but emboldened. Only the bold succeed, right? Sandy needed a man who wasn't afraid to wrestle with lions, and right then under the influence of three margaritas and a plate of nachos with too much hot sauce, that was me. I took the bait like one of the salmon trying to leap the dam next to where we were sitting.

"Yeah? Well consider yourself asked," I said.

"What?"

"A date. You and me, pinkie."

"Really?" She grinned, shaking her head, her long hair streaming, backlit by the sun. "You are asking *me* on a date?"

"It's your lucky day. We're on one now, aren't we?"

"What would we do?"

"For starters, a long walk on the beach."

"Oh, but that's what lovers do," she said, gazing into my eyes in reproach. She still had that innocent schoolgirl look to her eyes back then.

"We could go to a concert instead," I shrugged. "Go dancing? Movie?"

She shrugged.

"Maybe you could bang a drum with me down on the dock and we could make some more money."

I was kidding with that last bit, but you never know what turns a bored rich girl's crank, and just then, I had found it.

"Seriously? We could do that?" She lit up like a kid who'd been promised a second Christmas that afternoon.

"I've got a djembe in my Jeep."

Sandy spent the next two hours hammering the drum while I banged out tunes. She was good, she had rhythm. But I kept imagining that I was hallucinating the most beautiful woman in all of northern Michigan, and one of the richest to boot, going boonga-bonga with me, a dead-broke street player and cosmetology student. I mean, what could she possibly see in me?

But that afternoon, we went for a long walk down the five-mile crescent of Good Harbor Beach on Lake Michigan, and then we were off on a whirlwind romance with a northern Michigan flavor. We hiked to Pyramid Point to gaze at the full moon atop a 300-foot sand dune. We nibbled on blackened marshmallows, chased with jello shots around bonfires on the beach. We danced on the decks of lakefront bars, rocking in each-other's arms long after the music stopped. And as for making love and long nights of steamy sex... well, I'm not a kiss-and-tell kind of guy, but let's just say it didn't happen. Ever.

"We're saving that, Dredd, saving it for sometime special," she said primly after our fifth date, well past the time most new couples get horizontal. "Momma always told me to keep a kopeck between my knees until I'm sure that you're a real Count Vronsky, and I always listen to my Momma."

"But..."

"Oh Dredd, you don't want our relationship to be just about nookie, do you?" Her eyes filled with consternation.

"Nookie? Oh hell no, but..."

But when? I wondered after our ninth date and no sugar. For when my balls turned so blue that they fell right off? I figured that a kopeck was something similar to a dime, but who was Count Vronsky? Probably some Mr. Darcy type that all the women go on about. But I didn't tell Sandy about the condition of my aching testicles and was smart enough not to beg. I figured I'd be cool and bide my time and she would come around once she realized I was Mr. Right, or Mr. Effing Vronsky, whoever that was. Then we'd have a pent-up, week-long orgasm and then another, and another, and, well... first comes love, then comes marriage, then comes baby in a baby carriage. That was my fantasy, anyway. Funny, I'd never thought about getting married before, much less having kids, but after a month with Sandy, I wanted her in a wedding gown the way Frodo wanted to hang onto his magic ring.

In the meantime, we carried on like any couple, going to parties, biking along the lakeshore and grilling dinner in the back yard of my rental place in Cedar. Sandy liked to kiss, at least, and have her back rubbed, and that gave me hope that soon we'd be lovers.

"Oh Sandy, your kisses are sweeter than cherry wine." I actually remember saying that while panting for air.

"Ooh, I know Dredd, I know." Kiss, kiss.

But oh, the pain. Sandy was free with her kisses and her body shimmied beneath my hands, which only made me ache all the more down below my waist until I was delirious with desire for her, delirious for the day we'd consummate our love. Within a few days I completely lost the ability to think straight and my friends started asking if I was alright. I wasn't. I couldn't sleep at night, couldn't think of anything but her. I was love-struck, in much the same way that one is struck by a speeding dump truck.

Mostly our time together was cool, sometimes, anyway. We'd drive down the two blocks of Leland in Sandy's Jag with the top down, blasting Russian death metal - the worst shit in the world - at high volume on her $2,000 sound system to the outraged looks of the local brahmins. Sandy didn't care; she lived life like she only had 30 minutes left on the meter.

But sometimes, Sandy's white-hot way of living made me wonder. "Where do you think this is going?" I asked her once. "I mean, with you and me?"

Sandy only shrugged and caressed my hand. "Don't be so serious, Dredd. It's, how do you say? You're killing my buzz. We're having fun, remember? Lean back and enjoy it while it lasts."

"While it lasts?"

"All things end, Dredd. It's only a matter of when," she said, her face clouding over. "You look at me and see a beautiful woman, but I know that someday my looks will end. I'll be an old hag with saggy breasts and wrinkles all over my face, and then..."

"Alright, alright already! Like you say, let's not get too serious."

"No Dredd," she said with a wan smile. "Let's not."

Of course, through all of this I was expected to pay for our revels. Sandy was an old-fashioned Russian girl that way, and had the expectation that she would be wined and dined. A bag of marshmallows? Sure, I could afford that, and the stick to roast them and the campfire were free. But when we stepped out for a perch dinner or a night of dancing, I soon learned that svelte Sandy could drink like a hippopotamus and she only ordered top-shelf liquor. "It's a Russian thing, sweetie," she told me. "We have vodka in our veins and I like the best."

But Sandy would also guzzle stuff like root beer-flavored whisky and peanut butter schnapps, so go figure.

I had $64 in my checking account on the day we met, all the money I had in the world at the age of 28. That evaporated on day two of our romance and then I started chugging down the road of debt and ruin with my only credit card, racking up hundreds of dollars in fling money at 19 percent interest. I didn't care, I was giddy, euphoric, drugged, completely submerged in Sandy's spell and the kisses she doled out like Halloween candy. What was a little debt when you had an angel on your arm? Like I said, ours was a whirlwind romance.

Too bad it turned out to be the kind of whirlwind where a flying barn crashes into a field full of cow doody.

Three months into our love affair I was walking around town with my head swirling in the clouds, wondering how I'd round up enough cash to buy Sandy a suitable commitment ring to prove that we were going steady and that she was my official girlfriend. The pawn shop had some rings... if I pawned my guitar I could snag one. With a girl like Sandy, I figured I'd better get a gold ring instead of one of those silver and turquoise jobs. After all, she was still wearing her engagement ring from Derek Smith and it was a 24-karat gold band topped by a diamond the size of a chickpea. I had to measure up in my own small way.

But I was also wondering why Sandy wasn't returning my calls.

The only call I got was from Smokey Williams. "Hey, don't want to alarm you, but I saw your lady out driving around town with Timothy Bottom," he said.

"Alarm me? Why would that alarm me?" I replied. "We're as tight as..."

"Dude!" he interrupted. "Smell the coffee, okay? This is *Sandy* we're talking about, lit up like a Christmas tree in Bottom's Tesla Roadster. Do you know how much one of those costs?"

"No." But I got a sick feeling in my gut when Williams told me. All of my friends had hinted - broadly - for weeks that Sandy was just a tin-hearted gold-digger having a fling with a boy-toy and that I meant nothing to her, but I'd been deaf to the message. I thought they were jealous, yet now the message was starting to creep in. Timothy Bottom and my Sandy? The sick feeling spread in my guts and crept up my throat in a wave of nausea.

"Just wanted to give you a heads-up, okay?"

"Yeah, thanks." I nearly puked on my phone as Williams rang off.

SANDY BOTTOM

True, I supposed that some women might think that Bottom was a handsome guy and he probably had enough money to reach halfway to the moon. But what woman would want a guy who'd made his money peddling baby powder compared to an up-and-comer like me? I had dreadlocks past my shoulders, for Christ's sake, and could play the guitar, including all of the songs that Sandy loved. Plus, I had just graduated from cosmetology school with a glowing recommendation from my instructor. I was going to be a barber! Sandy was my girlfriend, she'd even said so, and she'd met all my friends. I'd even written a song about her.

But I called her 41 times that day, once for every date we'd gone out on over the three months we'd been together, and all I got was a new message on her voice mail:

"Sorry sweeties," she said in her most trenchant Russian accent, "but I'm out having fun with someone exciting and new. I'll get back to you someday, maybe, but don't count on it."

Wow, that was cold, and I couldn't help thinking that Sandy meant her voicemail message for me in particular. Was she ghosting me? Seriously?

That night the message slid like a dagger through my heart as I stared at Sandy's Facebook profile on a laptop borrowed from Smokey Williams. It said she was "In a relationship," and not with me. Sandy had never posted anything about being in a relationship with me and that rubbed salt in the wound. Yet there she was on the Home page, cuddled cheek-to-cheek with my new nemesis, Timothy Frickin' Bottom, with a smile so big on her face that her eyes seemed to burn right through the screen. By the second day it was clear I'd been dumped. Canceled.

After things fell apart with Sandy, I decided to take the advice of various old bluesmen and country singers and head south. Way south. Way down to Mexico where I could be free, to quote Jimi Hendrix. Past where the train ran out of tracks, to quote Marshall Tucker. Down beyond the sun, to quote Robert Johnson. If I found a river of whiskey down there, I'd swim to the bottom and drink my way back up.

The tracks of life had led me nowhere so far, except to dead ends. After two years of beauty school I had a cosmetology diploma that was so fresh the ink was still wet, but after giving a haircut or two it turned out I no longer cared to be a barber. I'd been a star pitcher with a killer fastball on the Traverse City Central High baseball team when I was 17 and had tried out for the local Beach Bums minor league team, but never made the cut. Playing guitar on street corners had a certain *je ne sais qua*, but didn't pay the bills. At the age of 28, I was at a crossroads, and not the one where Robert Johnson inked a deal with the devil.

The next day I sold my Jeep to Smokey to cover my credit card debt and scrape up a little traveling money. I snagged a weathered tent from a garage sale, tossed a sleeping bag in my pack and hitched a ride out of town with my guitar.

I figured that if I couldn't have Sandy then at least I could outrun her. I caught a cheap flight from Chicago to Tijuana and then a series of buses to Ensenada, Loreto and La Paz down the 900 desert miles of the Baja California peninsula. From there I took the night ferry across the Sea of Cortez to Topolobampo and on south to Mazatlan, San Pancho, Sayulita, Puerto Vallarta, Barra de Navidad, Acapulco, Zihuatenengo, Puerto Escondido, Zipolite, Oaxaca, San Cristobel... all the way down to Lake Atitlan in Guatemala, always heading further south, further away from Sandy and the poison bathing my soul.

I wandered south of the border for months trying to forget her, but I might as well have tried squeezing my brains out through my ears for all the good it did. For me, Sandy was quite literally unforgettable.

I passed through a succession of hostels and campgrounds strung along the foot-burning sands of Mexico's southern coast. The hostels were all the same: a palapa roof or grove of palm trees just off the beach to shelter a dozen or so ragged tents amid a lace of sun-weathered hammocks. The price was right, $2 a night for those who were really going the spartan route, sand fleas included free of charge.

There were long nights at open-air beach bars, drowsing over beers in the amber glow of coconut shell lamps, trying to stare a hole through the bar's mirror lined with bottles of booze. Trying to forget Sandy. Times beyond count I woke up in flop sweat and naked atop my grungy sleeping bag in the arms of some backpacker chick, both of us still drunk or high from the night before, often with the taste of vomit or something fishy in my mouth. Turns out there were a lot of women down that way who were trying to escape their own version of Sandy; usually, the guy's name was Mike, though sometimes he was a she.

Lake Atitlan was more than the travel website promised. I arrived there to find 18 miles of deep blue nestled in the cradle of three volcanoes swathed in palms. Aldous Huxley had visited in the 1930s, calling it "the most beautiful lake in the world," equal to that of Lake Como in Italy. I caught a *launcha* out of the tourist trap town of Panajachel for a kid-ney-shattering ride across the bumpy waves to San Marcos and my new home, intending to stay there forever.

Walking up the pathway from the dock, I got the impression that the world had tilted sideways, dumping half the hippies on earth into the lanes of San Marcos. Heavily tattooed dudes festooned with dreads and ear spacers lounged on the narrow pathway into town, accompanied by thin-as-a-wisp neo-hip-pie chicks in sheer cotton and nose rings. There was blood all over the sidewalk from where some street mutt had throt-tled a chicken the night before, along with murals of Mayan gods, mermaids, angels and such, painted all along the dingy concrete wall heading into town. Little Mayan ladies with braids down to their waists and babies slung to their backs were tucked against the wall, selling hand-made textiles and necklaces, displayed on patches of brightly colored cloth.

Further on, two scarlet and emerald macaws were perched on a macramé ring outside an open-air coffee house, where the patrons lounged on pillows spread across the floor. An untended gringo toddler ran down the pathway, laughing and gurgling in his low-hanging diaper. The air was heavy with the skunky musk of good reefer and incense. At the time it seemed like my kind of place, and with my shoulder-length dreads and beat-to-shit guitar I fit right in. San Marcos was exactly the sort of place where I could live *la pura vida* and forget old whatshername.

I got a room at the cheapest hostel in town. It had a foam rubber pad for a mattress and plywood walls that were so thin you could hear a mouse squeak next door at night. The toilet in the room on the other side of the wall was adjacent to my bed, so every night I heard tinkles, grunts, groans and titanic cascades and splashes courtesy of *la turista*. This, along with the ruttings of college kids, which could go on for hours.

That didn't last long. I spread the word around town that I was a barber, but no one wanted a haircut in San Marcos where they'd been working on their dreadlocks for a decade or more. That, and it turned out you could get a haircut in Guatemala for about $2, not enough for a wandering gringo to live on. Down to my last ten quetzals, I got a job bartending at a yoga retreat, the Last Resort, trading two nights' work each week for a treehouse crib that offered a partial view of the lake. Interesting people came and went and I figured I was set for life, or barring that, at least ten years in the tropics.

I spent the next couple of years as a sort of big brother bartender, offering life lessons to kids who were only a few years younger than me. I got along well with the many trustafarians and rastaphonians in town, and they were generally free with their tips after getting buttered up with the kind of New-Agey jive talk that I'd grown up with. "Jah, mon, irie, etc. ..." I even got on a bit of an anti-hookworm crusade, urging the hippies to quit walking around the village barefoot through the squishy leavings of various dogs, chickens and pigs. I hiked the local trails, worked on my Standing Tree Pose, and crashed whatever parties and drum circles I could find in the string of villages along the lakeshore.

I also made a discovery that proved to be on par with a college education. In the resort's lending library of greasy paperbacks and inscrutable novels in French and German, someone had left behind a trove of old-school detective thrillers from the likes of Mickey Spillane, Raymond Chandler, Dashiel Hammett, James M. Cain, Elmore Leonard, James Elroy, Loren Estelman, John D. McDonald and Jim Thompson. There were even some Doc Savage pulps, two Nancy Drews and a few Hardy Boys hardcovers. Beneath a stack of old *Condé Nast Travel* magazines I found more than 60 novels on the lives and times of America's hard-boiled dicks and how to stick it to whodunnit. I found out later that most of these books were no longer carried in public libraries or book stores, so it was kind of like discovering the Lost Dutchman Mine of mystery fiction.

It was a slow warm-up, but by the time I finished Chandler's *Killer in the Rain* I was as hooked as a crack whore on pulp mystery novels. Something chimed within me and soon I couldn't get enough of the sleaze, the snappy patter and bent plot twists. I tore through the trove of books, mostly reading in a rope hammock strung from two palm trees overlooking the lake. While the retreat's customers were getting their chakras aligned and practicing Wheel Pose, I was mixing it up with mugs and molls on the mean streets of L.A., New York, Detroit and wherever tough guys hung their hats. Gradually, I picked up on the street smarts of shamuses like Marlowe, Spade and Hammer.

There was even some new stuff buried in the stash: a half dozen James Pattons, two Sue Graftons and one Barbara Cornwell. But it was the old stuff that got me hooked, the hard-boiled, underdog, tough-talking, name-taking private dicks who were just shy of being criminals themselves, forever getting blackjacked, shivved and beaten senseless when they weren't dishing it out themselves, stopping at nothing, getting played for saps, taking it on the kisser, busting someone's chops, blowing some perv's head off with a .45 and every so often, foiling a black-hearted, two-timing, blond femme fatale dame like...

Oh Jeezus! I found myself slowly seduced by the idea of slipping into those brogans, trading my dreads for a fedora, and wrapping myself in the snug trenchcoat of a hard-boiled dick, like a time traveling shamus straight outta' 1944.

Who could have been reading this stuff in a New Age hippie colony like San Marcos? I asked around but didn't get any answers.

Little did I know, my education had just begun.

In Which I Get Woke

Shaman Don Juan del Pedro was as wispy as a ghost with ginger-brown hair that fell in shreds to his armpits. He had a high, piping voice with a touch of rasp to it and my first impression was of poor Ben Gunn, the castaway in the *Treasure Island* flick from the '30s.

He looked like he weighed about 98 pounds and was as old as the Bible, though he claimed to be 68. He wore the dirty white PJs of a Guatemalan peasant with a sling over his shoulder and a sisal rope for a belt.

Shaman Don wafted into the bar one afternoon in the rainy season, just back from a three-month stay teaching nude yoga on the beach in Zipolite. It's a village on the Pacific Ocean in the state of Oaxaca, Mexico that attracts overweight, middle-aged Europeans who wish to sling their tubs in the sun, *au naturel*. There are some sights there that you can't unsee, including wrinkly old Don in his birthday suit, but I digress.

Shaman Don cocked his head at the door, looking sharply right and left, wary as a bird before floating up to the bar where I was wiping down glasses. He sat down beneath a string of Tibetan prayer flags and flipped a business card on the bar. It had a line of type alongside a picture of a grinning skull:

SANDY BOTTOM

Shaman Don Juan del Pedro, CSP • Crystal Skull Practitioner

"Stand me a drink, will you brutha'? Chivas Regal with a hint of lime. I'm thirsty as an old bone."

I was about to tell him that the patrons of the Last Resort had to lay down a credit card if they wanted to run a tab and there were no free drinks on my watch, but something in his eyes set me back. They were as clear as water and just as colorless.

"Sure, whatever you say." I pulled him a glass of our cheapest beer and added a lime wedge.

He gave a grimace. "Enh, beer," but he drank it, sipping as gently as a hummingbird at a lily. I went on wiping glasses, sneaking a peek now and then at the women practicing Warrior Pose across the way. I'd all but forgotten the old timer when he piped up ten minutes later.

"I got a feeling about you," he said.

"That right?"

"Yeah, and Don Pedro feels it too."

"Can't say that I know him."

"Yeah, but he knows you, friend. He is a powerful sorcerer embodied in a prison of stone and he has led me to you, here in the here and now."

"Hmm. The here and now, huh?" I should have cut him off right then, but I was more bored than usual that afternoon. I'd gotten a bit tired of skinny people and sunshine. Tired of lecturing college girls about walking barefoot in the dirt. Tired of the hare-brained plans of bare-chested young men in dhotis and man-buns.

I bit. "So who's Don Pedro?"

The old guy downed the last of his beer in a gulp and motioned for another.

"He's the Crystal Skull."

"That right?"

"That's right," he said with a touch of impatience, "and I am a Crystal Skull practitioner. If you submit, Don Pedro will have you as his neophyte."

"I don't know what that is."

"His student. His newbie."

By now I knew enough New Age talking points to keep up my end of the conversation.

"So you're a shaman, right?"

He nodded.

"You ever talk to dead people?"

"No, not much," he said in a growl. "Dead folks hold no attraction for me. I've tried now and then but they just want to send messages to their loved-ones. I don't have time for that. I have shamanic duties to attend to, such as tracking down neophytes for Don Pedro."

"What's my spirit animal then?"

Shaman Don answered in a blink. "A tapir."

"Wrong, it's a gazelle," I said. A passing witch from Argentina had told me as much. She called herself a *bruja*, but was hedging her bets by seeking a fine arts degree at the University of Buenaventura Aires in case the bottom fell out of the witchcraft business.

"Gazelle? Get real. That's the kind of thing some woman would tell you," he waved.

"You got me there."

The test went on.

"What's the Holy Grail made of?"

"Too easy," he said, "give me something harder."

"How did Gandalf defeat the Balrog?"

"How should I know? I'm a shaman, not a wizard."

"What's on page 138 of the I Ching?"

"Bean paste."

He got up and strolled over to the resort's free lending library of tattered paperbacks and pulled the 1965 edition of the *I Ching* from the shelf, the one with the plain gray cover and yellow letters on the title. It's a fortune-telling book of sorts: you toss three yarrow sticks, or coins, and the *I Ching* provides some inscrutable wisdom that's totally worthless, but sounds like a way forward.

"What'd I tell ya?" he said, holding the book open to page 138. Sure enough, there was a brown smear of *frijole* on the page.

That got me. It wasn't until months later that I realized that Shaman Don had a touch of bean dip on his thumb when he retrieved the book. He'd picked it up while nibbling on the nachos at the bar.

"One last question," I said uneasily. "What's the color of my aura?"

"Charcoal gray right now, though it could warm up plenty if you didn't have a broken heart," he replied.

Touché. Shaman Don Juan del Pedro had peered into the core of me, coming up with a nugget.

"Anyone could figure that out," I blustered. "Everyone's had a broken heart sometime or other."

"Yes my friend, but yours is bleeding a river and Don Pedro told me the bottom of the river is sandy, very sandy. You're drowning in the sand, being sucked down. Even your eyes are sandy with sorrow. Only Don Pedro can dig you out of your heartache and get to the bottom of your troubles."

Suddenly the bar grew as chilly as Greenland in the fall with a howling wind blowing up from the lake. Shaman Don eyed me with a *gotcha!* look in his eyes, sly, very sly, and suddenly I felt like a little boy, uncertain and afraid. *Sandy, very sandy....* How could he know about my unrequited love for Sandy? He hadn't said it but somehow he'd given me the shamanic whamma-jamma to show that he knew. And that last bit about the *bottom* of my troubles... Whoa!

Shaman Don leaned in and whispered. "I can teach you things friend, things that would blow Harry Potter's socks off if you let me. He who masters the Crystal Skull is master of himself. And he who masters himself is master of all masters."

"Master of all masters?"

Shaman Don nodded solemnly and motioned for another beer. "If you please," he said.

I had to admit, Don Juan del Pedro's shaman-talk went a step beyond the hippie drivel I was used to at the bar. Plus, he was freaky as a banana spider, but in a good way. And, like I said, I was bored that afternoon and everyone at the retreat had taken a *launcha* over to San Pedro to hit the ATM and the Sunday barbecue. I had plenty of time to listen.

Shaman Don launched into a long tale of his many adventures South of the Border. Back in '68 he and three women had rambled south along the Oaxacan coast in a Volkswagen van, stumbling upon the fishing village of Zipolite. It was a dump back then, the kind of place where chickens ran in and out of the palm huts and wife-beating was considered socially acceptable. But Don and his harem saw potential. Pooling $600, they bought an old hacienda that had been wrecked in a hurricane. The place was a nest of spiders and bugs with banana trees growing through the roof, but its cinderblock walls were still standing and they had been reinforced with rebar.

"We had that place all fixed up with a new palapa roof in three months," he recalled. "Then I made a call home on the only phone in town and told my friends that we'd created a utopia on the southern coast of Mexico. That's all it took to get the place rolling."

Thirty years later there were funky hotels, hostels and restaurants all up and down the mile-long beach of Zipolite. Then came the nudists, shrugged off as harmless by the Mexican army.

"It all got a bit old after awhile," Shaman Don said. "I moved on to the Guate and that's when I met Don Pedro."

"The Crystal Skull."

He nodded. "He was given to me by a shaman up in the hills along with the pathway to wisdom. His name was Shaman Salvadore Don Juan de LaMancha. Good guy."

"What kind of wisdom?"

"Insight, mostly," he waved. "Intuition. The nature of existence, that sort of thing."

The bar got busy and I moved on to filling orders. When I turned around Shaman Don was gone.

SANDY BOTTOM

But the next day he was back. He asked for another Chivas Regal. "The 18-year-old stuff if you've got it."

"Let's see some green first."

He shrugged. "A shaman does not need money. He lives on the charity of others as do the wandering gurus of India."

"I see. So you have a rice bowl, I imagine?"

Shaman Don gave me a sly smile. He reached into the long sling he wore over his shoulder and pulled out a tin plate. "You bet I do, brother. Can you fill this for me?"

That got me. It was a good trick pulling that plate out of his ass and I suppose that's why I went along with all that followed. I filled his plate with nachos and salsa and poured him a beer.

"You're going to get me in trouble if I keep giving you free beer," I grumbled.

"There's a way past that, you know."

"Yeah? What's that?"

"The way of Don Pedro."

"Crystal Skull."

Shaman Don nodded. "Don Pedro whispered to me last night that you get free classes here: yoga, meditation, levitation, even saltwater nasal douches and access to the sweat lodge whenever you want, am I right?"

I nodded. "It's part of my pay. Sometimes even a massage, if I'm lucky."

"Well then, my friend, Don Pedro says he will teach you the way of the Crystal Skull through me."

"And why would I want that?"

"Don Pedro told me you crave insight, direction, a way forward," he said gravely. "You're in the trap of non-existence here - you've lost your path. The one you're on is *sandy* and troubled, leading you to the *bottom* of the astral plane. Don Pedro can lead you back to your dharma."

Astral plane? My dharma? My one true path in life? If the old weasel only knew. An expression settled on my face like a dog that swallowed a toad as I thought of my lost love, Sandy.

As if reading my thoughts, Shaman Don leaned in and whispered, "He can help you with that too."

"With Sandy?" I whispered, breaking into a sweat. "No way."

He nodded, closed his eyes and clasped his fingers. "Even so."

"I'll think about it," I said glumly.

Shaman Don took a swig of his beer and gave a polite belch. "Well, don't think about it too long, because Don Pedro is a proud spirit and brooks no hesitation."

"So when do I meet Don Pedro?"

"First your answer my friend. First, your heart-felt answer."

"Like I said, I'll think about it."

That night terrible dreams came to me. Sandy was flying over my hammock like a witch in a long white skirt that kept smothering me as she careened and laughed, her toenails digging at my chest. I awoke in a sweat to find the mosquito net had parted and spent the next hour awake, swatting in futility at the air. A weird laugh echoed down from the hills about 3 a.m. and then some jackass ignited a bomb-sized firecracker over at the church yard. I finally fell asleep around 5, only to have a dream of Sandy again, crawling up my chest like an iguana, her impossibly long tongue flickering at me. Then the roosters started crowing as the sun cracked the horizon and a cat ran under my hammock, fighting with a rat. Oh boy, what a night. I crawled out of the sack and stepped on a scorpion with a crunch. Goddamnit!

Shaman Don was waiting at the bar when I hobbled in with my foot bandaged. I was working the day shift and wasn't happy about it. I had a hammering hangover from the night before and my foot was pulsing like I'd kicked a porcupine.

"I woke up this morning and I got myself a be-ah!" he sang.

I gave him a black look. "Don't start."

He turned and walked out of the bar without a word.

Much later I realized that Shaman Don was just playing the

fish, and that would be me. But I spent the rest of the day mulling over what he'd said. It was true, after more than two years in San Marcos my life had entered a state of stasis. I'd read a lot of detective novels and could do Standing Tree Pose effortlessly. I had a lot of girlfriends on Facebook and a steady gig playing old songs by the Eagles every Wednesday at the inn up the way, but I didn't have Sandy and still hadn't come to grips with the fact that I never would. Shaman Don Juan and his Crystal Skull friend Don Pedro, were right. I was in need of insight, direction, a way out of non-existence.

That afternoon after work I hobbled around the narrow walkways of the village looking for the old guy. Someone said he'd taken a *launcha* to San Pedro la Laguna and would be gone for a few days up in the mountains, doing whatever it was that shamans did up there. But I turned a corner down near the boat launch and there he was, sitting on a rock wall with one ear pressed to a coconut.

"Shhh..." he motioned, listening. He held up one finger and listened on through a hole in the shell. Two minutes went by and he handed it to me without a word.

I pressed it to my ear. "What am I listening for?" I whispered.

"The sound of the universe breathing," he replied.

I shrugged, put the husk to my ear and listened. At first there was nothing, just that hollow roar you get from a seashell.

"Really? That's it?" I handed him the shell.

"You didn't hear it? The keening? Try again."

I put the coconut to my ear and listened longer this time. We were in a quiet place on the jungle path and the wind had died on the lake that day. After a time I began to hear something; like Shaman Don said, it was a sort of keening sound, like a long *wheeeeee*... It kept growing louder and louder - *WHEEEEE!* - until I had to take my ear away.

"Damn!"

"Amazing, isn't it?" He gazed at me with his colorless eyes, looking quite saintly beneath a bougainvillea tree.

"Kind of," I admitted. "So when do I meet Don Pedro?"

"Are you ready for that? It's no small thing."

"I'm ready to switch gears, I know that."

"Then, little brother, you must know that there's no going back," he said gravely.

"Just don't call me little brother."

"Don Pedro will select your neophyte name."

"Whatever."

"From your heart."

I examined my heart and realized it was dying. What did I have to lose? I wasn't an old dog yet; I could learn new tricks.

I gave Shaman Don my most serious look. "From my heart," I said.

He gave me a goofy, sideways grin that went on for so long that I began to wonder if he'd fallen asleep with his eyes wide shut. Then slowly, he reached into the dirty sling around his neck and pulled out an object the size of a hand grenade.

"This is Don Pedro," he said.

It was a crystal skull. Well, not really. It was a crudely carved skull made out of pearly white alabaster, but Shaman Don called it crystal, so that's what we went with.

"This is just a silly-ass skull." I protested.

"And that was just a coconut with a hole in it, yet you heard the sound of the universe breathing, right? Trust me, there's about 50 gigawatts of power in this silly-ass skull, as you call it. You just need to learn how to summon it."

"What is it, like a Mayan chatbot?"

"Huh?"

"It's an app that talks back to you. It's a computer thing"

"Oh, you mean that online shit. No! This is old school, really old! Ancient. There's none of your online trickery or artifice. The Crystal Skull Don Pedro makes a direct connection to your body, mind and soul, right down your chakras to the lowest levels of existence itself, and..."

"Okay, okay, I get it. It's one of those cosmic deals."

"Exactly."

SANDY BOTTOM

Well, you can't live in San Marcos without some belief in Mayan magic rubbing off on you, and I'd heard enough stories and weird tales over the past two years of tending bar to start believing in some of it myself. That afternoon over shots of Quetzelteca, Shaman Don told me the skull was a pre-Colombian artifact that had been dug from a Mayan temple by his own teacher, Shaman Salvadore Don Juan de La Mancha, back in the 1940s. The temple was concealed under a moss-covered mound way out in the jungle past the far mountains, which Salvadore had found while searching for gold. He'd had it appraised by an antiquities dealer in Antigua and was told that it was more than 4,000 years old.

"There had been an offer to buy the skull for more than $10,000, but on a whim, Salvadore said no."

"Seriously? For this thing? I would have taken the cash."

"Then you would have been a bigger fool than you appear, because that's when Don Pedro began talking to him," Shaman Don said. "Not literally, of course, but in his thoughts."

"Bullshit."

Without a word, he handed me the skull and I rolled it around in my palm. It did feel a bit warm and I swear I felt a tingle. It had a comfortable heft to it, like you could bean someone pretty good if you gave it a fling.

"Do you want to get woke or don't you?" Shaman Don gave me a cockeyed look.

"Woke? You mean like up on things? Aware that you weren't aware in the past but are totally aware now? I'm already woke."

"Not by half," he scoffed.

For real? I twirled a tendril of the dreadlocks I'd been growing since the age of 12. I was the most happenin' dude in San Marcos, in my mind, anyway. Everyone in town knew me, even the *chapina* ladies who swept the streets each morning. Who was more woke than me? Still, Shaman Don had planted the seed of doubt in my mind and it grew faster than Jack's beanstalk.

"Okay, so?" I countered.

"You do yoga, right?"

"Yeah."

"And when you stand on your head, you believe it's charging up your chakras, am I right?"

"I guess so." Actually, I didn't remember my yoga teacher telling me that, but it sounded good.

"And you believe that somewhere on this earth you have one true soul mate waiting for you, am I right?"

I thought of Sandy and got a twinge. "Yeah, maybe."

"And when you do a three-day fast and get an enema, you believe it's cleansing all of the bad karma and toxins out of your body, am I right?"

"I don't do enemas."

"Well you really should try it! But let me think. Somewhere along the way someone did your astrological chart and you believed they nailed it, am I right?"

"Yeah," I said glumly, "but not with a happy outcome." An astrologer back in Traverse City had drawn up our horoscope and discovered that Sandy's Venus was conjunct my Mars in the sign of Libra. Plus, my moon was conjunct her sun in Leo. That meant we were total soul mates and that Sandy should have been madly in love with me, like I was with her.

"There was this woman back home and our charts showed that we were practically a jelly roll, all wrapped up in each-other like strawberry jam and pound cake, but it didn't pan out," I explained. "It was a real bummer."

"But still you believed it, didn't you?" Shaman Don insisted. "And your dreams of this woman may yet come true, because the stars never lie. Never! Trust me, the Crystal Skull will secure the jelly roll of your dreams."

The jelly roll of my dreams? That sounded pretty bent, but what did I have to lose? Maybe Shaman Don was right; it was time to get woke.

My training began at 4 a.m. the next day. Shaman Don arranged for a three-wheeled tuk-tuk to take us to the ramshackle village of Santa Clara and the trailhead to the Indian's Nose.

SANDY BOTTOM

It's a mountain overlooking Lake Atitlan with an elevation of more than 9,000 feet that looks like its namesake. Shaman Don called it by its Mayan name, Rupalaj K'istalin. "Sounds like RuPaul kissin'," he said.

There were a bunch of tourists up at the top who'd paid $90 each for the pleasure of watching the sun rise over Lake Atitlan, but Shaman Don motioned me down a goat path and we found a quiet place overlooking the lake ringed by volcanoes.

He pulled out the skull and held it out to me. "This is yours now."

"Seriously? I thought you said this thing was worth ten grand."

Shaman Don shrugged. "Money means nothing to a shaman, and you are on that sacred path now. Just remember, if you sell the skull, bad karma will land on you with the gravity of Jupiter. Why do you think Shaman Salvadore gave it to me? Someday you will pass it on to your own neophyte and its name will change to the Crystal Skull Don Bumpo."

It made sense, and again the skull felt warm in my hand with a bit of a tingle running down the base of my thumb. Frankly, it was a bit scary.

"So what do I do with it?"

"You meditate with this and over time, Don Pedro speaks to you, Grasshopper." Shaman Don said.

"Grasshopper?"

"That is your spirit name now," he intoned darkly. "But like a mantra of holy meditation you must not share it with anyone. It's an unnameable secret, a thing that only you and the spirits may know."

"Can't I have a better name than that?"

"What? Like Cricket? Salamander? Grasshopper is cool! Own it."

"What was your spirit name? Centipede?"

Shaman Don frowned. "Not funny. Shaman says: you can't share your spirit name. This is just between me, you and the skull."

And so I became Grasshopper, and Shaman Don taught me an ancient form of Mayan meditation that he said had been taught to him by Shaman Salvadore Don Juan de La Mancha and hundreds of shamans and sorcerers before him dating back thousands of years.

There was nothing special about the technique. You simply held the crystal skull to your forehead round about your third eye, also known as the light-sensing pineal gland at the center of your brain, and Shaman Don would utter a phrase to meditate on. At some point, the Crystal Skull Don Pedro would offer an insight and you were done for the day. Since my mind tended to wander, I tried to get Don Pedro to spill the beans within a half hour or so.

The talking points that Shaman Don gave me tended to be on the inscrutable side. He'd give me a single line to think about and I'd have to dispel all other thoughts, rooting around in my head for some key to the wisdom invoked. "Life is like a beanstalk, isn't it?" That was one, along with "One road, two journeys" and "the eagle with one wing flapping." Some had a non-spiritual bent: "three years in the Mexican army"... a black cat bone and a mojo too"... the flight of the ostrich"... "turtle feathers"... It would have all passed for drunken gibberish if it didn't have a shamanic edge to it.

One day I meditated on the world's longest word: pneumonoultramicroscopicsilicovolcanoconiosis, a lung disease that comes from inhaling particles of silica belched out of a volcano. "It's fitting, isn't it?" Don said, "considering we have so many volcanoes around here."

Of course, the Crystal Skull Don Pedro never spoke to me directly. After all, he was just a chunk of alabaster with his jaws permanently chiseled in place. But when I meditated, the answers to the daily riddles did arise in my mind.

We'd have a beer or three on my dime at the Last Resort's bar every night and talk about the day's lesson.

"The answers come unbidden, don't they?" Shaman Don remarked over his fourth Dos Equis on our second week of training.

"Unbidden? I guess so, though I did have some trouble with that black cat bone thing," I replied.

"Yeah, that's a tough one, but you can come back to that later when your shamanic powers have gathered like a storm."

"Mmm," I nodded. It was true, I did feel like I was becoming a bit more of a shaman under Don's tutelage because he had many wild tales of healing ceremonies, exotic drug trips, invisible beings and holy orgies to share. But I can't say that my shamanic powers were "gathering like a storm."

One thing that was gathering was Shaman Don's bar tab, which I marked with a line on a notepad behind the bar. My own beers were on the house, but management required me to pay for Don's at a buck a pop.

"Say, I've been meaning to ask you, why are we doing only one riddle a day?" I said, hoping to move the process along.

Shaman Don burped and gazed into the depths of his beer bottle with a bleary right eye, like it was a telescope to the spirit world. "You can't hurry the spirits, Grasshopper," he mumbled. "It may not feel like it, but this is powerful medicine you're soaking up each day and your mind is like a transistor. You don't want to burn it out."

The Crystal Skull Don Pedro never did reveal why life is like a beanstalk, but I figured out the rest of them, sort of. Take pneumonoultramicroscopicsilicovolcanoconiosis, for instance. After meditating on it for a bit, Don Pedro told me not to go breathing in dust particles from exploding volcanoes. It was simple stuff, really. Gradually, I began to fill up with insights and could feel my sense of intuition growing stronger.

But sometimes I cheated, like with that black cat bone thing. I meditated on it a couple of times with no result and eventually looked it up online. It turns out that certain African sorcerers believe that black cats contain a magical bone that brings good luck. It's a hoodoo belief that worked its way into blues tunes by the likes of Muddy Waters. Also, a reminder to stay well-hidden if you're a black cat anywhere near a sorcerer with a skinning knife.

It sounds nuts, but my training was no crazier than what the New Age seekers were doing in the pyramids made out of PVC pipe and vinyl tarps in San Marcos. They believed in the power of the crystals hanging around their necks and the health benefits of aromatherapy vapors drifting around their hammock dormitories. I, at least, had some results that were clarifying my mind and enhancing my intuition, or so I thought.

Word got around that I was a Crystal Skull practitioner in touch the spirit world and had immense shamanic powers. Some of the girls hanging out at the bar said I had a new light in my eyes and that I had become a "peaceful warrior," which I quickly learned was code for "you're hot, let's ball tonight." The shaman thing helped considerably with my love life, easing the pain of Sandy's memory as one eager backpacker babe after another sidled up to me in the bar. Mostly, it was just holding hands and kissing down at the dock after long soulful talks at sundown, but a few wanted a touch of the magic wand, for which of course, I was grateful to oblige.

Strangely, Shaman Don wasn't happy with this latter bit. "Don't be a tool, Grasshopper," he fumed. "These women are taking advantage of you, draining your spiritual power. They are using you."

"That's a bit disingenuous, coming from a guy who taught yoga in his birthday suit in Zipolite," I said dryly. "As the saying goes, they can use me until they use me up, if you want to meditate on that one."

Don snorted. "Do not abuse your power, Grasshopper. I sense that Don Pedro has grown strong within you, but do not test him, or me."

"I just don't want to lose my sense of humor."

"Trust me, women can drive you crazy, even if you're a shaman," he said bitterly.

"I thought you said I'd end up being the master of all masters."

"Yeah, but that doesn't mean you're not human. You can still end up on some gal's little finger like a pinkie ring. It's simple biology. As soon as a man gets an erection, his brain blows a fuse and he loses the ability to think straight. Understand this: your dick is one big on-and-off switch."

"Whatever you say, Obi-Wan."

But I had to admit, that's exactly what Sandy had done to me.

To his credit, Shaman Don never asked for any payment. He went on begging at wood-fired pizza joints and for tacos and beans at the few restaurants around town. Sometimes he'd scrounge bananas or get handouts from the church.

"Oh, no worries, mate. But if you like, you can keep the beers coming," he said when I asked what I owed him. So I kept on pouring. Every afternoon he'd come by and tank up, bringing an insightful phrase or riddle for the next the day. He quoted Rumi, Schiller, Buddha, Whitman, Jesus, Crowley, Dylan, Lord Byron, Nietzshe, Goethe, Kipling, Lennon, Ringo, Marx (both Groucho and Karl), various angels, bodhissatvas and Muhammad. Every day there was something new to think about in the company of Don Pedro. Later on I learned that it had all been lifted from a paperback called *Shamanism for Ding-Dongs*, but at the time it all seemed quite profound and I felt that my inner man was being nourished with spiritual wisdom.

In some ways, meditating with Don Pedro made me feel like a toddler prattling on a toy telephone, like I was talking, "Ba ba boo boo?" to amuse my parents. But I kept at it. At one of our nightly sessions at the bar, Shaman Don explained that I was storing up wisdom in my spirit battery that would transform me into a powerful shaman and the "master of all masters."

"But aren't I supposed to be learning how to heal people and talk to the dead?" I protested. "I thought that's what shamans did in primitive societies."

"Primitive societies? Bosh! Does it look like we're living in a primitive society to you?" Don waved grandly and sipped his beer.

"Well, kind of," I said, thinking about the hippie denizens of

San Marcos, the chickens and feral dogs in the lanes and the general anarchy of the place.

"No, no, forget all that. You're a *Mayan* shaman and their tradition is all about building insights to help the befuddled. Now, if you want to get involved with actually healing people, you can do a sort of shaman 2.0 course, but we'd have to beat the bushes to find someone at that level. Sadly, my own master never imparted the healing magic to me."

"Makes sense," I replied, "and I like the insight part."

"Let's have another beer and think on it."

We did, and I actually intensified my practice because meditating with the Crystal Skull Don Pedro seemed to be eroding my memories of Sandy, washing that bad witch out of my head where she'd been swanning around for more than two years now. No matter how many women I met, no matter how many late night kisses on the dock or village dances, there would be friggin' phantom Sandy Bottom lying in my hammock at the Last Resort after midnight, waiting for me to brood over her again and again. Where had I gone wrong? Was she really in love with Timothy Bottom, or did she secretly pine for me? Would I ever see her again?

"Hope not," the Crystal Skull whispered to me in my dreams.

This went on for more than six months and I got as silly as the locals, walking around bare-chested, dressed in dhoti pajamas and sandals with my dreads piled high in a big guru man-bun and with a necklace of seed pods hanging around my neck. Then I got full arm tattoos with intertwining vines, flowers, a hummingbird and some Mayan symbols and hieroglyphics inked in from my wrists to my neck. Plus the flying monkey bearing thunderbolts on my chest. I was only about a month away from strolling around town barefoot with a parrot or an iguana on my shoulder, and then I'd be truly lost.

If I seem relatively normal now, then you've got to understand that I was raised as a feral hippie child, so getting a boatload of tattoos seemed a perfect fit for my plan to spend the rest of my life as a bartender in a yoga retreat.

SANDY BOTTOM

Status-wise, I was a rock star in San Marcos, even though the whole town was only about two hundred yards square. I caught lithe women of the very attractive sort casting sideways glances in me in the cafés as they sipped their bubble tea and nibbled at their bean sprouts. Some would sidle up to me and initiate conversations and I'd respond like a wise, all-knowing guru. I was shaky on my credentials as a part-time shaman and secretly I thought it was all bullshit anyway, but it was fun for a couple of months until I learned that shamanism runs more along the lines of psychotherapy.

Gradually, the weight of being a local celebrity became too much for me. I got tired of hearing the sound of one hand clapping and being called a peaceful warrior by gullible young women in full goddess mode. I got tired of playing "Tequila Sunrise" and "Hotel California" at my Wednesday night gig at the bar. Tired of chicken tacos and *frijoles*. Late nights talking about the corn goddess Chicomecoatl and other Mayan deities had me yawning instead of enthralled. I even got tired of smoking weed.

It also turned out that the women who wanted my services as a shaman were mostly interested in finding a shoulder to cry on about their ex-lovers, their issues with their mothers, their time in foster care, and other gist for therapy that wasn't in my wheelhouse. Thoughts of hanging up my shingle as a shaman evaporated after the third foxy lady confessed that she had slept with her step-brother and didn't know what to do about it. As it happened, neither did I.

Even San Marcos got old. You could walk from one end of town to the other in five minutes and that's where you had to stay, since it was risky walking around in the jungle outside of its limits. Dozens of gringos had been robbed on the jungle trails by impoverished peasants bearing machetes and that tended to be a buzz-kill. There's only so much free time you can spend in a hammock reading detective novels and despite my plan to stay on forever, my feet started itching to wander.

Thoughts of Sandy came back to haunt me: she was real,

she had brass, an unapologetic Russian gold digger with a tin heart who was more of a mercenary than a goddess. If I had become a peaceful warrior and a shaman thanks to the sorcerer Don Juan del Pedro and the Crystal Skull, then Sandy was the Valkyrie bitch goddess I still longed for.

I upped my consumption of hard-boiled detective novels, reading them in my hammock at night on my e-tablet. I prowled the mean streets of the Bronx, L.A., Hollywood, Newark, Detroit and the East End of London in my imagination, riding on the shoulders of a series of detectives. Carl Jung called it "running toward the opposite" and it provided a much-needed break from the shaman bit. It churned up a tug-of-war within me as the hard-boiled dick of my imagination did battle with the peaceful warrior of San Marcos. Gradually, I began to shed my skin.

It all came to a bitter end about nine months after it started as the result of a day trip to the Thursday market at Chichicastenango.

Strange to say, but I'd never been to Chichi in the three years that I'd lived in Guatemala. It's a big tourist destination easily reached by chicken bus or the pricey shuttle vans that cater to gringos. The streets of the town are filled with hundreds of vendors selling textiles, ceramics, wood carvings and the like. Hand-dyed clothing is spread across acres of the marketplace in colors that would make a rainbow envious.

All that, and crystal skulls.

Threading my way past dozens of vendors, I wove through the market past the old colonial cathedral, the steps of which were blanketed with flowers for sale. Did I want a hand-carved frog rattle? No thanks. Did I need a hash pipe carved like a red penis and a set of balls? No, gracias. "Hey longhair, you want some weed?" Got some already.

I turned a corner past the cathedral and a glut of stalls, seeking to get away from the hustlers for a few moments of peace.

Stepping around a trickle of leaking sewage, I made my way

into a narrow alley in back of the cathedral, and there, standing amid a patch of weeds, was a rickety stand, groaning under six shelves laden with hundreds of white alabaster skulls that were a spitting image of Don Pedro, who happened to be resting comfortably in my hemp man-purse.

A handwritten sign on the table said it all: "Unleash Your Hidden Skull Power, 20 quetzals." That was about $2.59, U.S.

"Senor, senor, would you like a skull?" An old woman parked next to the stand with a skinny cat between her knees gazed at me with pleading eyes. "No buy, just look. Just look!"

Well, what could I do but laugh? Hollowly. I walked out of town's hubbub down a dusty dirt trail and sat on the wreck of an abandoned car next to the stream of sewage, the sour smell of chicken shit lingering in my nostrils. I dug Don Pedro out of my bag and placed him at my forehead adjacent to my third eye.

"What does it all mean?" I asked.

The answer came quickly, faster than it ever had before:

"Free beer for Shaman Don."

"You asked for insight and I gave it to you!" he protested when I got back to San Marcos that afternoon. "Admit it, you have intuition now, women, power, respect. You're a shaman now, Grasshopper! Have mercy!"

"Don't ever call me fucking Grasshopper again," I said coldly. I'd looked it up online and learned that it was the name given to the actor David Carradine in a TV western from the '70s called *Kung Fu*. It was about a young guy who goes karate-chopping his way around the Wild West under the tutelage of a blind guy named Master Po. Grasshopper is a term for a neophyte, in this case, me.

That, and I had discovered that the Crystal Skull shtick was a boatload of BS invented by Victorian shysters back in the 19th century. The alleged mystic skulls of Mayan sorcerers had in fact been carved with jeweler's tools in Europe. Some had even been planted in Mayan ruins by unscrupulous "archeologists," finding their way back to places of honor in the British Museum in London and the Musee de l'Homme in Paris.

"Haven't you ever watched 'Kung Fu' on Hulu?" Don asked. "I thought you knew."

"We don't have Hulu in Guatemala! And I figured no shaman worth his frijoles would watch TV anyway."

"That's not true, Grass... I mean Dredd. Shamans have a lot of time on their hands and watching TV sharpens our social skills. I myself watch a number of soap operas, when no one's looking, of course."

"You made a fool of me just so you could get free drinks," I sniveled.

"Oh come on! Every shaman starts out as a fool," Don said kindly. "How else would you learn to hear one hand clapping?"

"Like I'd want to."

"Only fools are eligible to be shamans."

"Seems to be the case."

"Admit it. It's brought you rewards," he said in reproach.

"Yeah, I guess." It was true. Shaman Don Juan del Pedro had livened up my life in a sleepy little hippie town. I don't know how well he had sharpened my powers of intuition, since it took me a ridiculous long time to suss him out, but I'd had plenty of practice and the final lesson of Chichicastenango had taught me to embrace a sense of cynicism from now on. Like Marlowe, or Bogart.

For starters, I finally noticed that Shaman Don was no longer a wispy, thin-as-a-cracker bar fly. He had a beer belly now, thanks to the payback for all of the "lessons" he'd been doling out. How did I miss this? Talk about cosmic insights.

"And the meaning of existence?" I asked. "Free beer? That's it?"

Shaman Don shrugged. "Works for me. Buddha said the peak of existence was being reincarnated enough times to reach Nirvana, followed by the reward of being snuffed out for eternity. Poof! Goners! No more pain or suffering on the wheel of life because you're non-existent! How do you like them apples? I vote for free beer instead. Chivas Regal if you can get it."

Don interlocked his fingers and made a steeple of his index fingers, symbolizing *Uttarabodhi*, the Buddha's hand signal of supreme enlightenment, also known to little kids in the West as "here's the church, here's the steeple, open the doors and here's the people." He rocked back and forth on his hams with a satisfied half-smile on his face.

"So what do I do now?" I asked.

His eyes twinkled. "I got a little present for you on my run over to Panajachel last week," he said. Reaching into his sling, he pulled out a small stack of business cards wrapped in a rubber band.

"Here," he said, "I made these up for your graduation ceremony. Don Pedro told me your time had come."

I took the cards, printed on hard stock by a copy machine. There was a picture of a grinning skull with the legend:

Shaman Nathaniel Dredd Bumpo, CSP • Crystal Skull Practitioner

"Did I get your name right?"

I nodded. "You did. Thanks Shaman Don." Despite myself I was touched, a little bit weepy. I was a shaman now, after only nine months of study. Some yogis took a lifetime of sitting around meditating in a cave to get their guru credentials, but Shaman Don and the Crystal Skull had given me a shortcut and I was grateful.

We got roaring drunk that night on caipirinhas made from Guatemalan sugar cane and the dismal truth came out about Shaman Don Juan del Pedro. His real name was Don DuBois, the one-time owner of a second-hand car lot in Bakersfield, California which had been foreclosed due to bankruptcy. Don's wife had left him for his business partner and, heartbroken, he'd taken the Taco Trail south along the same path I'd run, seeking to reinvent himself.

"I have a 401k, but hardly ever use it," he said. "My idea was to live like those businessmen in India who give up everything to become monks, gurus, that sort of thing," he waved. "Sadhus, I think they call them."

"Uh-huh. And what about Shaman Salvadore? I take it he's not real either?"

"No, he's real alright, but let's just say his story was a bit embroidered. He was hiding out from the death squads during the revolution down here and found an old Mayan ruin out in the jungle. It prompted him to style himself as a shaman and he came out of the jungle crazy as a loon. He bamboozled me real good with that one." Shaman Don laughed at the memory. "I was such a fool."

"Like you bamboozled me," I said miserably.

He cocked an eyebrow. "I prefer to think that I enlightened you, Grass..."

"Don't."

"Okay, okay." He lifted his glass to his lips, spilling his drink down his shirt. "Holy crickets!"

"So what happens now?" I asked.

He shrugged. "How old are you, almost thirty-two? Buck up, you're a shaman now! The world's your oyster. Go out and multiply, live long and prosper, that sort of thing," he waved grandly. "Ask Don Pedro what you should do."

"He already told me," I said.

"And?"

"I'll send you a postcard. I'm leaving tomorrow."

"We'll miss you kid."

"Yeah? Well I'll be back someday, I suppose. But there's one thing I'd like to know before I go. Two things actually. When we met you gave me that bit about the sandy river and my bleeding heart; how did you know about Sandy?"

"Oh that," he waved. "I knew about Sandy even before I got back to town. Half of Guatemala was talking about the bartender in San Marcos who couldn't stop blabbing on about some broad named Sandy Bottom. Listen, if you're going to be a shaman, you've got to learn to keep your trap shut."

Fair enough. Philip Marlowe might have given the same advice. I began to flush under my collar, thinking of what a sap I'd been. I wouldn't make that mistake again. From now on it would be strictly mum's the word, zip the lip when it came to Sandy or any other woman.

"The other thing..."

"The coconut?" he said. "The sound of the universe breathing?"

"Yeah. How did you do it?"

Shaman Don leaned over and bathed me in his beery breath. "A ladybug," he said.

"Ladybug?"

"Yeah. I stuck a ladybug in the coconut shell and you heard it roaring to get out. The shell amplified its voice."

Return to Neverland

At the dock in San Marcos, Shaman Don gave me a black cat bone as a parting gift. It looked like a chicken's leg bone to me, but who was I to argue?

"Consider this a little *buena suerte*, buddy," he said. "This magic bone and Don Pedro will come through for you when all else fails."

"Sure, thus sprach Zarathustra," I said, "but thanks."

We exchanged the top secret shaman handshake and I gave Shaman Don a ring carved out of a sea shell that had set me back 75 cents on a trip to the beaches in El Salvador.

"It's a magic ring that can make you invisible in times of trouble," I said. "But you must throw into a volcano if its burden grows too heavy."

"Really?"

I nodded. "Shaman's honor."

"You have learned much, Grasshopper," he winked.

I caught a chicken bus and headed north through Guatemala to the port of Livingstone on the Caribbean. At a stopover in the island town of Flores, I took a side trip to the Mayan ruins at Tikal. Standing atop the Grand Pyramid at dawn, I could have sworn I heard a squawk from the bag that held Don Pedro, but when I looked within he was the same blank-faced piece of tourist trash as I remembered, carved out of white alabaster, as inscrutable as a book-end.

I caught the ferry to Belize and then a series of ramshackle buses to the Mexican border at Chetumal. A day later I was in Cancun, mulling over whether to catch a cheap five-hour flight home, or take a nasty two-week bus ride through Mexico, Texas and the Midwest. I chose the latter.

I had to think. I had a plan in mind, but it wasn't even half-baked yet; it was more like a mush of oatmeal and evaporated milk. In all of the detective novels I'd read, there wasn't anything that the likes of Marlowe, Spade and Hammer knew that I couldn't manage; mostly they just nosed around a lot and cracked wise. True, some of them were good at beating people up, which didn't happen to be one of my specialties, but I had the benefit of my shamanic training and the intuition it provided. Maybe it was my ego talking, or just Don Pedro, but my intuition told me I'd make a great detective. I took the long bus ride home, hashing out scenarios for my return to northern Michigan as a private investigator. Natty Dredd Bumpo, P.I. - that had a nice ring to it.

The Neverland of Traverse City had changed by the time I hit town. The Great Recession was over and local developers were bulldozing every vacant lot, sunlit field and forest glade in sight with the kind of frenzy you'd expect from a school of starving sharks. Two-bedroom $800,000 condos for wealthy retirees from Chicago and the Detroit suburbs were sprouting on every corner like dandelions in a spring weed patch.

The imprint of old Traverse City with its ballyhooed "small town charm" was almost impossible to see now, buried beneath a landslide of condos, pricey restaurants, swarms of tourists and traffic jams backed up for miles. The hills outside of town were being nibbled away as if by colossal ants, their forested slopes replaced by rows of townhouses.

There'd been an earthquake in the social landscape as well.

SANDY BOTTOM

The last of the Baby Boomers and Gen-Xers who once owned the dance floors of the local bars had been chased out by a new generation. It was the Millennial's scene now, a generation that lived with their parents into their mid 30s and could afford $12 cocktails and farm-to-table organic kale that cost four times what you'd pay down at Food Fare. Talkin' 'bout my g-g-generation... sheesh. As for the Boomers, they were now consigned to a miserable existence, with hordes of them corralled in a smattering of gourmet restaurants where they were stuck ponying up $38 or more for their entrees, salad not included. If they weren't packing the high-priced restaurants you'd find them dancing to crusty old Motown tunes and torpid classic rock bands playing endless versions of "Sweet Home Chicago" and "Sweet Home Alabama" at happy hour gigs. It was an ignoble end for the generation that invented sex, drugs and rock & roll, but we're all heading in that direction, *comprende*? and for now, my generation was more than happy to take over the party until our own time came to blow.

I took stock of the local scene and decided it was a good fit. I was a Millennial, and as Shaman Don had said, that made the world my oyster, or at least my clam.

Problem was, I didn't have a degree in criminal justice or any experience as a private eye. My status as a detective was lower on the dick scale than that of a security guard at a shopping mall. True, I had an online certificate from a police academy in Pakistan, but I needed some hands-on experience before I hung out my shingle.

Fortunately, I had friends.

Beanie Winkelstein had played short-stop at TC Central back in the days when I did my stint as a pitcher. We'd been friends since the 10th grade and he'd been my strongest supporter when I tried out for the Beach Bums before the minor league team changed their name to the Traverse City Pit Spitters. He even sent me a get well card when the team passed on me. Now, 15 years on, Beanie was manager of the largest department store in Traverse City, and as it happened, there was an opening for a house detective, or as he called it, a "loss prevention specialist."

Basically, he was the owner of a meat market, and I was a dog begging for a bone. Lucky for me, he liked dogs.

We sat in Beanie's office at the back of the store, a small airless room barricaded by pallets of cardboard boxes and crates full of merchandise destined for the shelves. Small talk ensued about old flames from high school and such. Beanie had flown to Amsterdam and married the captain of the cheerleading squad straight out of high school; I didn't even know he was gay. He'd hit the retail jackpot after 10 years of slaving as a stock boy and then a cashier, and now he was set for life as a store manager working 75 hours a week. I gave him a fingernail sketch of my own small accomplishments, leaving out the Crystal Skull bit.

"You ever bust a perp?" he asked at our interview.

"That's classified," I said. "But no."

"What would you do if a 14-year-old girl stuck a load of jeggings in her underpants and walked out of the store?"

"I'd read her her Miranda rights to save the cops the trouble."

"Seriously, that's what goes on here."

"Bust her in the chops?"

Beanie gave a dry chuckle. "Do you know how to watch TV?"

"I've seen it a time or two."

"You're hired."

It turned out that being a department store dick mostly involved sitting in a suffocating room at the back of the store, monitoring a bank of videocams. Was it you that lifted the pair of socks made up of 75% acrylic, 10% merino wool and 15% recycled materials last spring? Well, that was me, looking over your shoulder from a roving camera planted ten feet up in the ceiling.

The fun part, if you can call it that, was accosting tearful shoplifters in the parking lot after trailing them around the store via the eyes in the sky. Some of them were sassy and unapologetic, demanding to be allowed to pay for the stuff they'd stolen at a five-finger discount in lieu of getting a free ride in a cop car. Those were the ones who encountered the full weight of the law, which often as not, was getting let go by the cops after an all-too-gentle, politically-correct talking-to out in the parking lot.

Snooping on camera was easy enough: I'd count how many garments were taken into the dressing room and how many came out. The shoplifters were almost all women, some using babies for cover and packing tin snips to cut off the security tags that triggered the door alarm. One woman stuffed an entire bedding set under her clothes, including a comforter, sheets and pillow cases. She came out looking like Mother Waddles.

But there were professionals too, men and women working as teams. The guy might act really suspicious in the electronics section, hoping to engage my attention, while his girlfriend plundered the jewelry counter. Those were the scores I savored the most. Alas, they were all too few.

Six weeks after I signed on, Beanie got fired for embezzlement and Don Pedro whispered to me in my sleep that my job sucked. *"You are destined for bigger things, amigo. Own it, hombre. Grow some cajones!"* He was always saying stuff like that, speaking more and more often, though only in my dreams, thank God.

So I quit after a couple of months and after my last check two weeks later, I had 35 cents in the coffee cup that served as my secret stash. Fortunately, I also had a brick of top grade Guatemalan hashish packed into the bottom of my backpack, another parting gift from Shaman Don and another reason why I took the bus north. This was a year before marijuana was legalized in Michigan, and even thereafter, hash was a prized commodity. I sold it to Beanie for $3,000 - a very good deal for him, plus, he had the retail skills to move the stuff.

I took $35 of my grubstake down to the trophy shop and bought myself a desktop shingle:

Nathaniel Dredd Bumpo, LC, CSP, PI

Traverse City was in an uproar the week that I set up shop. Someone had nabbed a kid from a mall parking lot, little Rebecca Jabbers, only six years old. The cops were ripping the town from top to bottom and every service club, scout troop and sports team piled on the search. There was a statewide Amber Alert, bloodhounds, nightly news reports, the works. The FBI went door-to-door to every house in town, canine patrols combed the countryside and citizen volunteers rummaged through dumpsters and swept through the fields outside town in long horizontal rows. Nothing turned up.

Four days later, a woman walked into my office a half hour after I'd pinned one of my business cards on a supermarket's bulletin board. It was Rebecca's mom, Gloria Jabbers. She looked like she'd been mainlining hi-caff energy drinks for a week. Her hair was tangled in wires, her skin was stretched across her face like a starving deer, she was just a mess. A country gal, gone to seed.

"You gots to find her, Mr. Bumpo," she said, tears running down her cheeks. "You gots to find my Becky! I seen your card down at the market. The cops ain't turned up nuthin' and I'm just... just worried sick!"

She looked it too, standing there caved in upon herself like a child shrunken with fright.

As for myself, I gazed back like I'd been poleaxed between the eyes. Gloria Jabbers was my first client and I didn't know what to do.

"Okay, have a seat," I said, offering the plastic chair I'd snagged down at Goodwill. "Tell me what happened."

"Oh sweet Jesus! I's loading groceries in the back of my truck and when I turned 'round Becky was gone!"

I knew that already.

"At the mall." I knew that too, but said it anyway.

"Yes! Right in the middle of the parking lot with cars all around. At first I thought she was just playin' and I ran up and down the rows lookin' all over, but then it sunk in — someone took her! I just knew it. I got that cold, dreadful feelin' in my bones. I knew Becky been took!"

SANDY BOTTOM

It shook me up, Gloria Jabbers sitting there, shivering and wailing like a ghost, making me feel more like a *poseur* by the minute. What the hell? Nothing in the detective stories I'd read had prepared me for this. In the tales of Mickey Spillane and Raymond Chandler it was always about some guy getting bumped off or some dame in a jam, never about a missing kid, unless it was a creepy, child-abusing grandfather, like the one played by John Huston in *Chinatown*.

Suddenly, I was a deer in the headlights, not knowing what to do. Don Pedro was sitting on the table as a paperweight, a little joke I'd indulged in. On an impulse I grabbed him as a worry stone. The alabaster of his polished skull had an instant effect, calming me, smoothing out my face as flat and expressionless as Joe Friday's in *Dragnet*.

"Okay, what's your kid, I mean Becky, look like?"

She pulled out a photo of a plump little girl in a plaid skirt, wearing round black specs and a chin-length bob hairstyle of the sort worn by 100 million Chinese schoolgirls.

I mused on the photo. "Anyone got it in for you?"

"No, no way," Gloria shook her head. "It had to be a stranger, it had to be."

"Ex husband?"

"No! Becky's a love child. We haven't seen her daddy since she was born and he's dead anyway."

"You sure about that?"

"I spoke at his funeral."

I looked at the photo again and then gazed out the window, wondering what to say to Gloria Jabbers. What was I thinking? I was in too deep. I wasn't a real detective, how could I take her on as a client? She needed the State Police or the FBI, both of which were already on the case, getting nowhere. What could I do that they couldn't? I'd just be wasting her time. I started fidgeting inside, getting ready to spill my guts, but then something caught my eye.

Down on the street below, the slow crawl of tourists was passing by in shades of pastel with some of hipsters wearing black M-22 t-shirts extolling the highway of the same name looping north of town. One couple stood out. It was a guy with a beard that looked like a couple of ragged gray bird nests glued to either side of his chin. He was wearing army fatigue pants, a dirty wife-beater t-shirt and a black baseball cap. Wrinkly gray old-guy arms. That, and he was holding the hand of a fat little boy with a really bad haircut.

The cosmetologist in me studied the boy's hair. I looked like it had been hacked with hedge clippers. Even rednecks had better haircuts than that - they go for buzz cuts that look like they've been trimmed with dog shears - but this was another thing entirely.

Gloria Jabbers had been in my office less than five minutes. I'd spent less than 20 seconds gazing at the pair walking down the street below.

The kid with the bad haircut was squinting. His eyes were all pinched like he needed glasses.

Something clicked.

I pointed out the window to the street below. "Is that your kid down there?"

Gloria shot out of her seat, craned her neck, bugged out her eyes and screamed. "Becky!"

I ran pell-mell down the stairs after her, taking the steps four at a time. Down the block, the dirtbag and Becky were already lost in the swarm of tourists, so we took to the street, weaving in and out of the slow-moving cars.

Did I say running fast? We reached the intersection of Front and Union just as Weird Beard and the kid were turning the corner. By then, the mob of tourists trailing along behind were in full battle mode, smart phone cameras blazing, snapping photos in bursts worthy of machine guns and shooting video.

Who knows? Maybe it was the intercession of the Crystal Skull Don Juan, but instead of politely tapping the old dude on the shoulder and inquiring as to whether he was a maniacal kidnapper, I tripped on the curb and launched an accidental flying tackle straight into his paunch just as he was turning around to see what all the hoo-ha was about.

SANDY BOTTOM

Sprawled on the sidewalk on top of him, I recoiled at his baloney breath at about the same moment that a thought ran through my mind that perhaps I'd misread the situation. Perhaps he was just some loving grandpa out for the day with a grandkid and I was about to get charged with assault and sued to boot. Not to mention making the kid cry.

"Um, this is really awkward," I said, gazing into his uncomprehending eyes.

But as it turned out, Jacob Maywether was a schizophrenic cut from the same mold as the religious kook who abducted Elizabeth Smart back in the '90s. Nuttier than squirrel poop, he was the edgiest character in the Church of the Praying Prophet, Traverse City's most mental of fundamentalist churches. Big believers in Satan, those folks - always looking over their shoulders in fear that Lucifer might be sneaking up on them in the grocery store or at the gas pump.

Maywether had been holed up with Becky in his cargo van just four blocks from the police station the entire time that the manhunt was underway. He'd been struck by the idea that he was going to bring a sinner to Jesus one soul at a time and Becky just happened to be walking past his van at the mall when that lightning bolt flashed through his brain. He'd passed the time reading the Scriptures to her in his own made-up version of ancient Aramaic. They'd exited the van in search of a public restroom when their pee jug began to overflow.

But as for myself, spectacular footage of my flying tackle went viral, earning me 45 seconds of fame on the *Today Show, Good Morning America, CBS This Morning* and all the rest of it. In the follow-up interviews I neglected to mention that I'd simply tripped on the curb. Why ruin a good story? And it turned out that Gloria Jabbers "gave good interview" as they say in the news business, going on and on about how I'd solved the case within minutes of her appearing in my office. ("Within five minutes, I tell ya! Within five minutes!") She even broke into tears on camera at the thought of it, which of course resulted in even more air time on TV. There was even some talk about telling the story on *48 Hours*, but the producers couldn't cook up enough material to fill out a show, considering I'd solved the case in less time than it took to boil an egg.

Again, I didn't mention my cosmetology background or the fact that any beautician could have "solved" the case, what with Becky's bad haircut.

But the upshot was that I became Traverse City's most celebrated detective by the time the paper came out the next morning. No, make that Michigan, if not the entire country. I expected the phone to start ringing off the hook with new clients, but after the last reporter called it remained curiously silent. The only call I got was someone looking for a lost dog and when I told the guy my fee, he hung up. Celebrated or not, my new gig as a private dick remained as slow as skiing down a sand dune in cement galoshes, 'til Sandy walked in, that is.

I don't know if Sandy would have ever given me a second thought if it hadn't been for all the publicity over the Becky Jabbers' case, but now we'd come full circle and she was single again. That meant I had another chance with her. But did I want to take it? Should I? Could I? I'll be damned if I was going to consult with the Crystal Skull Don Pedro, because I already knew exactly what he'd say.

Bigfoot Unbound

Not everyone was happy with my big score. That Monday I got an invite to stop by the detective bureau at the Traverse City Public Safety Department. It wasn't quite a summons, but it wasn't something I could blow off either.

I made it through the metal detector and was led downstairs into a labyrinth of cubicles, stale air, and a ring of tight offices in the basement. Beyond the next door, I knew, was the jail. I'd been to the cop shop once before back in high school when I got busted for drinking a wine cooler at the Clinch Park Beach and I didn't relish reliving my time in a cell.

SANDY BOTTOM

I expected to be hailed as a conquering hero, but things soon got ugly.

At first, Chief Inspector Bruno "Beef" Wellington was as gracious as a lady in waiting while we settled in over Styrofoam cups of tepid coffee, the kind of syrupy stuff that's been sitting in a pot half the day.

"Mud," he smacked his lips, raising his cup. "Here's to you Mr. Bumpo."

"Cheers."

Wellington looked like what you might expect from a guy nicknamed Beef. He was roughly the same size and shape as the Thing from the Fantastic Four, stuffed into a too-tight uniform. He was heavily jowled with a red face, a sweaty forehead, and a few strands of sandy hair crossing the top of his arid skull.

We made some small talk about the weather and the Detroit Tigers. I said that I'd been a pitcher in high school, while Beef said he'd played tight end on the TC Trojans football team, an unfortunate metaphor if you ask me, but I kept mum.

Then things in the office got a bit warmer. Wellington's office was a windowless room with lots of paper lying around in shambling piles and more paper and photos tacked up clear to the ceiling on a bulletin board. A four-by-six-foot whiteboard occupied the wall behind him, covered with scribbles and arrows in red and green, following up leads in the Becky Jabbers case. The same case which was kaputzo now, thanks to yours truly.

"You know, I'm just wondering," Wellington said, cracking his knuckles. "I read in the paper about how you solved this case, and I've seen it reported on TV. Gloria Jabbers says you found her daughter in under five minutes."

I nodded. "I think it was more like two minutes."

"That's amazing."

I shrugged. "What can I say?"

"Simply amazing."

"I guess."

"What are you, some kind of Sherlock Holmes?"

I could play stupid too. "Yeah, just like Sherlock Holmes," I replied. "Doctor Watson arranged a lucky break for me."

Wellington nodded, gazing into his cup, like there was something down at the bottom, a bug, perhaps.

"Lucky break," he mused.

"Yeah."

He gave a weak grin and a chuckle.

"I suppose you know where Jimmy is buried too?"

"Jimmy?"

"Hoffa."

"As a matter of fact I do."

"Seriously."

"Uh-huh."

"And where might that be?"

"In the pages of hundreds of true crime books,"

Wellington sighed. "So you're a smarty pants on top of a private detective. A Mr. Know-it-All. A wise guy."

"Seriously? A smarty pants?"

"Could be." He raised his eyebrows and leaned toward me, all moony-eyed.

"If you insist, but I prefer to think of myself as an ace detective with a heightened sense of awareness. They said as much on the 'Today' show. And Jodi Brown called me a hometown hero on the Six O'Clock News."

I regretted that last bit. It was bragging. Not cool.

"I see," he knitted his fingers together and eased back in his chair, gazing up at the ceiling. An ugly silence filled the room.

"The arm tattoos. What's up with that, mister hometown hero?" He pointed at my arms, which were covered with vines, Guatemalan wildlife, Mayan hieroglyphics and tribal symbols.

"I'm a colorful guy," I shrugged.

"You look like a criminal, you know that?"

Suddenly, I felt as uncomfortable as a dude at a Taylor Swift concert.

"Not even close," I glowered. "Mild-mannered, upstanding

citizen, that's me, Check my rap sheet."

Wellington cleared his throat and pushed his chair back a few inches, giving the floorboards a loud scrape. I knew he had nothing on me but a high school dalliance drinking soda pop wine on the beach, but he didn't mention it.

"You know, Mr. Bumpo, we had the entire force out working this case," he said after a moment. "Four detectives, along with myself, and every patrol officer on the force, including our bicycle and motorcycle officers. We burned a lot of overtime on this one."

"That so?"

"Guess how much?"

I squirmed in my seat. "I don't know, maybe seven hundred bucks?"

Wellington picked up a spread sheet from his desk and pretended to read it in mock surprise.

"Thirty-eight thousand dollars," he said, looking up at me.

I whistled. "That's a lot of coin."

"Yeah. The mayor's pretty teed off about that last bit."

"Pardon?"

"The overtime."

I shrugged again. "Shit happens, am I right?"

Bruno "Beef" Wellington gave me a look on par with that of a severely constipated bulldog getting ready to blow.

"Yeah, shit happens," he sneered. "And I don't mind telling you that I smell bullshit here."

I felt myself shrinking in my chair. Despite myself, I gulped.

"Bullshit, huh?"

"Yeah, bullshit. You got something to tell me, Mr. Bumpo?"

"Whattayou mean?" I gulped again. My tough guy persona, honed by countless hours spent turning the pages of detective fiction seemed to be deserting me in Beef's presence. I made a mental note to work on my shtick, but in the meantime, he had my knees shaking and I was glad that there was a desk between us so he couldn't see.

"I mean come clean, right here, right now!" he went on. "Because something stinks about how you pinched this punk in minutes when my whole department got nowhere. Not to mention the State Police and the FBI. You embarrassed the force, Mr. Bumpo. You embarrassed me, and I take that personally."

"I guess the force was with me."

"What do you mean by that?"

"You know, the force. Like in Star Wars."

"We're not kidding around here, smart guy!"

"Tell me what you really think, Chief," I said as casually as I could manage. "I can see you've got your panties in a bunch over this thing."

I forced myself to choke out the words. I had rallied, giving my shaking legs a hard pinch. It was my turn to talk tough, even though it came out kind of squeaky.

Wellington slammed his palm on the metal desk. "You embarrassed me, boy! You put my job at risk! You think I like that, mister smart guy?"

Jeezus, was Wellington whining? I suppressed a giggle, choking in the process. I felt a wave of hiccups coming on...

"So what? Are you going to sweat me now?" I said (*hic*). "Bare light bulb, beating with a rubber hose? (*hic*)"

Wellington's eyes narrowed to slits as thin as slivered almonds.

"I hope it doesn't come to that Bumpo, but we're going to keep an eye on you. If you had anything to do with Becky Jabbers' abduction, we'll sniff it out, see?"

I gave a disdainful snort. Wellington had nothing on me and I didn't give a damn if he had a bee up his dress. I looked at my nails, channeling my inner tough guy. What would Sam Spade do?

"You know, I think I could use a manicure," I said slowly.

"What?"

"But I can't afford one because Gloria Jabbers is poor as a cockroach. She couldn't even pay the twenty-five bucks on my prorated fee (*hic*). I did it pro bono. What do you think about that?"

Wellington could tell what was coming. I went in for the kill.

"Your department offered a five-thousand dollar reward for information leading to the resolution of Becky Jabbers' abduction," I said. "I want that money. I earned it fair and square."

Wellington leaned over and gave me a blast of his coffee breath. "Why do you think you're sitting here, Mr. Bumpo? I think you rigged this whole thing for the reward. I've got you figured for a sheep in wolf's clothing."

"You've got that bass-ackward, Beef," I pointed out.

"Come again?"

"I earned that reward with my heightened powers of detection. You owe me the dough and I expect to see it delivered, pronto, or I'll..."

"Or you'll what?"

I cast my thoughts around for a possible threat, coming up with snake eyes. "Or I'll sic the media on you," I said at last.

Wellington chuckled at that one.

"Oh, you'll get your reward alright," he said, "but only after we run this titty through the ringer. And if we find out it was you who set this up... well, prepare yourself for a nice long stretch in Oaks Prison."

"I'll remember that." I got up to go.

"Keep your nose clean, Bumpo."

"It's clean as a whistle, Chief. Saline douche."

"What?"

I turned at the door. "It's a holistic thing. Big ju-ju. You wouldn't understand."

That afternoon I got a call from a friend at the Oryana Food Coop. She said a couple of detectives stopped by and purchased a whole shelf of saline nasal douche, including all three gluten-free, organic brands.

"They mentioned your name and they looked seriously pissed off," she said.

It was a few weeks after my big score with the Becky Jabbers case that Timothy Bottom was found recumbent in a Benzie County outhouse. The bigfoot theory was hot around town, egged on by wild tales rocketing around Facebook and talk radio. Men bearing shotguns and AK-47s combed the swamps and forests for miles around, searching for murderous yetis in the hope of achieving some sort of minor celebrity.

But that all quieted down after a bigfoot expert noted in the *Eagle* that a sasquatch has full color vision and anyone wearing blaze orange out in the boonies was likely to be the target of a club-wielding monster. The alternative was wearing camo and taking friendly fire from other hunters.

Then, Fox News ran a little laugh-of-the-day blip about Traverse City's bigfoot connection and a certain pumpkin-headed doofus in Washington, D.C., misheard the bit and tweeted it as gospel to his 65 million Twitter followers. The tweet went viral, rocketing around the echo chamber of the nightly news until Traverse City was fingered as the epicenter of America's bigfoot population.

Quicker than you can say Alley Oop, an advance team from the reality TV show, *Bigfoot Unbound*, flew in, armed with infrared night scopes, parabolic microphones and a makeup assistant.

I got a call that afternoon from a television studio in Burbank, California. Was I doing anything tomorrow evening? Well, no, except for maybe shaving my nose and ironing my underpants. Would I like to join Bigfoot Hunter Buck Bayers and his team for some quick cash? Well, I think I might be able to pencil that in...

Being a newly-minted minor celebrity, I was invited along to provide local color and serve as the team's guide. I was cool with it; being on a cheesy cable show meant my star was on the rise. I even suggested the search area along Boardman Lake a half-mile south of downtown. There's a skirt of woods and marshland between the lakeshore and an adjacent bike path that I figured would be prime bigfoot territory.

"You sure about this?" the show's producer asked. "The map shows that this area is still in the city limits."

Truthfully? I was pretty sure there wasn't a bigfoot any-where within 500 miles of Traverse City; they lived up be-yond Hudsons Bay, most likely. So why make the search any more painful than necessary?

"Listen, if there's a bigfoot in Traverse City, this is definite-ly where he'd hide out," I said, looking as earnest as I could muster. "The bike path along here is a wildlife corridor, like a greenway. Word has it that the yetis in the area use this route to get through town after midnight."

I didn't know if this was true, but it sounded good. "Plus, there's a brewpub less than a quarter mile from the woods," I added. "The alternative is wading around the Cedar Swamp ten miles west of town, which is full of bugs, leeches and crazed poachers armed with shotguns."

That cinched it. The next morning, square-jawed reality TV star, Bigfoot Hunter Buck Bayers, flew in on a chartered jet for lunch with the Rotary Club, a quick tour around town and some local news interviews. It was very big stuff for Traverse City, as you can imagine. We snuck away after dinner and spent the evening quaffing drinks at Side Traxx, the gay bar at the north end of Boardman Lake. It was a stone's throw from what I called the "bigfoot bypass."

Then it was show time, and we went weaving down the adjacent bike path some time after midnight, making enough noise to wake up the south side of town.

"Shh!" Bayers said. "Look, people, it's time to get in char-acter. We're looking for hominids here, big ones. Let's keep frosty, people!"

Bigfoot Hunter Buck Bayers pulled himself together and re-peated "Let's keep frosty, people" for the benefit of the night-vision camera. He also liked to say, "Stay liquid" and "Watch your six," just like the detectives on various TV dramas. On the monitor, Bayers appeared as a big green ghost in a safari jacket and Australian digger hat. But I had to admit, he was a pro. Bayers had downed half a dozen margaritas yet appeared to be stone-cold sober and on point. If anyone could stay liquid, it was Bayers.

"Stay liquid! Watch your six, people!" he called out as we headed down the bike path past the city's sewage processing plant.

We were poking around in the weeds paralleling the railroad tracks at one in the morning with Bayers, a cameraman and a sound guy, when we heard a rustling in the bushes. All four of us were wearing infrared headsets, with the bushes and trees flaring a fuzzy green. There were a lot of bugs flying around that night - a blizzard of them, actually - and some of them got in Buck Bayers' towering hair, giving him a jump.

Bayers was straight out of L.A. where bugs are an afterthought and I could see the sheen of his hair gel melting down his forehead, glistening in the moonlight. He had a big dragonfly trapped in the crest of his hair, stuck in a follicular tarpit. It looked a bit like a barrette.

"This place is like Jurassic Park," he said, swiping at his head. "You sure these aren't bats?"

"Little ones, maybe."

Just then we rounded a low bluff and heard something big moving in the night. We heard a low moaning sound and then something akin to a fart, followed by a groan.

"Ohmigod... oh Jeezus! This looks like it could be it!" Bayers said in a stage whisper, fumbling with his microphone. "Keep frosty, people!"

He'd been talking my arm off all evening about the bigfoot scat he'd found out in Idaho and other curious matters, but I got the feeling he wasn't a true believer. He was a bit too well-staged to be a bigfoot hunter, a bit too slick. I got the feeling that *Bigfoot Unbound* was just a whistle-stop on Bayers' way to bigger things, like a fourth remake of *Knight Rider* or something.

But now he had the real deal as a huge form leapt up from the bushes, rising like a green ghost in the night. The creature let out with a roar and tossed something that looked like a boulder straight at Bayers' chest.

"What da fug?! What da fug?!" it raged.

"We're gonna' have to beep that shit," the sound guy muttered.

But, like I figured, it was just some homeless guy, and the rock I'd seen flying past my nose turned out to be a gallon of orange juice and vodka in a plastic milk jug that hit Bayers square in the chest, making a mess of his safari jacket.

"Who the hell are you?" Bayers exclaimed.

"Well ahm jus' Jim Dandy," our host shot back. "The question is, who the hell are *you*? An' whut are you doin' in my living room?"

Living room? Yeah, sure. He had a tarp spread out on the ground in a thicket by the lakeshore with some swag that included a greasy-looking sleeping bag, a broken lawn chair and a Styrofoam cooler with half the top torn off. A downed tree limb served as a couch.

It was a tense scene for a few moments with the four of us gaping at Dandy like we were in a Mexican standoff. It was him who broke the ice, waving us into his camp. "Oh you chuckleheads can come sit down fer a bit, I s'pose."

All eyes turned to Buck Bayers. "Might as well stay a bit," he shrugged. "This could be interesting." He walked over and sat down on the tree limb.

"Nice place you got here," I said to Dandy, taking my own seat on a weed-shrouded grocery cart that had been tossed sideways in the grass.

"Suits me," Dandy replied, shuffling over to his lawn chair. "This is the big rock candy mountain. Lakeshore frontage and no mortgage."

Jim Dandy looked like a gaunt Charlton Heston portraying Moses in *The Ten Commandments*. He was scrawny as a Mexican chicken with a raggedy beard halfway down his chest. He also possessed a bouffant hairdo with a gray streak like a skunk sweeping back over the top of his head. He was maybe 40 years old but he looked 60.

"So what's your real name?"

"I'd tell ya, but then I'd have to kill ya. Some things are personal, know what I mean?"

I did. Dandy scratched himself under his left armpit and motioned for the sound guy to toss him his jug of screwdrivers. Then he gave a look around as if to say, what now? I was wondering the same thing.

"Look, Buck, I think we might have better luck if we pushed on a little further south," I said.

"Whoa, Dredd, whoa! We've got a teachable moment here," Bayers replied. "Truth is, the show gets a little stale at times and this makes for a nice dogleg. This fellow lives tooth-by-jowl in the wilderness. I'm sure he could tell us a great deal about the local sasquatch population."

Dogleg? Wilderness? A pile of twenty new condo units was less than one hundred yards away, just beyond the bike path. But who was I to argue?

"You're the boss, Buck. I'm just here to serve."

We hadn't bagged a bigfoot, but all of us agreed that the uproar in the night made for great footage and Bayers was thrilled to have something bigger than a squirrel on camera for a change. He got Jim Dandy to sign a waiver as a walk-on extra, promising him $100, cash.

Jim Dandy made a face. "Make it a thousand and you got a deal," he said.

Bayers grimaced and motioned for the cameraman to stop filming.

"Jim, be reasonable," he said. "I'm going to put you on TV for Christ's sake! I'm going to make you a star."

"Do I look like I got a dang TV?" Dandy said, waving an arm in a majestic sweep. "Look around ya. Do you see any satellite dish out here?"

"Look, I can go two-fifty," Bayers said. "Two-hundred-and-fifty dollars, hot cash, right here, right now."

"Okay, eight-fifty," Dandy countered, spitting in the palm of his hand and extending it to Bayers. "That's my final offer. Eight hundred and fifty bucks, cash."

Bayers looked stricken, realizing that he was playing with

an empty hand while Dandy held all the cards. "Whoa, Jim! Seven hundred is as far as I can go," he said. "That's taking it to the max."

Dandy frowned, giving Bayers a hard-luck stare. "Look, Buck, I'm gonna' do you a solid, okay? I'll let you slide for seven-hundred-and-fifty dollars. That's my bargain rate."

Bayers' eyes narrowed in the moonlight. "You sure you never worked in Hollywood?"

"Final offer."

Jim Dandy had Bayers by the short hairs and he knew it. "Okay, okay, but no handshake." Bayers said. He fished eight one-hundred dollar bills from his wallet, snatching the bill-fold away before Dandy could dig his mitts in for more.

Dandy tucked the bills in the thicket of chest hair down the front of his shirt and we kicked some trash out of the way, settling in for an interview in his squalid camp.

"You owe me fifty bucks change," Bayers said with a pout.

"Yeah, sure, I'll write you a check," Dandy cackled.

Before the shooting started, Dandy insisted that he be introduced as the King of the Hobos, "locally, anyway."

"I thought hobos were men out looking for work, like riding the rails during the Depression," Bayers said.

Dandy spat off to the side, wiping a dribble off his chin with his sleeve. "I'm workin' now, ain't I? If you can call what you do 'work' that is.

"Whatever. Watch your six, people, we're going to interview the King of the Hobos," Bayers said sarcastically. The sound man pulled several LEDs out of his pack and set them up on fiberglass poles. Then, with a storm of moths and insects flittering in the lights by the lakeshore, Bayers grilled Jim Dandy, King of the Hobos, for the camera.

"Have you come across any yetis in your life as a wayfaring stranger?" Bayers asked, thrusting his mic in Dandy's face.

"A what?"

"Bigfoots. They're bipedal hominids covered with fur, about seven or eight feet tall. Primates of course."

"Yeah, we got a guy kinda' looks like that, but he's out shopping for supplies. We run outta' toilet paper. But that other thing you mentioned, I..."

"Wayfaring stranger? It means a gentleman of the highways, a walkabout fellow. An indigent chap with time on his hands."

"Yeah, yeah, I get it," Dandy said with a dismissive wave. "Yeah, sure, I seen all kinds of 'em."

"Bigfeet?"

"Them? Oh, hell no! I mean indigents. You don't got ta' look far to find 'em these days. And I s'pose there might be a few bigfoots among 'em, if you know what I mean."

And so it went. After an hour of chit-chat on life in the bush, including a number of retakes, we were good to go. The camera loved this guy; he looked like hell and came up with a lot of snappy patter, inventing his own bigfoot encounters on the spot. Bayers was so impressed that he gave him a card after the interview and told him to contact his agent. "Something might turn up."

Then the lights were on me. I passed on the talk radio scuttlebutt about yetis roaming the forests of northern Michigan, saying they generally kept to the swamps, "looking for swamp hogs."

"Swamp hogs?" Bayers was intrigued.

"That's right," I nodded, trying to look grave. "You don't see many of them around these days because the yetis have a taste for them."

I didn't know if it was true, but I'd heard that some wild boars had gotten loose from a hunting preserve back in the early-'00s and now large numbers of them were said to be busy tearing up golf courses and scaring the bejabbers out of hunters. A conservation group at the state capital claimed that a plague of wild boars was going hog-wild in Michigan with their "razor sharp tusks" and belligerent ways, though no one seemed to have actually seen one.

By now, half a dozen other homeless guys had joined us, sitting around a circle, sharing ciggies and what was left of the vodka and orange juice. After that, Jim Dandy pulled a big jug of Mogen David wine from behind a stump and passed it around.

"You're in the heart of Michigan's wine country and you're drinking Mad Dog 20/20?" I was incredulous. "I can't believe you're drinking this stuff."

"This 'stuff' as you call it is a time-honored tradition," Dandy said in a huff, wiping his lips with his sleeve. "It's not like that fairy juice you high-tone types drink. It's fortified with extra alcohol and has a crisp bite. Plus it's cheap."

As an afterthought he added, "But we will sample the local vintages if you care to provide them."

The margaritas at Side Traxx and then the orange juice and vodka and the MD 20/20 started separating the men from the boys. The sound man and the camera guy stumbled off into the bushes to puke their guts out. I had held back some with the imbibing so I wasn't reeling yet, while Bayers seemed to be a virtual sluice when it came to booze. He could have drained Thor's bottomless mead horn.

In fact, he was still in full interview mode after drinking enough to fill a pickle bucket. I guess that's what made him a pro. He started badgering me about swamp hogs and hobos and I kept dissembling, trying to explain in a nice way that I didn't know jack about either. Finally, with the first gray shades of dawn creeping over the east side of the lake, Bayers noticed that some spooky looking guy was tugging the camera man's wallet out of his jeans as he lay passed out in the grass. Bayers walked over and nudged his crew with his foot a couple of times until they roused themselves.

"Get frosty guys," he mumbled. "We got to go."

Then we beat it for the airport.

"Don't you want to search out a few more places?" I asked on the ride to the plane. "Rumor has it there's a few bigfoots running around the vineyards north of here."

"Stomping grapes, I suppose," Bayers said. "Ha, ha, Dredd, you can't shit a shitter."

"But we barely got started," I protested.

"Yeah, listen. We nailed it tonight and that means a bonus of two weeks off for me and the crew," Bayers said. "We're flying down to Saint Barts over the next few days to soak up some sun and cocktails while the home office thinks we're still out beating the bushes. But mum's the word on that one, okay sport?"

Waving farewell, I felt the $500 cash for my walk-on appearance glowing in my pocket. Life as a small town detective was finally paying off.

More than a few homeless dudes got rousted from their camps by amateur bigfoot hunters over the next week as word of Bayers' interview spread, but the search was half-hearted at best, more of joke than anything. The enthusiasm for mucking around out in the woods died down after a week of heavy rain and its resulting mosquito hatch.

That was a couple of weeks before Sandy Bottom drifted back into my life. She saw an interview with Bigfoot Hunter Buck Bayers on the nightly news and a reference to the Becky Jabbers case and put it together with our long-gone days of splendor in the grass. I doubt she would have even remembered me otherwise. How wrong that turned out to be.

More Snappy Patter

So how do you crack a case like the death of Timothy Bottom? Beats me. I knew my cosmetology skills wouldn't amount to squat on this one and I'd long since fallen off my meditation practice with Don Pedro, who mostly sat grinning on my desk or rode around in my fanny pack as a sort of worry stone.

Bottom had a lot of friends on either side of the economic divide in town. I called on everyone from his hoity-toity pals with deep pockets to the stone-broke activists of the Wildlife Warriors. Everyone was in a state of sorrow and confusion. Best guy ever, they said, everyone missed him, even his enemies had nothing but praise. Some claimed that Bottom had been iced by a hit man hired by the Michigan Snowmobile

Federation, but they were already raising money to erect a statue of him on a trail he'd saved from development.

Then there were the claw marks on his body, like he'd been ripped six ways to Sunday by a cougar. I still had my dog theory, but it didn't seem to be going anywhere. Bottom had been clawed, but not bitten. A dog would bite, right?

I spent another day on the phone and pounding on doors. Same-same but different after three days on the job with nothing turning up. That afternoon, I stopped by Smokey's garage, thinking he might have some ideas.

Smokey Williams had a line of repo'ed vehicles, boats and motorcycles edging out the door of his garage and filling the lot. But apparently, there were plenty more of them out in the boonies waiting to get retrieved.

"I've got work if you want it," he said. "I think there's a couple of young bravos out there who'd love to hear from Alison Beckons."

"Thanks, but I'm working a case." I filled him on Sandy's visit and the search for Bottom's killer.

Williams gave a long whistle at the end of my story.

"Don't you know that little boys shouldn't play with matches?" he said, cocking an eyebrow. "You got burned once before with this gal, torched to a crisp as I recall. Napalmed! Stay away from her Dredd, because chances are she's the one who killed her husband. Don't you know that cops always look at family members first when there's a homicide?"

"Duh, I hadn't thought of that one. So obvious," I replied. It didn't seem possible, but maybe Sandy had screwed my head up so much that I couldn't see straight. For her, that would be as easy as twisting a cap off a bottle of soda.

"You're thinking she's a Russian witch instead of a good fairy, I take it."

"She's a black widow. Remember Derek Smith?"

"She was out of town when her first husband died."

"Uh-huh."

"Besides, Sandy doesn't need to kill anybody to get what she wants. She just wiggles her little finger."

"Yeah, that and her money-maker. But you told me she wasn't entirely happy being married to Bottom, remember?"

"Well, yeah..."

"So listen, have you ever seen 'Body Heat' with Katherine Turner, or 'Wild Things' with Matt Dillon? They're all about these femme fatale types setting up some doofus to take a fall. He gets blamed for murder while the shady lady gets away with millions."

"Hmm. 'Wild Things' was a pretty good movie," I admitted. "I didn't see the other one."

"So who's been the biggest doofus in Sandy's life since you've known her?"

"Uh..." It was a gobsmack moment.

"Who, for instance, would make the ideal patsy?" he went on rhetorically. "Oh, I know! How about some guy who scraped together a living as a street musician until, what? the age of thirty? Yeah, that's the ticket - *that* guy would be an ideal chump for a smooth-talking babe like Sandy. The cops would be all over that guy."

"Yeah, well for your information, I quit banging tunes on the street when I was twenty-eight," I said sourly. But I knew Smokey was right. What a sap I'd been. Sandy was hiding in plain sight and I'd been blind to her as a suspect. I'd read about the sexy psychologist Charlotte Manning in *I, the Jury* and Cora Smith, the unfaithful wife in *The Postman Always Rings Twice*. Both were femme fatales, what the French called, "the fatal woman," so luscious and alluring that they made pigs of men, leading them to their doom. Sandy had certainly made a doofus out of me, if not a pig. A chump. A patsy. Suddenly, I was looking at the woman of my dreams in a different light, from a different angle, sideways. Could it be true?

I began to wonder if Sandy owned a killer canine along the lines of a mastiff or a Rottweiler. Knowing her, she probably owned a tiger.

"For my information?" Williams snorted. "How do you know that Sandy didn't set you up three years ago? For all you know, she's giving you the honey pot treatment."

I hadn't ever sampled Sandy's honey pot, but wasn't about to admit that to Williams. "So what do you think I should do? I can't just drop the case. I've already taken some of her money."

"Ah, the root of all evil."

"Yeah, something I've been rooting around for."

"Well then, since we're spreading the cliches around, consider that two heads are better than one, even if one of them is a cabbage head."

"I take it I'm the cabbage head."

"Who else?" Williams poked me in the chest. "I've got a little secret for you. You see all these repos out there? It's not just you scouting around playing Alison on Facebook or working the phone lines that brought them in. I've got plenty of eyes on the street."

"A street team?"

"That's right. I tell them what cars to look for and they get back to me. They get twenty bucks for every deadbeat they track down."

"I get it, you've got your own Baker Street Irregulars."

"Who?"

"Sherlock Holmes had a gang of street boys who got a shilling a day to keep an eye out for him. They'd get a guinea for every clue they turned up."

"What's a guinea?"

"I think it's like a pound."

"What's a ... "

"It was like twenty bucks back then," I interrupted. "Point is they helped him out with a couple of big cases."

"And these were homeless boys?"

"Yeah, urchins, but lovable urchins, or so it's said. They're in a story called 'The Sign of the Four'."

"Interesting, because my squad is in the same demographic, but older. Look, Dredd, you need your own team of Irregulars out there beating the bushes and maybe my guys can help. There's a guy I know named Dandy..."

"Jim Dandy?"

"You know him?"

"Hell yes, everyone knows Jim Dandy."

Williams gave me a skeptical look. "You'll find him out at Railroad Point. It's down the lakeshore near..."

I held up a hand. "Been there."

"Well then, I see progress! Maybe you're a real detective after all."

"I don't think you ever doubted me, Smoke."

"Not for a minute. Check in with Jim and see what he can do," he said, reaching for his guitar propped up against a file cabinet.

"Consider it done."

Smokey started looking a bit antsy and I braced myself for what was coming.

"Say, let me play you my new song, see what you think."

I suffered through Smokey's new tune about a misunderstood bear who's seen trouble all his days and is hitting the road in search of love. It was the least I could do. I had to admit, Smokey was getting better; this time he wasn't that far off-key and he wasn't as wordy as usual. He'd even toned down the death-metal vocal stylings. But my thoughts were like that bear, far, far away.

Early that evening I made my way to Railroad Point, partway down the west side of Boardman Lake. Back in the Great Depression through the 1950s it used to be a place where poor men from Detroit and points south would arrive in search of migrant farm work, mostly picking cherries. The train would slow at a point on the lake where it curved toward the train station and they'd jump off into the brush. For a long time, it served as Traverse City's hobo jungle, but a new bike path and a slew of condos had pushed the camps of the homeless to the woods further to the south and west. Jim Dandy seemed to have the last thicket of brush within which to hide.

I rode my bike down the pathway and crept into the bushes where Bigfoot Hunter Buck Bayers and I had been entertained only a few weeks ago. Dandy wasn't home, but his swag was still in place. I wrote out a note, wrapped it around a twenty dollar bill, and stuck it in a branch over his lawn chair.

Sandy gave me a call on the afternoon of my fourth day on the job, which happened to be my fourth day of discovering nothing at all.

"So what have you got?" she demanded.

"Pizza for dinner if you want to stop by. But you'll have to bring the wine."

"Is this more snappy patter?"

"I'm working on it, Sandy. I'm following up on some leads." I didn't tell her that one of them was her.

"So? Like what? I'm two thousand bucks in the hole with you so far. I thought you would have solved this by now," she fumed. "It's not good, Dredd, not good at all."

"It's confidential," I muttered. "Strictly hush-hush at this point." I wanted to ask Sandy if she had a dog of the more vicious sort, but that would be tipping my hand. Still, there had to be a way...

There came a long pause at the other end of the line.

"Hush-hush? Remember Dredd, natural causes," she said. "All you have to do is discover that my dear Timothy died of natural causes. So simple."

"Yeah, dear Timothy, I got that. I was heading out the door just now to follow up on a lead. Oh, by the way, did I tell you I'm thinking of getting a dog?"

"A dog?"

"Yeah, an Irish terrier maybe. Just a little one. I love dogs, don't you? Some people like really big dogs, but not me. Do you like big dogs?"

"Oh Dredd, that's so sweet, but I'm more of a cat person myself." Sandy gave a merry laugh over the phone. "Would you like me to get you a dog, Dredd? I don't have much to do this afternoon and I could stop by the animal shelter and..."

"Oh, no, no, no. I'd need to get a bigger place first."

"Well, it's really no problem."

"I was thinking more about you, Sandy. You don't have a dog? I thought I heard you had a dog."

I could sense Sandy's ears pricking up over the phone, suspicious now.

"Why do you keep asking me about dogs?"

"Oh, just making small-talk, thinking about getting a dog myself someday, and..."

"No, not me," she cut me off with a touch of frost to her voice. "It must be one of your other girlfriends."

"Girlfriends? I..."

"Don't. I don't want to hear it," she said before I could say something stupid and needy.

There was a long silence over the phone and then, "You know, Dredd, there could be something very special for you if you can sort this out by the weekend," she said in a slow, breathy voice. "Call it a bonus. Something *very* sweet and special, just between the two of us."

I could feel a bonus coming on at the thought of what Sandy was suggesting.

"What do you have in mind?"

"Oh, I can't tell you Dredd. That would be like spoiling Christmas," she teased.

Could it be? The weekend was three days away. I felt my chest constricting, felt it getting hard to breathe. My thoughts of Sandy as a suspect had evaporated with the words "something very sweet and special."

For a moment anyway. Then it settled in that Sandy was playing me like a salmon on a 30-pound line. What if Smokey was right and she'd hatched this whole crazy set-up three years ago?

"Dredd, are you still there?"

I summoned my inner Batman and gave her the straight-arm.

"Yeah, Sandy, look, I got no time for dames right now, get it? Not even you. I got to go. The meter's running and it's your dime, *capiche*?"

"But Dredd..."

"And don't count on anything by the weekend. If this is what I think it is, it's going to take awhile to track down."

I hit the button on my phone, grabbed my fedora and headed for the city's Animal Control office. If Sandy did have a pit bull or a rottweiler, maybe the pooch also had a license.

The Gobbling Gator

The old guy was plenty hungry. A month ago he'd been receiving a healthy serving of chicken guts, augmented by the occasional fish or turtle, but something had gone dreadfully wrong. He'd been lassoed and tied, tumbled into a dark box, and jostled up and down for three days and nights before being dumped into unfamiliar waters without anything to eat for ever so long.

He'd made a stab at a seagull. Nothing. Fish? Very few, and those he saw darted away lickety-split. All he could do was wait, just as his ancestors had done for 100 million years, blending in with the logs floating in the shallows.

Down the shallow river came a squadron of eight kayaks and the sound of hooting that reminded him of tasty waterfowl. He'd seen kayaks before, of course, but had never had the nerve to go for one. Yet now the fury of his empty belly inflamed his brain, or what counted for one, anyway, it being about the size of a peanut. And the hooting, it was confusing... He saw feet dangling in the water, and one of the smaller paddlers began drifting his way. Yum-yum! The river was too shallow to attempt a swim, so he rose up on his legs and made a run for it, his two-foot long jaws snapping in anticipation...

Who knew an alligator could run that fast?

The snatch made the front page of the *Eagle* the next day:

Gobbling Gator Nabs Coach Pipers

By A. Tucker Jakeway

High school wrestling coach Petey Pipers had the scare of a lifetime yesterday when a ten-foot-long, 800-pound alligator severed his left foot while kayaking with his team on the Crystal River outside Glen Arbor.

"I saw that gator coming and thought it was a g-_____ dinosaur," Coach Pipers said from his hospital bed at Munson Medical Center, where his foot was reattached after a seven-hour surgery. "I'm just grateful that my boys were with me, otherwise I'd be in that gator's gut right now."

Pipers hailed his team as heroes for piling into the water and wrestling the thrashing alligator into submission after it bit off his foot. Several of the teammates suffered lacerations and claw marks before the reptile dashed into the cattails along the shore.

"Fortunately, they were able to retrieve Mr. Piper's foot," said orthopedic surgeon Mike Nighty, M.D. "If it had been swallowed, I'm afraid that the digestive juices of the alligator's stomach would have made our job far more difficult."

Pipers said it was his "a-__-kicking foot" that was severed. "The doc says it's going to be a bit stiff when I get back to walking again, but I hope to be hobbling around soon."

Indeed, I thought, reading on. There was a five-column photo of the dead alligator at the top of the page, along with the game wardens from the DNR who'd shot him 27 times in the resulting melee. They'd found him chasing a homeowner's labradoodle around the front yard of a riverfront home. It had been a close call for the pooch, since it had been staked on a long chain in the center of the yard, just like the goat in *Jurassic Park*, and it turned out that an alligator can run faster than one might think.

I looked it up online: 15 mph in short bursts.

Over the course of the next few days, some 46 letters to the editor about the incident appeared in the *Eagle*, most of them complaining that the terms g-_____ and a-__ didn't belong in a family newspaper, even if the naughty words had both been blanked out.

I heard through the grapevine that reporter, A. Tucker Jakeway, was now up shizzle's creek, fearing for his job for raising the dander of the geriatric readers of the *Eagle*. Apparently, the paper hadn't hired a new copy editor yet and the gol'darned offending blanked-out language squeaked through.

But I didn't take Jakeway for a pushover. Somehow he'd heard of my shamanic background and had come snooping around after I solved the Becky Jabbers case, hoping to expose me as a New Age dick and shamanic shamus. I'd laughed him off at the time ("You crazy?"), but now it was my turn to snoop and I knew right where to find him: at the far end of the bar at the U&I Lounge.

If you sit in the U&I long enough, you'll see everyone who ever lived in Traverse City passing through its long, narrow corridor. Always packed elbow-to-elbow with locals, the "U" is one of those places like Cheers, where everyone knows your name. Eleven big-screen TVs shine endless sports coverage down from up near the pressed tin ceiling, but they're mostly ignored amid the roar of gossip and deals going down.

But the guy I was looking for wasn't chatting away or yakking it up with friends; he was sitting forlorn and miserable at the bar, staring a hole through the mirror beyond a row of liquor bottles.

"Tough times, eh Jakeway?" I piled into the seat next to him in the darkness of the bar. "What's that you're drinking? Root beer? I'll be goddamned. Hey, how about a couple of capirinhas for me and my buddy?" I addressed the barkeep.

Jakeway wore coke bottles glasses - goggles, really. He had a wide jaw shaped like a trench shovel and a big galumphing Adam's apple that bobbed up and down when he talked, kind of like when you see an ostrich at the zoo bobbing its head. He gave me an sideways look with a wooden smile and said nothing, but when our drinks arrived he grunted a grudging thanks.

"Goddamn is right," he muttered. "I try to be accurate, I try to keep it real, and what do I get?"

"Doodle-squat."

"Yeah."

"Bony fingers."

"Damn straight."

"You need to write online, like for a blog site."

"They don't pay."

"So a newspaper does?"

"Better than nothing," he shrugged.

"I guess."

We sat there a moment, me reflecting on the nothing I was likely to earn after the clock ran out on Sandy's case. I knew she wouldn't pay me if I didn't find what she was after.

"Well, it was a damned good story," I said at last.

"Thanks."

"You saw that gator?"

He nodded.

"You think he was the one that got Timothy Bottom?"

"I doubt it," Jakeway said. "I did a little research and it turns out that alligators like to drag their prey underwater, going round and round in a death spiral and biting the whole time. They hide the corpse under a log the bottom until it rots out and gets nice and tender. Then they swallow it whole. That doesn't fit with what happened to Bottom."

"What can you tell me about him?"

"Timothy Bottom?"

"No, man, the gator."

"He was big and green and had a peaceful smile, even in death."

I took a sip of my drink. "I think he's tied in with Bottom's murder."

"You think?" Jakeway gave a bleak smile. "Brilliant deduction, shamus. But what's it to you?"

"I've got a client who's asked me to look into how Bottom died."

"Sandy Bottom." He stared into his drink.

"I can't say."

"Who else could it be?"

"Well, yeah, but..."

"You know what they found in that gator's stomach?"

"A human skull."

"What the heck?" Jakeway gave me an arch look.

"Just kidding."

"Guess again."

"Oh, I don't know. A pair of wingtips? An old Sears catalog? A yoga instructor, maybe."

"Funny guy, Bumpo. They found chicken bones."

"Yeah?"

"Yeah. Almost completely digested but still identifiable as the leg bones and skulls of at least three chickens."

"So?" I craned forward, spreading my hands as if to say, what of it?

Jakeway gave me a somber look. Behind him, Indiana U's basketball team was pounding Ohio State into ground beef on the TV mounted up near the ceiling.

"You're the detective, you figure it out," he said, rapping his empty glass on the counter, waving for another round.

It took a moment for eureka to hit me. I didn't need to ask Don Pedro what chicken bones in a gator's gut meant. That reptile had been someone's pet.

Just then there was lull in the bar's music, and I heard a voice wafting from over my shoulder. It was, as they say, strangely familiar.

"... you want to see skeeters, you should check out Wrangell some time," the guy was saying. "They 'bout carry the caribou away."

It was the same smoky voice I'd heard going on about the Cedar Swamp bigfoot on the radio. In a thunderbolt, I realized it was the same voice as the guy who blackjacked me outside the back door of the bar, warning me to stay away from Sandy.

I looked up in the mirror over the bar and saw a big ginger-haired dude with a red face and a bushy red beard to match. He was wearing a set of brown coveralls of the sort that duck hunters wear over a green flannel shirt that was torn at the elbows. He was talking to a couple of young guys alongside the railing against the wall, both of them wearing tight grins, black baseball caps and black t-shirts.

"Hey, don't turn around, but who are those guys behind us?" I asked Jakeway in a low voice.

He lifted his glass to his lips and glanced at the mirror. "The two young guys are members of the Wildlife Warriors," he said. "I don't know the big guy, but those two were arrested last fall on suspicion of vandalizing the fish weir in town. Bottom bailed them out and nothing came of it."

I hadn't been in town, but I'd heard the story. The Wildlife Warriors had crowbarred the big fish weir across the Boardman River just west of downtown Traverse City, allegedly to keep thousands of salmon from being turned into pet food, fertilizer, or whatever the DNR did with them.

"Why bother?"

Jakeway shrugged. "They got away with a couple thousand pounds of fish," he said. "No one knows what they did with it."

I glanced back in the mirror and my eyes met those of the big guy, whose peepers flashed in recognition, flaring with hostility. Casual as I could manage, I went back to paying attention to the ice in the bottom of my glass, pretending I hadn't seen him. I pulled out my phone, switched the camera feature to the reverse lens, and pretended to make a phone call, figuring I'd get a photo of the guy.

But he was gone, and not to the men's room. I saw him disappearing out the front door, moving fast.

I ordered two IPAs and placed them on the counter alongside the dudes. They looked to be in their early 20s and had interlocking Ws on their hats and t-shirts along with the imagine of a running wolf, outlined in white. Both had dark hair and looked like they spent a lot of time in the gym.

The guy on the left looked like a frat house jock with a Princeton haircut tapered down his neck, like he'd just pledged to Alpha Delta Phi. The guy on right had a hairdo like one of the chimps in *Planet of the Apes*, looking more like a stereotypical Earth First! or Greenpeace radical. Just a couple of fresh-faced, college grads who liked to torch bulldozers.

They looked up at me, wary as wolves, and then down at the two pints of beer.

"You boys look thirsty. Mind if I join you?" I said, channeling my best Bogart impression.

Frat boy sniggered. "Sorry, we don't swing that way. The men's room is down the hall."

"Yeah, I'll forget you said that. I'm looking for information, that's all. The name's Dredd." I held out my hand and got a fist-bump in return.

"I'm Mac and this is Cheese," he wise-cracked.

"Yeah, I already know your names are Luke and Ben."

Their mouths gaped open in surprise. "How did you know?" Ben said.

"You've got name badges on."

"Oh, right. We had a presentation on stream management at the Rotary Club today."

"Is it true you guys carry sheath knives in your boots?"

"Why don't you ask your buddy there," Luke nodded. "He wrote the story about us."

Over at the bar, Jakeway hunched a little lower, but didn't turn around.

"I'm sure he did you justice, but I'd like to know what happened to your friend who was just here? I think I know that guy."

"Yeah? If you know him, then why ask?" Ben said. "What are you? Some kind of cop?"

I showed them my license. "I'm a P.I. looking into the death of Timothy Bottom, just checking out every angle."

"You've been sleeping on the job then," Luke said with a snort. "That's Anky Al. He's the groundskeeper at Bottom's place out on the peninsula. Or at least he was."

"So what's Anky stand for?"

"Anchorage. He's from Alaska," Ben said, raising his glass. "He helps out with Tim's mother-in-law. She's a roly-poly meatball type who needs a lot of TLC. Anky drives her around to go grocery shopping and out to the mall, stuff like that. He's her day care provider. She calls him her butler."

"So he knows Tim's widow, Sandy."

"Obviously. He probably spends half his time peeking in her bedroom window. You sure you're a detective?"

"Sometimes I wonder, but thanks for noticing," I said dryly. "So how do you know Anky Al?"

"We don't, really," Luke said. "He's not in our tribe, that's for sure. He's more of a poacher type, though he did work for Bottom, so go figure. We were just playing nice to keep an eye on him, like when Republicans and Democrats get together and act nice to avoid slugging each other in the face."

"Keep your friends close and your enemies closer."

"Now you're getting it." Luke raised his pint and took a long pull. "Plus, he's spending time with the militia."

"The Sons?"

Luke nodded.

"Doing what?"

He shrugged. "Who knows."

"Does he have a thing for Sandy?"

Ben smirked and raised his beer. "Are you kidding? Everyone has a thing for Sandy."

"Amen to that. We call it the S.O.S. club - losers who are Stuck On Sandy - and there are a lot of members," Luke said. "But she's way beyond our pay grade. She's high maintenance - way high."

"Yeah, amen to that," I said. "Thanks."

So that was it. I figured Anky Al was a jealous caretaker, a loser smacked silly over Sandy, just like me. Smitten enough to try breaking my skull with a metal baton. That would call for some payback if I was a real hard-boiled dick, say in the mode of Mike Hammer or John Wick, but at best I was still at the soft-boiled end of things.

After the Warriors left I made a little more small talk with Jakeway and paid the tab. It was time to play detective. But first I had to stop and see Smokey Williams.

"What happened?" I pushed through the door to his garage and found him bent over the engine of an old Chevy.

"Oh, you heard," he said, tossing a wrench on the work bench.

"Sure, it made the *New York Times*."

"No, really."

"There was an item on page three in the *Eagle* that said you were arrested on a BATA bus yesterday for disturbing the peace."

"Was it a big story?"

"It was only two paragraphs, but I thought I'd better check in."

"Kind of you," he said, turning his attention back to the Chevy and jiggling a spark plug wire.

"So what happened? I thought you tried to stay out of the press, what with being in the repo business."

"Yeah, well the truth is, my garage sale gigs didn't go so well," he said with a stricken look. "They chased me off, the homeowners, I mean. I cleared about thirty-nine cents with my tip jar and was playing my heart out, but they said I was driving customers away."

"So you figured you'd try playing on the bus."

"Yeah, it was like a hail Mary pass with my music, know what I mean? You told me about those mariachi dudes playing on the buses down in Mexico, and I figured I'd give it a shot here in town."

"So how did it go?" Like I needed to ask.

"Well, I got on the bus over to the mall and played a tune and then passed a tip cup around and this guy - this friggin' passenger - got really cheesed off about it. There was like no respect at all, know what I mean? So I went back to playing a little more and that's when the bus driver started in on me, like actually *yelling* at me. And after that, it was a matter of principle. I lost it - I started sing louder and kept on playing until the cops came and dragged me off the bus."

"That's Americans for you. No patience, not like in Nicaragua or Honduras."

"Yeah, I've been schooled on that one. No respect, none!"

"Good thing they called the cops instead of the guys with

the butterfly nets."

"Maybe that's where I belong," he muttered, turning back to the engine. "An insane asylum."

"Don't stop believin'."

"I couldn't even if I wanted to."

"Smoke, listen, why the desperation? Why the tip cup? Why bother with venues at all? Why not just play in your living room? You don't need the money."

"It's validation, Dredd. The payment of money validates my music. Why bother if I'm not getting validated?"

"Just tell yourself you're validated and that will solve everything. Declare victory and rest on your laurels."

"Have you seen my laurels?" he said bitterly. "They've got frostbite, wilted, like boiled spinach."

How could I help Smokey with his disease? I searched my memory for the wisdom imparted by the Crystal Skull Don Pedro and came up with a nugget from *The Art of War* by Sun Tzu. "You know, when an army is in retreat, a good general calls it 'attacking to the rear,' rather than a defeat."

"Huh?"

"Forget it."

We talked a bit about the difference between alligators and crocodiles, of which neither of us knew a thing. Then Smokey told me he was going the spoken-word route with more of his music, owing to success he was having with his belligerent rendition of "I Am a Rock." He'd been covering more hits from the '60s, including "I Love the Flower Girl" by a singing family called The Cowsills.

Smokey had been scared off from reviving folk music after some guy laughed so hard at his cover of "Hang Down Your Head Tom Dooley" that his friends had to call 9-11 to fetch some EMTs. The guy couldn't stop laughing and was literally in danger of splitting a gut.

"I thought the guy was having a seizure," he said. "Scared the shit out of me. So I said screw it and ditched the folk revival."

"So what now?"

"I'm digging up the Swinging Sixties," he said, "all done in the style of the talking blues."

"Sounds horrible."

"Yeah, but people love that shit. Have you heard 'The Beat Goes On' by Sonny and Cher? Or 'Windy' by The Association? Stuff by the Monkees? That shit is magic."

"I guess that's better than trying to jump-start folk music," I said, trying to be encouraging. Even so, I didn't think that exhuming the corpse of '60s pop music would move the needle on Smokey's fantasy.

Smokey had stopped tinkering on the car and was standing there with the promise of musical glory gleaming in his eyes. I was afraid to ask where he planned to play next, considering he'd run out of options. Underneath the Union Street bridge, perhaps? Maybe stick to nursing homes where the audience couldn't run away? But I wasn't about to pee in his beer mug with the hard truths of musician's disease. He'd confessed to me once that tracking down deadbeat loans as a repo man was spiritually-draining. "It's sucks the soul out of you, shaking down these poor bastards for some bank loan. The music keeps me going, it regenerates my soul battery."

So why should I care? The guy wasn't hurting anyone, except for the eardrums of bus passengers, and everyone needs a little juice in their soul battery, even me.

Contrary to what you might think, not everything is on the internet, in particular gator snatchings.

I figured the alligator in the river had to be tied in with Timothy Bottom's death. That was a no-brainer; everyone in town came to the same conclusion. But how? Why? Obviously, a gator that big must have been imported and I figured it was raised on a farm down south. I scoured the online news for reports of missing gators in an arc ranging from Brownsville, Texas to the Florida Keys.

Nothing. So what would Marlowe do? He'd exercise some shoe leather, or in my case, get on the phone. I started calling every alligator breeding ranch, sideshow and wildlife preserve along the Gulf Coast, starting with Texas and working my way east. It turned out there was a missing gator in Apalachicola, Florida, but he was only a four-footer. I kept punching.

Thirty-seven calls later I was halfway through the state of Florida. Yeah, there were a few missing alligators here and there, but all of them were two-or-three-footers who were most likely eaten by their pen pals.

Then I got a bingo.

"You might try Tater's Gators down in Istachatta." It was a lead from the foreman of an alligator breeding operation outside Brooksville, Florida.

"Tater's? I don't have that one on my list," I said.

"Oh, he ain't in no directory," the guy said. "He's a small-time wrangler down the Withlacoochee River. Gets most of his stock from local farmers who get tard of shooin' gators 'way from their cattle. Specializes in big 'uns, and jus' between you and me, this cat flies a bit under the radar, know what I mean?"

I didn't, but I was all ears anyway. We chatted a bit longer and I learned that Istachatta means "man snake" in the Seminole language.

"Tha's a good 'un, doncha' thank?"

"Yeah, man snake, I like that." I got the number and made the call.

Chum Bugley answered on the third ring.

"Tater's." The voice on the other end of the line was as weary as dirty laundry.

"This Tater?"

"No, this is Chum."

"I was hoping to talk to Tater."

"Tater's a cocker spaniel. This is Chum Bugley, proprietor. Now whut can ah he'p you with?"

I started in with my spiel, but Bugley cut me off.

"Now hol' on right there," he wheezed. "Are you a cop? 'Cause you got to tell truth if yer a cop if we gonna' keep tawkin."

"No, no, I'm a private detective," I said.

"Fish and game? Wildlife detective?"

"No, none of that."

"'Cause you got to tell me if you are. Tha's the law here in Florida."

I don't know if that was true, but I spent the next few minutes trying to convince Chum Bugley that I was legit.

"I'm just trying to find out who dumped a ten-foot-long alligator in the river up here in Michigan," I said at last, exasperated to the point of hanging up.

"Mich'gin, you say?" I could sense Bugley perking up at the other end of the line. He gave a long pause and I could hear him hawking a loogie.

"Well then, I 'speck yer tawkin' 'bout Gramps."

"Gramps?"

"Yep, Gramps. Been around here for forty years 'til last month. You say this feller's 'bout ten foot long?"

"Yeah, at least."

"Does he have a missing right front tooth on the lower jaw?"

"I don't know, maybe. Can you hold on?" I called up a photo of the dead gator on my laptop. The same photo that ran on the front page of the *Eagle*. A photo of an alligator with a missing tooth.

"Yeah, that sounds like him," I said. "Do you want me to email you his picture?"

"Nah, I got no truck with email. Just tell me, is he missin' a tooth?"

"Yeah, lower right side. But he had a nice smile, otherwise."

"Well, I 'speck yer tawkin' 'bout Gramps."

"I 'speck so."

"Mah baby boy, he was."

"Big guy."

"Oh, naw. Gramps is jest a pup as fer as big gators go," Bugley said. He lowered his voice to a hush, as if we were sharing a dark secret. "They can grow up to fourteen feet, you know. The Florida state record is seventeen-and-a-half feet. Big enough to eat ol' Gramps, I reckon."

"Is that right."

"A'yuh. And if'n Gramps was any bigger we never would'a got him in the truck."

"Truck?"

"A'yuh, tha's right." I could almost see Bugley nodding at the other end of the line.

"What truck?"

"Well, jus' between you an' me, an' you didn't hear this from me, understan'? A feller came through and bought ol' Gramps about a month ago. Paid two thousand dollars for him, the most I evah got fer a gator. I loved that old boy, but money's money, am I right?"

"You're damn right!" The realization that I'd actually gotten somewhere made me giddy.

"Paid cash, all in hunnerd dollah bills."

"Did you get this guy's name?"

Bugley laughed on the other end of the line. "Friend, when yer sellin' gators at two grand a pop, you don't ask fer the feller's name. You jus' want to know if he's a cop, get my meaning?"

"I do, but is..."

"Now hol' on, 'cause I ain't sayin' nuthin' more!" he shouted over the phone. "The missus here is wavin' over my shoulder like I's sayin' too much already. I'll jus' tell you one more thing and that's it, understan'?"

"Yeah sure."

"This cat that bought ol' Gramps?"

"Yeah?"

"He had Mich'gin plates on his truck."

"No shit?" For some reason, I wasn't all that surprised.

"Tha's right, he drove a big ol' silver Silverado with a truck-topper on the back. We got Gramps all doped up an' snug in a roll a' polyvinyl house wrap and tossed him in the back of the truck with a bag 'a chicken innards and off they went. I could hear that ol' boy snappin' his jahs all 'way down the road."

SANDY BOTTOM

I said so long to Chum Bugley and savored the moment. I had no reason to believe that Gramps was connected to Timothy Bottom's death other than my so-called heightened intuition, but that particular sensitivity was smokin' red hot. All I had to do was connect the dots.

Sandy was getting impatient, but at last I had something to report. We met for dinner at a ritzy place downtown and I filled her in on Gramps the gator. For a change she was wearing a tailored pantsuit of black linen over a red blouse, a jarring juxtaposition from her usual man-killer outfit. It was a side of her I'd never seen before, kind of scary.

"I just came from my lawyer's office," she explained, thumbing through the menu. "And what about you?" she gazed down her nose at my outfit. "Don't you ever wear anything but t-shirts?"

"I was going to wear my Che Guevara but I thought you might like Peter Tosh instead," I replied. My shirt bore a photo of Tosh's glowering face along with the legend, "Wanted: Dread and Alive."

"And who is this Peter Tosh?"

"He was in Bob Marley's band, The Wailers. He got shot, like a lot of other reggae dudes. It was an occupational hazard."

"And you think this is smart, wearing a t-shirt with Peter Tosh to a fancy restaurant?"

I shrugged. Truthfully, it was my best t-shirt and I thought Sandy would be impressed. It wasn't like I had a closet full of spiffy duds to wear, after all.

"Hmm, I think you should buy some new clothes with my money," she said tartly. "You need to look more professional, Dredd. Those hippie clothes were fine when you had your dreadlocks, but now, not so much. That shirt and those tattoos... what are you thinking? Your mind, it is mixed up."

"Point taken."

It had been a long time since I'd been to a gourmet restaurant, at least fifteen years in fact, back in the days when Dad used to take our family out to dinner for Christmas. Back then, fancy restaurants in Traverse City had just two things on the menu other than chicken, those being sirloin steak and pecan-crusted whitefish. Since then, whenever I went out to dinner it usually meant a choice of burritos or pizza. Now, I couldn't make heads or tails of what the restaurant was serving.

Even before I'd left for Guatemala a horde of foodies had begun popping up in Traverse City like shiitake mushrooms in a herb garden. Former hippies, now in their 60s and 70s, packed the restaurants in town like cattle in an Omaha feed lot, browsing on micro dishes of lamb *etouffé* and sauteed salmon cheeks. Millennials enriched by the burgeoning tech scene jammed organic restaurants, coughing up $34 or so for entrees of kale and farm-to-table navy beans garnished with free-range chicken shreds, jamming high-priced cocktail bars and overflowing the brewpubs that occupy every other corner in town

I wasn't one of them.

"Charcuterie," I said, scanning the menu, "I've heard of that, I think."

"Is pig meat," she replied.

"Beurre blanc?"

"Butter."

"Mujadara? Halloumi? Polpo? Huckleberry mastarda? Conch toast points? I see Indonesian spiced pig ears on the menu, but can't figure out the rest of it."

"Oh Dredd, you're such a savage!" she teased, waving a finger. "You need to spend more time with the foodies. They know all of these things. But I'll tell you this, don't order the pork belly unless you want a mouthful of pig fat."

"I don't eat meat."

"No? You used to."

"I went vegan in Guatemala."

Sandy pursed her lips and pretended to study the menu.

I checked out the wine list and discovered a selection of whites that seemed to have everything but grapes: A Pinot

Grigio with aromas of white flowers, green tomatoes, sugar snap peas and butter cream. A Sauvignon Blanc called Chic Bait with notes of chocolate and chicken broth, clearly marketed toward women. A Chardonnay with a licorice nose. "I didn't know wine had a nose," I said.

"You're so crass, Dredd," Sandy replied. "It's got a nose so the wine can breathe."

"You know I was kidding, don't you?

"It's all about beer for you Millennials."

"But you're a Millennial, Sandy. Born between 1981 and '96, right?"

"Perhaps. But my goal is to be a tsarina."

"Now look who's being crass."

I went with a BLT with tempeh bacon on a gluten-free chapati from the lite menu along with a brown ale. Predictably, it was horrible. Sandy had a glass of Chic Bait and a plate of stuffed gremolata mushroom caps, of which she ate just one. "My figure," she explained.

"I thought Russian women let themselves go after the age of 30 or so."

"Yes, but I am no longer Russian now, am I? Now I am American girl-next-door."

I gave a snort at that, but said nothing.

Things quickly turned nasty.

"So you're working for some alligator now instead of me?" she snapped, swirling her wine in its glass.

"What? No," I protested, "but it's all connected, see? It's got to be." I filled Sandy in on my talk with Jakeway. "My theory is that whoever killed your husband was working with an animal, starting with that alligator."

"I thought you got all of your training from detective novels," she mused.

"Yeah, so? What's that got to do with it?"

"I do my research too, Dredd, and in a detective novel, your alligator would be what is called a red herring. It's a thing that leads the detective down the wrong path and fools the readers into thinking they know what's going on. I would think that a shaman like you would know the basics of misdirection, no?"

A small smile and a look of triumph crossed Sandy's face as she took a hummingbird sip of her wine. "What we have with your alligator is simply a matter of an invasive species and nothing more," she said. "You said yourself that the alligator couldn't have killed Tim and it's your job to find out what did."

Sandy couldn't see a pattern, and maybe I couldn't either, really, but I wasn't about to give up.

"I still think there's a connection," I said. "I found out that someone hauled that gator up here from Florida and maybe he had something to do with Bottom's murder."

"Oh yes, there's a connection, but not what you think. Timothy was obsessed with invasive species. He hated them! Purple loosestrife, quagga mussels, zebra mussels, spiny waterflea..." Sandy ticked them off.

"Spiny waterflea?"

"Oh yes, that and flowering rush, the round goby, sea lampreys, Eurasian watermilfoil and the rusty crayfish. Oh, there are so many of them and they are all so nasty!"

What the hell? "Sandy, how in the world do you know all of these?"

"Timothy made me repeat them each week before he'd give me my allowance," she said miserably. "There were times when he even blamed me for invasive species."

"What? Why?"

"Because I'm Russian. Where do you think the zebra mussel comes from, darling? From the Caspian Sea in the ballast of ships passing through the Great Lakes. Many of the nasties are from there."

"Foreign freighters dumping their ballast water in the lakes."

"Yes, in the old days. Not anymore."

I gave a whistle. "So being a mail order bride has its downside."

"Don't be cruel," she sniffed, "but yes, yes it does."

I tossed her a linen napkin to dry her eyes.

"Did you know, I ate a lot of herring back in Russia? Canned herring. It was gross, I hated it, but Momma and I had nothing else to eat. We were so poor, I had to cut blocks of ice on Lake Baikal in the winter when I was only ten years old so we'd have a few rubles to buy food. One year, Momma gave me a crosscut saw for Christmas." Her eyes glistened at the memory.

I tried to imagine ten-year-old Sandy, bundled in rags, sawing ice in the Siberian winter. I'd always assumed she was a Russian supermodel type who grew up eating beluga cavier and sipping Stolichnaya, but apparently, not so.

For the first time, it occurred to me that the reason Sandy was such a rapacious money grubber was because she'd grown up poor as dirt in Siberia.

"So what did you do with the ice?"

"Don't be stupid, Dredd. We sold it to people so they could keep their refrigerators cold when the power went out."

"Where was your dad in all this?"

"Dead in Afghanistan with the Russian army," she said grimly, "back in the '80s when you Americans were supplying the Taliban with machine guns and rocket launchers. Now they have come back to haunt you, but my papa, no. They never even found his grave."

That was ancient history to me, so I kept my lips zipped.

Sandy composed herself, drained her glass and then dropped a bomb.

"Look Dredd, I didn't mention this before, but if you don't solve this, half of Timothy's money goes to a wildlife fund and the other half goes to his brother, Billy."

"Oh? And you forgot to mention that little tidbit?"

"It didn't seem, what's the word? Relevant, at the time. But my lawyer just reminded me."

"His brother stands to inherit $30 million and you didn't think that was relevant?"

"I want you to focus on Timothy's death, not his screwed-up family."

"You don't need to draw me a picture, Sandy. If Billy was involved in Timothy's death then you can't claim your ex died of natural causes."

"Oh Dredd, you're a genius," she said dryly.

"Do you think Billy had a hand in Timothy's death?"

She shrugged. "Who can say?"

"So tell me about him."

"He's a dick."

"Details," I waved. "Give it to me."

Sandy gave a deep sigh, and for once she looked a bit sad and vulnerable. Old, even. It gave me a twinge.

"Billy has a big place out near Leland. It's practically a palace out north of Good Harbor Beach on Lake Michigan. It's totally contemporary, with a wall of smoked glass facing the west, Brazilian rosewood floors, gold leaf toilets... "

"Sandy!"

"What?"

"Focus on Billy."

"Oh. Well, like I'm saying, he's such a dick. What we called a *hui* in Russia, a *mu-dak*. He and Timothy got in a terrible fight years ago, long before we got together. They were co-owners of the baby powder company they inherited from their father, Marcus."

"So what was the fight about?"

"Well, it was so stupid."

"Most family fights are."

"Yes, I'm thinking the same thing."

"So tell me."

"Well, Tim was the older brother, so he was the company's CEO, by tradition, you know? And Billy was the financial officer and vice president of operations. But they had this break-up over what to call the company. Billy was all about branding. He wanted to rename the company Better Baby Bottoms."

"But that's what its called. I've seen it on the shelves."

"No my dear. The name of the company is Better Baby *Bottom*. Timothy was very clear in this; he did not want an 's' added to the company name. He said the family's name was *Bottom*, not Bottoms."

"And that's what broke up the company? That's crazy."

Sandy waved dismissively. "Oh, you know how stupid men are, but that was just an excuse, you see. It was the old story: Timothy came home to find Billy in bed with his first wife, giving her the stiff one. The big hoo-ha about the company name was just something they put on the press release when Bill resigned."

"But Timothy left his brother in his will? You told me before that your husband left all of his money to wildlife causes."

Sandy shrugged. "I tell a little white lie."

"What do you mean, white lie?"

"About leaving half his money to Billy."

"What, $30 million?"

Sandy gave a wan smile. "No my dear, that was also my little fib. You see, Timothy was actually worth $120 million, not sixty. It's $121.6 million, to be exact. And now I think, why should Bill have half of that? I am Timothy's widow. I want it all."

I gave Sandy a hard look. She didn't look so old and vulnerable now.

"You know Sandy, that gator they found in the river..."

"Yes?"

"I think you could give him a run for his money."

"Oh Dredd, you make me want to cry when you say such a thing." She gave a mocking smile.

"Go ahead, I'll get you a beach towel."

Sandy poked at her appetizer with an coral nail, but didn't pick one up.

"What do you want out of life, Sandy?" I strained to think of the most banal things possible. "A villa in Provence? The deed to a platinum mine? A diamond iWatch? A gold coffee pot?"

"Oh, Dredd..."

"A mahogany yacht in Roatan? A million followers on Instagram? A poodle with..."

"No, Dredd, no," she grimaced, waving her hands.

"What then?"

"I don't need the Instagram thing, Dredd. I value my privacy. But the rest? You think you know me, Dredd, but I think you don't know me at all."

"Huh?"

Sandy handed me the bill, $68 for lunch, not counting the tip. "Here you can put this on your expenses, but get the receipt."

"I've got nothing but moths in my wallet, babe."

"You think I carry money?" she sniffed. "Look at my handbag." It was the size of a peanut dish, big enough for her lipstick and car keys.

"Then we'll run out the side door and pay later, maybe."

"What? Dredd!" Sandy looked around the restaurant where other diners were sipping their wine and frowning over their pork belly and paté, but I could see that she was game.

I dug my emergency twenty dollar bill out of my shoe and left it on the table as a tip for our waiter. Then, when the staff wasn't looking, we tip-toed out the side door and ran down the sidewalk. Sandy was graceful as a gazelle, considering she was running on high heels.

We turned a corner a block away and stood there panting. "Oh Dredd, you're so daring!" Sandy exclaimed. "You've done this before, haven't you?"

Actually, I hadn't, but before I could answer, she clasped my face with both hands and gave me a long, deep kiss. Her tongue was warm and searching and I nearly blacked out from the shock of it.

"Uh..."

"You always were a good kisser, Dredd. Goodbye and good hunting! My car is just there."

I could see that Sandy's face was as flushed as mine as she rounded the bumper of her roadster and opened the door. She stood there for a moment and looked at me with her lips slightly parted. "This thing between us isn't over yet, is it Dredd?

SANDY BOTTOM

"Uh..."

But before I could answer, Sandy's car had slipped away from the curb and was running silent and fast down the street to the south.

I gulped hard and thought it over. That kiss, those lips. Whether Sandy was guilty of killing her husband or not, she definitely had me in her honey pot, and I wasn't sure that I'd be able to find my way out.

That night I went to a barn party out in Leelanau County, hooking up with some old friends I hadn't seen since I'd left for Guatemala more than three years ago. A flurry of back-slapping, man-hugs and fist-bumps ensued and I was invited to get up and play "Wagon Wheel" with the band. The scent of hay and righteous reefer was heavy in the air and jelly jars of ginger mead were flowing free for the asking. Dancing broke out under a cloud of white Christmas lights strung from the beams and soon enough it was like a scene from the Hall of the Mountain King.

I had just finished describing my encounter with Bigfoot Hunter Buck Bayers to a group of friends when I turned and saw Witchy-poo swimming through the dancers in my direction. She was gazing intently at me, wearing a black tank top with the silver spangles of the Eye of Horus outlined across her chest.

"Hi Dredd, been a long time," she said softly, nuzzling up against my shoulder. I breathed in her hair and felt her warmth flooding me right down to my toes.

"Way too long," I answered in a husky growl, giving her a bear hug that was a trifle too long. "You look amazing."

"You look different," she replied, not exactly a compliment. "What happened to your dreads?"

"I'm in a new line of work and had to clean up a bit."

"Oh."

I couldn't read her face as to whether that was a sign of approval or disappointment, but then I'd never been good at reading women and she was more inscrutable than most.

Speaking of which, I'd had my fill of women professing to be goddesses in Guatemala; they reminded me of little girls pretending to be princesses. It was okay playing along if you were trying to get laid, but otherwise, it was hard to bear some privileged 28-year-old carrying on about being the incarnation of Lilith or the half-sister of Diana the Huntress.

But Witchy-poo was something entirely different.

That was my pet name for Frankie Taylor. We used to make out in her bedroom as high school sweethearts in the late '90s, back when I used to climb a ladder to the second floor of her house, just like Romeo and Juliet. We parted ways when she went off to Michigan State University, while I launched my career as a failed street musician.

I don't know why I thought Frankie Taylor was a witch. She had mentioned once that she was a Wiccan, but I think she regretted it, because unlike some people who can't help talking your arm off about their gayness or their race or how depressed they are, Frankie never spoke of being a witch again and that's what convinced me that she was one. After all, I figured a true witch is self-sworn to silence and would never dream of spilling the beans.

Frankie had also owned a black cat named Coogie back in the day and she always wore the same thing: black tights or jeggings with a black t-shirt or tank top. I also happened to know that before she left for college she got a tramp-stamp tattoo, the cool thing to do in the late-'90s. Hers was of a pentagram with a smiling goat in the center, lying just north of her very supple and slender buttocks.

Then there was the faintly goth application of her mascara... It all went into a feeling I had about her. Kind of stupid, really. I'd never dream of asking Frankie if she spent her nights dancing in circles around a ring of stones with a coven of addled sisters. That would be rude, and possibly dangerous.

Tonight she was wearing a short tiered skirt of mauve organdy, which fell just a breath below her bottom over black tights and high-heeled ankle boots. With her chestnut-red lipstick and dark eye shadow she had me smoldering at a glance. Other than Sandy, I'd barely even talked to a woman since I'd gotten back from the Guate almost five months ago now, and Frankie had my total attention.

We wandered out of the barn and leaned up against its wall, sharing a doob. It was a warm night and a halo of moths were flitting around a gas vapor lamp off to the side.

"So how's Coogie doing?" I exhaled a dragon stream of smoke from where it had wrapped around my brain.

"Oh he's still around. He's got nineteen lives, you know. I stopped counting after ten."

I let that pass and we played catch-up for the next half hour. Frankie had been married for a year to a stock broker, but it didn't work our. No surprise there. She'd taught English in China for two years and then made her way to Kerala in southern India for training as a yoga instructor. That's what she was doing now, teaching Vinyasa yoga, the hard stuff. No surprise there, either.

Frankie was the polar opposite of Sandy. Whereas Sandy was all curves and rolling topography, Frankie was as willowy as a plume of smoke. Sandy had waist-length blond hair, while Frankie was a tussled, gold-flecked brunette whose hair ended at her shoulders. Sandy wore flashy, primary colors, but Frankie opted for a figure-hugging darkness, like Catwoman or Modesty Blaise. Sandy was brassy and could be crude, while Frankie chose her words with care. Both of them were hotter than a barn fire, sexy as hell, and apt to be walking through my dreams on any given night. And if they would only whistle...

"I heard you on WNMC a while back," I said. "You said you thought Timothy Bottom got done in by aliens."

"Oh that," She blushed under the lamp light. "I was just kidding around because there was so much bullshit on the air that day. Stupid theories about bigfoot and cougars."

"So what do you really think?"

Frankie shrugged. "Probably aliens."

"I'm working that case, you know."

"So I heard. You're a big shot detective now," she said with a little laugh.

"Working on it."

I waited for her to press me for details on the search for Bottom's killer, but Frankie seemed as ambivalent as Coogie the cat, Instead, she remarked on the conjunction of Jupiter and Mars, shimmering overhead. "They look like purple and red crystals, don't you think?"

I threw my head back and looked up at the sky, feeling a bit dizzy.

"Oh yeah..."

Maybe it was the premo Indica we were smoking or the ginger mead or the holistic vibe of the party, but like an ass I let drop that I'd been a student of the Crystal Skull down in Guatemala.

Truthfully, I wanted to impress her, and it worked. Frankie was all ears, peppering me with questions, and for the next ten minutes I blabbed on about the spiritual insights I had received from my Crystal Skull meditations. It was the kind of B.S. that had worked so well with gullible hippie girls in San Marcos.

"This is way off the deep end," she said at last, her eyes rising to meet mine; hers were as skeptical as the eyes of a cat. "So you're a shaman now?"

"More like a part-timer."

"So do something magical," she ordered. "Shake the bones."

"Uh... I'm more of a detective than a shaman," I said, feeling my cheeks flush. "I never really got engaged with that shaman stuff beyond the Crystal Skull thing. Truth is, I've never done anything magical."

"Uh-huh." I could see enchantment dimming in Frankie's eyes, along with confirmation that she knew I was a phony.

"Have you ever talked to the dead?"

I hesitated a moment, straining to think of when I might have talked to my deceased Aunt Mary. "Maybe."

Frankie gave me a cock-eyed look, like she knew I was lying, but said nothing.

Suddenly, it all seemed a bit lame and, even worse, it felt as if the air had gone out of the love balloon. At best, I'd managed to convince Frankie that I was a fake, something I'd suspected all along.

Getting metaphysical was the kind of New Age-y rap that the hippies down in San Marcos used when they were hot to get into each-others' pants, but Frankie wasn't that naive or needy. I felt a pang of regret, imagining that Frankie must surely possess some exquisite carnal pleasures that I'd never managed to experience in our high school make-out sessions. The rule back then was that one of us had to keep our underpants on while we were wrestling on her bed because she was saving the good stuff for marriage.

To a friggin' stock broker!

Frankie was soulfully beautiful in the moonlight, casting a spell on me, whether she intended to or not. I remembered those times in her arms, and then the ache in my chest when she'd gone off to college. She seemed a touch restless, maybe even willing.

But even though I was buzzed far around the bend, I knew that Frankie wasn't the kind of girl who did one-night-stands, and I didn't want to sign that kind of contract anyway. Sleeping with a cool woman like Frankie would likely mean committing to a full-time girlfriend, and like I told Sandy, I didn't have time for dames right now.

Okay, just kidding on that bit, but maybe there was some nagging hope buried deep in my subconscious that Sandy and I would get back together again, against all common sense. It was better if I didn't get in a tangle with Frankie until I had that sorted out, assuming she even wanted me in her life. If Frankie really was a witch, she could cast a spell on me or drop a love potion in my latté and I'd be helpless to resist. But until then I was a free agent.

As if reading my thoughts, Frankie said, "Are you back to seeing that Sandy again?"

"Seeing her? No, it's not like that. She hired me but..."

"My advice? Stay away from her Dredd. She's a vampire."

There was an undercurrent of heat to her voice.

"That's a bit harsh, don't you think?"

Frankie paused, as if trying to decide whether to tell me.

"Sandy met Tim in my yoga class three years ago and she latched onto him like a lamprey eel goes after a sturgeon," she said after a moment. "She'd stand right in front of him, doing Downward Dog and waggling her butt like a stripper, only slower, you know? Twerking. Do you know what that does to a man?"

"I get the picture," I said glumly.

"He caved after the second time they were in class together."

That gave me a twinge and a hard twist to the heartstrings. I'd never known how Sandy met Tim.

"Sandy told me that Bottom was mostly celibate."

"Mostly?" Frankie raised an eyebrow.

What could I say? I didn't want to talk about Sandy with Frankie, or about Frankie with Sandy, for that matter. If romance was in the air under the eaves of the old barn, it had made a quick getaway.

"Sandy didn't mean much to me," I lied, hoping the subject would just go away. "We were kind of a train wreck and I'm way past that now."

Frankie gazed at me under the lamp of the gas light and the orbs of her eyes flared the color of chestnuts, pulling me in. For a moment I thought we were going to kiss, just like the kiss that Sandy had planted on me that afternoon. I'd be batting 1,000, sleeping with a smile on my face that night.

But it was not to be.

"Goo-od," she cooed, her breath tickling my nose. "I'm glad you got away from her."

"It was the other way around."

"Same difference," she shrugged, making motions to leave. "Call me sometime. We could do lunch, or go running."

"Yeah, I'd like that," I replied, not mentioning that I wasn't much for jogging. "Or roller blading maybe, like in the old days."

"No one does that anymore Dredd. Too many people broke their wrists." She leaned in, planted a kiss on my cheek, squeezed my upper arm and said, "See you 'round sometime." Within a few steps the darkness drank her in and she was gone.

Shaken and Stirred

The bear was almost dead from exhaustion and stress. One moment it had been diving for fish for the amusement of others in its spacious enclosure and the next thing it had awakened in a cage to darkness and diesel fumes along with a crushing headache that accompanies being shot in the rump with an animal tranquilizer.

Then had come four days and nights of a jarring sensation, followed the smell of the sea and a week of swaying, followed by ten more days of rocking and exhaust fumes.

When the truck finally stopped, the bear found itself caged in the middle of a pine forest with a foreign scent in the air. It let out a cry of anguish and slammed at the steel bars, roaring and confused, all to no avail.

At first there had been buckets of fish to eat, but when that ran out a rain of a strange granular substance had been dumped into the top of its cage. It was horrible, but there was nothing else to eat. The bear bellowed its rage at the shadowy figure that filled its water dish each day, but nothing changed.

Then one morning the bear awoke to find its cage door standing ajar, and a line of fish leading into the forest. It pushed free and started down the pathway, gobbling as it went. The trail of fish ended a hundred yards or so into the woods, but now there was no going back. The bear smelled freedom, and that night it continued on toward the north, disturbed now and then by a barking dog or a set of distant headlights.

So it was that rental car associate Bobby Johnson was awakened the next morning by a rumpus going on downstairs in the unfortunately-named suburb of Acme, just east of Traverse City. It sounded like his kitchen was being torn apart, with the sound of cans crashing out of cupboards and then the heavy thump of his refrigerator being tossed on its side.

Bobby grabbed the baseball bat that he kept by his bedside in one hand and scooped up his Chihuahua, Pico, in the other.

"Shhh." he whispered as the two of them crept down the stairs.

Rounding the corner of his staircase, Bobby was surprised to find that there was a brand new pillar rising from floor to ceiling in his kitchen. The kitchen itself looked like it had been tossed by a tornado, with boxes of cornflakes, pancake mix and canned food lying all over the floor.

"What the hell?"

At the sound of his voice, the pillar slowly turned on its hind legs to reveal an eight-foot-tall polar bear with its jaws dripping with leftover potato salad.

That's when Pico went nuts, leaping out of Bobby's arms, "just like a friggin' flying squirrel," as he recalled later, to land yipping, barking and nipping at the monster's feet.

"Pico, no! Bad doggie!" Bobby yelled before deciding that a rapid retreat was called for. He ran bare-assed back up the stairs to lock himself in the bathroom just as the bear crashed through the shattered front door and headed for the woods with Pico in hot pursuit.

The bear made it to the cover of the woods and turned to make its stand in a grove of maples, at which time Pico came to his senses and departed with a yelp.

The bear galumphed deeper into the woods alongside a trail, licking its greasy chops. But something was terribly wrong with its heart, which had been weakened by three weeks of diesel fumes, engine noise and a diet of cheap dog food. The bear was old and homesick, its fur yellowed by age, and the run-in with Pico had taxed it beyond endurance. It began weaving, its legs buckling as it stumbled forward. It stopped, panting hard in confusion and fright. With a long, mournful groan, it looked to the north, took two steps, gave a few more huffing breaths, and died.

Two hours later, a cohort of mountain bikers came rolling down the two-track next to where the dead bear lay and noticed flies buzzing in its open eyes and its tongue lolling out.

"Looks like someone dumped their sofa out here in the woods," one of them observed.

"Sofa, hell!" called out a rider who took a closer look. "That's a polar bear rug!"

After that, hell itself rose from the grave with wild rumors of everything short of dinosaurs running around, biting the tails off of house cats.

Some joker dressed up in a gorilla suit that Sunday and ran down Front Street grunting and shrieking. He scared the hell out of a barbershop quartet on tour from Ohio who wandered out of a restaurant just as he ran past. One of them crapped his pants and had to go to the hospital with heart palpitations.

A group of open-carry enthusiasts poured out of the restaurant and riddled the windows of half a dozen stores with bullets, trying to kill the run-amok "gorilla." The gunfire was so loud that they never heard the guy screaming that he couldn't get his mask off his head. Then a couple of bicycle cops rolled up and nearly shot mister monkeyshines, thinking he was a rampaging silverback. Fortunately, one of the officers realized that the beast was wearing a pair of running shoes and they backed down.

Then there were fish stories, and not the kind where you brag about the size of your catch. Local chapters of Trout Unlimited went on red alert, patrolling area rivers for signs of piranha. But the big one was when someone mistook a muskellunge for a shark at the Clinch Park Beach downtown and caused a stampede out of the water, just like in the film *Jaws*. A muskellunge is a type of pike that can grow more than five feet long. It's a scary looking fish if you're going eye-to-eye with one underwater, and it has needle-sharp teeth. But a shark? Come on.

But by then, the whole town was in a panic, worried about

vampire bats, electric eels and rabid bobcats. And why not? After all, there had already been a grumpy gator, a dead polar bear and reports of a bigfoot stalking the city. Somehow, the story of the guy in the gorilla suit got twisted around to be vouched as the real thing over lunch counters and vaping breaks. ("Did you hear about the gorilla downtown? It nearly killed some guy.") Shades were drawn around town and kids were ordered to stay inside to focus on their digital devices and video games instead, as if they needed any encouragement.

But even bigger than the rampaging gorilla was a tiger-sighting on the Vasa cross-country ski trail east of town, not far from where the dead polar bear had been found. There was credible evidence: two bird-watchers had seen it darting through the underbrush.

Then a mountain biker named Mark Mobley said it had stalked him down a single-track trail through the forest near dusk. "It was like getting chased by the Headless Lumberjack," he told Jodi Brown in a live, in-the-studio report on the Six O'Clock News the next day.

Jodi had taken to calling herself "Downtown Jodi Brown" to gin up some urban sass in little old Traverse City. To her credit, she'd quit wearing those large, clunky necklaces, which had gone out of style with female anchors, quelling rumors that she didn't have a neck.

"So tell us, Mark," she said. "It sounds like you had a terrible ordeal out there in the woods, far from any help. Weren't you frightened?"

"I totally was, Jodi," Mobley replied. "Totally. I could feel him breathing down my neck and I'll never forget that terrible growl!"

"My goodness, how did you ever get away?" Jodi asked.

"I was mashing my pedals like my life depended on it," Mobley replied. "I could hear it thundering along behind me just as I hit the crest of a hill and then I shot down that sucker like it was a roller coaster to get away."

Mobley said the tiger looked to be about nine feet long from tip to tail. "I never did get a good look at it because it was running through the brush, but that was my impression."

"Well Mark, you're just so brave," Jodi gushed, "you're one of our hometown heroes!"

The headline in the *Eagle* the next morning kicked off a week of tiger phobia:

Orange Menace Stalks the Woodlands

The story noted that several hundred people are devoured by tigers each year in India; the beasts have fangs four inches long; and they can jump out of nowhere since they blend in with tall grasses. Plus, tigers need to devour a lot of meat each day to get by. It was heavy stuff.

There was an emergency meeting of the county commission and one of the more unhinged commissioners called for bringing in the Michigan National Guard to track down the orange menace. The governor nixed that idea, but did send in a SWAT team from the DNR, who combed the woods east of town all the way from Traverse City to the village of Kalkaska, twenty-five miles away.

Soon, the forest rattled with gunfire as shaky DNR marksmen mistook frightened deer, raccoons and turkeys for a 600-lb. tiger. Up to four news choppers circled the forest each day, producing footage of miles of unbroken pine canopy along with breathless reports on the nightly news. The whole town was on edge, and the sound of tumbling dice was overwhelmed by the rattle of gunfire at the Turtle Creek Casino, just north of the woods.

It made the national news, of course, and the governor arrived with an armed motorcade to show solidarity with the besieged people of Traverse City. Moms armed with shotguns accompanied their kids to bus stops, and schools in proximity to the forest were closed. So too were roads leading into the area, with barricades manned by the sheriff's department. A lookout command post was established nearby at the Holiday Hills ski area, with officers scanning the forest perimeter with high-powered binoculars.

There was even talk of bringing in some tiger hunters from India if the DNR's SWAT team couldn't get the job done. It turned out that the Sikhs of northern India were pretty good at tracking down tigers and they reportedly came cheap.

It was almost as if little old Acme had been turned into a military camp.

But on day three of the search a team of commandos flushed out a scared-silly collie named Laddie hiding in a pine thicket. The pooch had run off from his home in the burg of Fife Lake, 15 miles to the east, and got lost in the woods. Staring down the guns of the DNR, a body-cam video of Laddie shivering with fright went viral, getting more hits on social media that week than Ariana Grande's latest fling.

Speculation on the orange menace carried on for another week or so, but with no more sightings, the DNR packed up its guns and drove back to Lansing. Mark Mobley's story was also discredited after plaster casts of the "tiger" which had chased him were found to be those of a dog about the size of Laddie.

But that wasn't the only shocker. At a press conference later that week, Chief Inspector Bruno "Beef" Wellington announced that it was the polar bear that killed Timothy Bottom.

"We believe that this terribly disturbed bear had an accomplice," Wellington said on a live TV newscast. "The bear's murderous activities were clearly guided by a criminal mastermind who had something to gain from Mr. Bottom's death. As head of the joint task force I'm ordering the apprehension of a person of interest to investigate further."

It turned out that person of interest was me.

That night, a team of Traverse City police officers, sheriff's deputies and undercover detectives from TNT, the Traverse Narcotics Team, kicked in the back door at my boarding house on Eighth Street, getting every kid in the place screaming his head off.

"Why didn't you assholes just knock?" demanded Shirley, a single mom of two toddlers who had the room next to mine.

It was like a scene out of the war in Iraq as helmeted cops in military gear trooped into the house with all of the kids and moms crying in the hallway.

"Hey, don't I know you from Leland?" I asked a long-haired detective in camo fatigues. He was the same undercover cop who'd tried to coax some weed out of me about five years ago.

"Shut up perp and get your hands behind your back," he said as I felt the cold steel clasp of a set of handcuffs. "You and your animal buddies are going down."

"Speaking of which, you'd better check the basement," I whispered conspiratorially. "But be careful down there. You never know what might jump out at you."

The cops slapped a bullet-proof vest on me and lead me none too gently to a black Suburban on loan from the State Police. It appeared I was getting the full Hannibal Lector treatment. I heard from Shirley later on that they spent the next three hours hemming and hawing at the basement door, waiting for a K-9 team and a robot crawler with a camera attachment to show up. Too bad there was nothing down there but a washing machine and piles of dirty clothes. But in the dark, those overflowing laundry baskets looked a lot like polar bears.

Down at the station, Chief Inspector Wellington was strutting like a rooster that just bagged the barnyard's biggest worm.

"We got you now, boy, and you're going to confess even if we have to sit here all night," he said.

"I confess that you're all a pack of keystone kops," I said. "Someone get me a cigarette."

"I happen to know you don't smoke," Wellington said.

"Yeah, but I'm playing out a scene here and it helps to get in character."

"Okay, wise guy, let's play out your little scene then. Take a look at this."

Wellington plunked a sheath of photos on the table between us. They'd been blown up to 8-by-10's and they were all of me and Sandy, shot three years ago. There was Sandy and me snuggled cheek-to-cheek; Sandy and me lying close together on a beach towel; the two of us hugging, smiling. Who could forget those days? I wish I could. Like in the Bob Seger song, "wish I didn't know now, what I didn't know then."

"So? What's this?"

"These landed on my desk today, and from what I can figure, these prove that you and Mrs. Bottom are in cahoots," Wellington said triumphantly. "You conspired with that polar bear to murder Timothy Bottom for his money. I don't know how you did it, Bumpo, but you're in the deep doo-doo now."

"Conspired with a polar bear? Like I had it on a leash or something? Hidden in my basement over on Eighth Street? Yeah, I don't think so. Someone's playing you for a sap, Chief."

Wellington brought his eyes down level with mine. "Then prove it, wise guy."

"Give me my phone and I'll prove it in the time it takes to flip a pancake."

Wellington nodded and a cop came forward with a bag full of my personal effects.

"I'll need my handcuffs off."

The cops glanced at each other around the room, registering doubt, like I might go all Jackie Chan on them, but Wellington gave a grudging nod and the cuffs came off.

I opened my phone, typed in the password, and called up my photo file. "See? These are the same photos as on your desk."

"I don't see how that helps your cause," Wellington said warily.

"These were all shot more than three years ago before Sandy even met Timothy Bottom," I said. "In your photos, my dreads have been Photoshopped out to make it look like they were shot recently. But in the original photos you can see that I still wore my hair down past my shoulders. That, and there's a time signature on each photo file from more than three years ago."

The news settled in and I could hear Wellington swallow hard behind my shoulders.

"So you and Mrs. Bottom had a fling," he said. "An affair. You dirty, dirty dog..."

"She was Sandy Smith back then. She wasn't married to Tim yet and it was a romance, not a fling. She was my girl-friend, or so I thought. But it didn't last long. She dumped me after three months."

"That must have hurt," Wellington said. A look of concern passed over his face.

"Yeah it did."

"Maybe it hurt so much that you decided to come home and kill her husband in hopes of firing things up again," he said with a note of menace.

"That's one possibility, but I didn't. I've been employed by Mrs. Bottom to find out who killed her husband and right now, I'm thinking that whoever dropped these photos off is in the picture himself, trying to throw you off track by impli-cating me."

"Let me tell you the picture I see, Bumpo. You got home from three years out of town and suddenly Timothy Bottom is dead. And then this."

With that he pulled a final photo from the bottom of the sheath. It was a telephoto shot of Sandy kissing me the lips a few days ago on Cass Street. Even I had to admit it looked pretty damned suspicious. Had Sandy set me up to be her pat-sy? And who had dropped off those old photos? They were all on my Facebook page, easy enough to download. All ex-cept the shot of her planting one on my kisser.

Smokey and Frankie's warnings about Sandy started creep-ing back into my thoughts.

I played my only hand.

"You got nothing on me, Beef," I said slowly. "Nothing but some photos that prove that I once dated a single woman known as Sandy Smith more than three years ago and that last week she gave me a sisterly kiss to thank me for my services.

"A sisterly kiss?!" he sputtered.

"That's right. Very chaste and innocent. That's all you've got chief, along with my promise that I'll find Timothy Bottom's killer before you do. You can take that check to the bank and cash it today if you like."

An hour later I was back on the street, both shaken and stirred.

But that wasn't all. An hour later I got a call from Jakeway at the *Eagle*.

"You'll never guess..." he began.

"You got a stack of photos of me and Sandy Bottom," I ended his sentence.

"How did you know?"

"Because Beef Wellington got the same package. I just got back from him sweating me over at the cop shop. They had me trussed up in wrist bracelets and apprehended by a SWAT team, the whole bit."

Jakeway whistled at the other end of the line. "Now don't get mad, Dredd, because I'm going to be quoting you," he advised.

"What? You think this is a story?"

"My editor told me to look into it."

"So I take it the august *Eagle* is a scandal sheet now."

"Look, Dredd, speaking as a friend instead of a reporter, you've got to admit, these photos make you look dirty."

"Wrong, Jakeway, and you know as well as I do, there's an old saying that a good newspaper has no friends, and that includes reporters."

"Yeah, well."

"So what are you going to do?"

"This story is too big to ignore," he said. "I've got to ask you some questions, on the record."

"Then start out with this. Those photos were taken three

years ago. All but one of them, anyway, and someone out there is trying to frame me."

"You're saying that you and Sandy were a thing?"

"That's right, before she married Bottom."

"Sandy Bottom was your girlfriend? *The* Sandy Bottom?"

I could tell that Jakeway thought my relationship with Ms. Smoking-Hot Sandy Bottom was as unlikely as an alien abduction.

"That's right, Jakeway, and we had long nights of unbridled passion and steamy sex like you wouldn't believe," I lied. "Tell that to your readers."

Uh-oh. That's when I clicked off my phone. There was no sense digging a bigger hole than the one I was already in.

The Nuclear Option

I was summoned by Sandy the next day and figured it had to do with that morning's story in the *Eagle*. Chief Inspector Wellington was quoted as saying I was still a "person of interest" in Bottom's murder and that he had possession of "compromising photos" of me and the widow, Sandy Bottom. But the paper didn't run a photo, and I could hear Sandy yawning about it over the phone when she invited me to lunch. If anything, she thought it was funny.

"I don't read the paper," she said, "but I love that it's all over Facebook! Everyone's talking about us!"

"Yeah, great. Our lucky day, I suppose."

We met at the food truck court in the parking lot at the Little Fleet bar on the east side of downtown. Sandy was wearing calico slacks of thin cotton in a purple, red and black tribal print that made her bum stand out, along with a wispy silk tank top that had a decided jiggle. Her sunlit hair flowed down her back to her waist and her ears dangled with hoops of gold. A table of frat boys nearly got whiplash craning to see her as she walked by. Lucky none of them broke their necks.

"You look good, Sandy, real good."

"I feel good, Dredd, and so does my lawyer now that things are settled." She was as sunny as the day, and it was in the mid-80s.

"How so?"

"I'm sure you heard the press conference," she said primly. "Detective Wellington said the polar bear killed Timothy, meaning he died of natural causes. I guess I won't be needing your services any more."

"But..."

"But I haven't forgotten that bonus I promised you Dredd," she said, wiggling in her seat and giving me her seductive, bedroom eyes. "I've got that sweet thing just for you."

What the hell? Was this really happening? I was about to ask her if we were going to her place or mine, when she reached into her beach bag and drew out a jumbo box of Junior Mints.

"Do you remember?" She was ecstatic. "This was *our* candy!"

Hope drained out of me like a punctured tire. "Sure, who could forget? Give."

So we shared out a handful of mints each, with Sandy babbling on about how happy she was that her husband's killer had been identified and then about the trip she planned to take to Morocco to celebrate now that it was all over. As for myself, I sat there numb through it all, barely hearing a word.

"Do you know there's this company that will take you on a camel safari through the Sahara and the Atlas Mountains outside of Marrakesh? They even set up the tents and... Dredd? Are you listening to me, Dredd?"

"Yeah, Sandy, sure, Morocco sounds good. Hope you enjoy your camel ride, but there's one thing you and your lawyer are forgetting."

"Oh?"

"The fur they found on Timothy's body was brown - deep, dark brown. And a polar bear's fur is white."

The light in Sandy's eyes dimmed a little with that news.

"Well we won't let that get in the way," she said petulantly.

"Yeah, but the probate court might not be as blind."

"But Wellington said..."

"He's a doofus, Sandy. What you call a *mu-dak* in Russia. He thinks you and I are in on this together."

"What do you mean?"

"He thinks you and I conspired to kill your husband. He thinks we have a thing going on."

"You and me? That's a laugh."

"Yeah, pretty funny."

"Then who, Dredd? What?" Her eyes searched mine.

"I don't know yet," I said, thinking of the photos down at the jailhouse and the implicating kiss she'd given me. *I was thinking that it might be you,* I thought, but didn't say it. "I need more time, just a little more time."

Sandy's eyes flared, then she groaned, screamed, and shook her head violently side-to-side with her blond hair whipping in the sun like a head-banger. "Oh, I hate this! When will it end? When!"

One of the frat boys got up from his seat and swaggered over to our table. He was a young, dumb body-builder type in a skinny-strap muscle shirt slashed down either side to show his well-tanned ribs.

"Is this guy bothering you, ma'am?" he asked, chest puffed out and hands on his hips.

"Ma'am?" Sandy's face went dragon-red. "You think I'm *old?* GET THE HELL OUT OF HERE!" she screamed at him, shooting daggers from her eyes.

"Damn!" He scuttled back to his seat, sat down a moment, gave a worried look our way and then got up and ran out of the parking lot.

"So, more time? Of course, you can have it," Sandy said, returning her composure. "But this can't go on forever, Dredd. I'm going broke and the bill collectors are knocking at my door. Timothy had some expenses I never knew about and they're starting to land on my head."

"Yeah? Like what?"

"Oh, stupid things like auto payments, credit card bills, the usual," she waved.

We had ordered sushi, but the rolls sat there mostly un-eaten, oozing soy sauce as both of us stewed in our private thoughts.

"Is there anything else you're holding back from me?" I asked. "Like the stuff about Tim's brother Billy? Do you know of anyone who might be interested in photos of us?"

"Photos? No! Who would care about such a thing?"

"Anything, Sandy, anything at all to give me another lead."

Sandy chewed on her gloss-pink lips, eyes cast sideways in reflection. "Well..."

"Well what?"

"The night before Tim died, when we made love for only the second time, he said we were celebrating something big. He called it the nuclear option."

"The nuclear option? What did he mean?" I leaned in close, drinking in those eyes despite myself.

"I don't know," she shrugged. "Something atomic? Like Chernobyl? A big boom, maybe? He called it Operation Black Fish."

"Uh-huh." I felt a tickle in my memory.

Speaking of Chernobyl, the day after our lunch date, the *Eagle* broke the story on the bear's Russian roots. Everyone in town figured it had wandered all the way down from the Arctic Circle through northern Canada in a mix-up of migration. But as it turned out, the bear's origins were far more sinister.

Polar Bear Roared Straight Out of Siberia

By A. Tucker Jakeway

IRKUTSK, RUSSIA: An *Eagle* investigation has deter-mined that the polar bear which terrorized the region last week was stolen from the Zoogalereya zoo in Irkutsk, a prominent city in eastern Siberia. Russian authorities are calling the heist a bear-napping by a group of domestic terrorists.

Last week, this reporter emailed a photo of the bear found dead outside of Traverse City to zoo authorities in Irkutsk, who confirmed that it was Sasha, a 43-year-old female, which had been in captivity since the mid-1970s. It's believed that Sasha was hijacked by a shadowy organization of poachers known as the Wolverine Pipeline, which funnels exotic animals from Russia to zoos, hunters and collectors around the world.

The Russian news agency Tass reported that the bear's cage was found empty on the morning of June 23, with the zoo's lone security guard incapacitated by a bottle of vodka laced with barbiturates.

"How was I to know?" said the guard, Grigory Shermanov, in media accounts. "I found the bottle in my locker and took one sip only, and the next thing it was morning and I was lying on the pavement."

Local authorities allege that the bottle had been drained and that Shermanov lay unconscious for a day and two nights before frustrated zoo-goers pushed in the gate and found him lying amid more than two dozen animals which had been released from their cages. "I was lucky the wolves like me," he said. "Otherwise, not so good."

Initially, authorities believed that the zoo's beloved polar bear had climbed over a wall and escaped to the swamps and woodlands outside the city. But an intensive two-week search turned up nothing..."

Wow, Jakeway was smokin' hot on this one. Maybe he should be playing detective instead of me, I thought while browsing the story over lunch. Later I found out that he'd simply Googled for news of suspicious polar bear incidents in Canada and then in Finland, Norway, Greenland and Russia, going down a list just like my phone search for the gator. He'd found a photo of Sasha online, which had the same small nick in her nose as the bear found outside of town.

Still, it was good work, and there was talk around town of

Jakeway winning a Pulitzer for this one, especially since the story went national. Bigfoot Hunter Buck Bayers weighed in on the *Nightly News* that Traverse City was rife with wildlife and that a polar bear or a ten-foot alligator turning up was, "a bit unusual, but not unusual."

Downtown Jodi Brown even did the unimaginable by interviewing Jakeway on the Six O'Clock News. Usually, the media in Traverse City ignored each other as if there were no other news outlets in town.

The story gave me a clue leading to my own search online. I'd seen photos of Sasha's carcass and even in death, the bear had looked old and haggard with its fur going yellow around its jowls. How long does a polar bear live, I wondered? It turned out that 45 years was the top end of longevity for a polar bear held in captivity. Sasha was 43 years old. If you considered that bears are distant relations to dogs, that would mean 301 human years — pretty old, I'd say.

An old polar bear on its last legs and an elderly alligator in the same fix. There had to be some kind of connection, but what? That afternoon on a whim I pulled the Crystal Skull Don Pedro from my table top and gave it a meditation go-round. But perhaps DP was mad at me for having ignored him for so long because not a single thought came to mind except that the bear and the gator were united by just one thing: old age.

That night I called the bar at the Last Resort in Guatemala.

"Buenas noches, how can I serve you, mate?" the barkeep said. He was a young guy with an Australian accent.

"Let me talk to Don Juan del Pedro."

"Don't know him."

"You must be new."

"Not really, been here a week now."

"He's the guy in the dirty white pajamas with the red nose sitting at the bar, begging for a Chivas Regal."

"Ah, Shaman Don. Si, amigo, he is teaching me the way of the Crystal Skull."

I felt like telling the kid to watch his back, but what did I know? A few seconds later Shaman Don was on the line.

"I knew you were going to call," he gushed. "I had a tingling."

"I need your help."

"I figured as much."

"Have you heard of the cabbage head?"

"Like two heads being better than one, even if..."

"Yeah, that's right and I'm the cabbage head here," I said. I gave him the lowdown on all that had happened since Sandy walked into my office a couple of weeks back, including the decrepit animals and the clues that led nowhere.

Shaman Don brushed all of that aside. "I saw you on 'Bigfoot Unbound'!" he said. "We get that show down here in the Guate, you know. All the girls here were super impressed. They want you to come home to mama."

"Did you hear anything I said at all, Don? I'm dying here. My credibility is on the line."

"Credibility? That's a bitch."

"It's paying the bills for now, but once I lose it, I'm out of business."

There was a long pause on the phone.

"What?"

"I'm intuiting," Don replied. "Give me a second."

There was another long pause. It was at least four minutes before Don came back on the line.

"Apologies, but I can't think without a drink in my hand and they said I was past my quota. I had to cadge another with the promise that you'd be good for it upon your eminent return to San Marcos. It's a Chivas, I'm afraid. Hope you don't mind, Grasshopper."

"Tell them not to hold their breath."

"Gullible kids here," he replied, "but good-hearted, very good-hearted kids."

"So what have you got for me?"

"Have you been keeping up with your practice?"

"Hell no."

"Well that's your problem, then. The Crystal Skull is like a rechargeable battery. You've got to keep juicing him if you want him to work. Otherwise he gets mopey."

"Yeah, listen, I haven't really believed in the Skull since I saw that pile of trinkets in Chichi," I said. "This is bullshit, meditating with a tourist trinket."

"So bitter, so disillusioned!" Don exclaimed at the other end of the line. "I fear you have lost the path, Grass..."

"Please don't call me Grasshopper."

"Look, you think the Skull is bullshit? All religion is bullshit, but its believers swear that it works," Don said, clearly exasperated. "You like to read detective novels? Well then, look at the thousands of books and movies that rely on magical relics, or people with supernatural gifts, or teenagers who save the world by levitating buildings and blowing things up with the power of their minds. That last bit alone is a huge genre unto itself! Carrie uses the demonic power of her mind to burn down the high school prom and makes a pincushion of her mother with flying butcher knives - you think that isn't crazy? Teenage mutants? Kids shooting lightning bolts out of their fingers and laser beams out of their eyes? Ridiculous, but people buy it."

"Yeah, sure, but that's in the movies. Communicating with an inanimate object is crazy."

"Not at all!" Don exclaimed. "It's not like we're living on old Babylon anymore, but idolatry never really went away. People pray to crucifixes and statues of Virgin Mary, Buddha and Krishna. They bury statues of St. Joseph upside down in their backyards, believing it will help sell their houses. Is the Crystal Skull any different?"

"Well, gee when you put it that way, I guess not."

"Atta' boy! So don't diss the Skull, mister hot-shot detective; he'll come when you call."

I couldn't help it. I was falling back under Shaman Don's spell. His juju was bullshit, but it was good bullshit.

"Shaman's honor, do you really buy it?" I asked. "I mean really?"

"Of course, but I've got no choice. For me it's a career. I'm a shaman for cripe's sake."

"So what's in it for me?"

"Just give the Skull a chance, Dredd. I don't know how or why or when, but I know that Don Pedro will come through if you just believe in him."

"Okay, what the hell, I'll give it another go," I said half-hearted.

We talked a bit more about how the Detroit Tigers were doing and Don said he was thinking of moving to Oklahoma City, of all places, to start up a new used car lot. I promised to visit him if he ever got stateside, crossing my fingers behind my back and then we clicked off. I felt better. Maybe Shaman Don was right.

I fished Don Pedro from my fanny pack and looked into his shallow alabaster eyes, thinking about giving the old meditation bit another try.

"Nah."

I had a troubled sleep that night. Do hard-boiled detectives have any other kind? I dreamed that I still had my dread-locks, but a nest of bees had taken up residence in their tangles and I had to move very carefully to avoid getting stung. That morning I woke up feeling bad that I'd spent another day on Sandy's account without turning up anything worth a dime. Oh well, she could afford it, for now, anyway. Plus, speaking of bees, it still stung a bit that she'd scoffed at us getting back together again. I knew that, but didn't need her rubbing my face in it.

I got my bike out of the garage that morning and rode the four blocks to downtown. Thoughts of elderly animals, Sandy's kiss, the Silverado used to transport the alligator and Beef Wellington's threats whirled around in my head without any connection. I was stumped, drifting around aimlessly. I decided to head for my office and meditate for a bit with Don Pedro like Shaman Don suggested. What could it hurt? Maybe he'd rev up my intuition.

But passing the post office I saw a black Ford 150 pickup

truck go by with Sandy's mother sitting in the passenger seat. Her nose barely cleared the bottom of the window, but you don't see little old ladies wearing kerchiefs tied around their heads these days and I spotted her in an instant. At the wheel was Anky Al, just being a good boy, driving Sandy's mom around like the Wildlife Warriors said. Al gazed in my direction, but his eyes passed right by like he hadn't seen me. I knew better.

I wheeled around and followed the truck down Union Street. Traffic was moving slow enough for me to keep pace with it, two blocks back. Then the truck took a right on 14th Street and sped out of sight, heading for Meijer's and some grocery shopping, most likely.

It started to sprinkle and then the sky gushed open and I was drenched in fat dollops of rain. Misery settled over me as I got soaked through. I was aspiring to be a hard-boiled dick, or at least a hot-shot detective like Magnum P.I., and here I was riding a bicycle around town in my sandals and an Outkast t-shirt, soaking wet without a clue. What kind of detective was I? I looked like a bum on a bike. A car whipped by just a foot away, splashing me head to foot in dirty water. Gloomily, I reflected that I was still just a Peter Pan neo-hippie living a pipe dream with no choice of solving this case or any other. Maybe I'd give Sandy a call later on and throw in the towel.

But first I had to get out of the rain and Smokey Williams' repo garage was just a couple of blocks away. The gutters along the curb were full by now and there were no fenders on my bike, meaning I got a face-full up front and a wet stripe down my back as I rolled toward shelter.

Shivering, I made it to the awning at the entry to Smokey's place and banged on the windowless steel door. No answer. Smokey kept the garage key in the dumbest place possible: under a potted geranium next to the door. I fished out the key and made my way inside.

"Smokey? You here, man?" No answer.

I nosed around the garage, expecting the worst. This is the

part in scores of detective novels and movies where I'd find my best friend Smoke lying shot dead in a corner, or possibly crushed beneath a Lincoln, dropped off a lift.

But there was none of that. Instead, Smokey had left me a note:

Dredd, had to leave town, will explain later. Keep an eye on the business, okay? And if I don't come back, it's all yours.

- Your Pal, Smokey

What the hell?! Keep on eye on the business? Was he kidding? I looked around the garage. Inside was a midnight blue Audi 3000, a '60's-era MGB with wire wheels and a rust bucket Ford Bronco that looked to be about circa 1987. But I knew there would another dozen vehicles in the back lot, none of which I had time for. What was Smokey thinking? I switched on the lights and started poking around. Crumpled up in an overflowing wastebasket was a travel itinerary detailing a one-way flight to Chicago.

Why would Smokey go to Chicago? And why would he fly when it was only a 300-mile drive? Maybe he was catching an ongoing flight... the hub at O'Hare Airport had connections to any point in the world.

Then I remembered: there had been longstanding rumors that Smokey Williams had connections to the Chicago Mob, whatever that was. You couldn't be in the repo business without coming in contact with organized crime, laundering money through vehicles sent to auction. That was the reason he carried a gun. I didn't know squat about the Mob, except that it dated back to Al Capone and hailed from the Windy City. Maybe the Mob didn't even exist; maybe it was just fodder for cop dramas on TV. But some of its members were said to have summer homes in northern Michigan. Supposedly, some of them even played golf with Timothy Bottom. Maybe he crossed them and got himself killed.

"Smokey, what the hell did you do?"

And what would I do with all of his vehicles? The banks would be expecting them to go to auction, not to mention issuing demands to go snooping around for more repos. I didn't know if I could cut it as a detective, but I sure as hell knew I didn't want a new career as a repo man.

That's when I looked out the back window and saw it: a late-model Silverado pickup truck parked alongside the garage. It had a truck-topper on the back, just like the one that Chum Bugley had told me about.

It was like seeing a ghost. "Not good. Not good at all."

Had Smokey been playing me all this time? Had he gone for the gator? I didn't recall him being out of town for an extended period, but then we hadn't been in touch for most of the past few weeks. It was a three-day drive to Florida from northern Michigan and three days back, but I knew that hard-driving Smokey probably could have shaved a day or two off the trip.

Then too, he'd made a point of warning me about Sandy, insinuating that she may have offed her husband. It had made sense at the time, but now I wondered if he'd been trying to throw me off track.

But it didn't add up. Smokey had his rough side - he had to be tough to make it in the repo business - but he was no killer, and I didn't see him inclined to smuggle an alligator across state lines, much less a Russian polar bear. Hanging out with gangsters? Stupid. As far as I knew he didn't have anything to do with Timothy or Sandy Bottom. His passion was music, not murder.

But what did I know? People are weird, you never know what the hell they'll do.

Smokey's living quarters were at the back of the garage. This time I didn't have the key, but I gave a good kick and the chintzy lock gave way as the veneer door splintered open. I paused again in the darkness of the doorway, wishing I had my dad's revolver. Once again it crossed my mind that Smokey might be lying dead inside; all of the pulp novels I'd ever read almost demanded it. But the room was empty.

SANDY BOTTOM

Smokey's battered Epiphone guitar was missing, but his bed was neatly made and it was clear that he'd tidied up the place before leaving.

I backed out of the room and pulled up a stool by Smokey's desk, sitting in the stillness of the garage. There was still half a joint in an ashtray on his desk and it helped settle my nerves. I pulled the Crystal Skull from his solitude in my fanny pack and held it to my forehead as the buzz washed through me.

What do you think? I wondered, breathing rhythmically and floating all other thoughts away.

I think you'd better stay in the detective racket a bit longer, shamus, came the reply, filtering through my thoughts. *If only to figure out what happened to Smokey.*

Fair enough, though searching around for Smokey Williams would be crossing the line on what Sandy had hired me to do. As it turned out, she didn't even need me.

That afternoon, Interlochen Public Radio announced that the Trace Evidence Unit of the Michigan State Police had finally determined what kind of animal killed Timothy Bottom nearly three months ago. Turns out it was a wolverine.

My heart sank as I listened to the news in my office cubicle because it would mean the end of my $500-per-day gig with Sandy. Considering that my investigation was just leading me deeper into a swamp of suspects and dead-ends, she'd probably demand a refund.

I leaned back and listened to the broadcast:

"... State Police investigators have been stumped trying to determine what sort of animal fibers were found on Mr. Bottom's corpse," the NPR reporter said. "Here's lab analyst Howard Caden with his take on the search."

"Thank you Daniel. Our unit compared a broad range of animal fibers using polarized light microscopy," Caden said. "Initially, we ruled out a wolverine because there hasn't been one sighted in Michigan since 2004. Before that, wolverines were thought to have been extinct in Michigan since the early 1800s."

"This is ironic, since Michigan is considered to be the Wolverine State," the reporter came back.

"Yes, it wasn't until we determined that our fur sample was hydrophobic that we realized it could be that of a wolverine. Hydrophobic fur is thick and somewhat oily, offering protection from frost and the cold. Native hunters use it as an insulating material for their clothing. We compared our sample with that of wolverine fiber collected in northern Canada and got a match."

A wolverine, huh? Hmm. I gave it a google and learned that the wolverine has a bad reputation as a vicious killer. Scientific name, gulogulo, but also known as the carcajou, glutton, skunk bear and the quick hatch, noted for its ability to run up to 15 miles per hour and rip its prey from limb to limb.

There had been a few cases of wolverines harming human beings, but deaths were extremely rare, if any. A full-grown wolverine was about as big as a medium-sized dog, topping out at 55 pounds.

For the most part, it was human beings who were doing the killing, since wolverines were almost extinct in the lower United States.

I read on. Wolverines had been known to jump out of trees to attack an unsuspecting moose, and one reportedly killed a polar bear by clamping its jaws around the bear's windpipe, but when it came to tangling with human beings, it was the wolverines that were on the run.

I spent the rest of the day waiting for Sandy's kiss-off phone call and playing video games on my laptop, but the phone never rang.

That evening, I was settling in with some microwave popcorn, watching *S.W.A.T.* on TV when there came a knock at my door.

"Oh Dree-edd, you've got a visitor," my housemate Mary Jean called out in a musical lilt.

I opened the door. "Yeah? Who is it?"

SANDY BOTTOM

"I think its Goldilocks," she said with a wink.

I groaned. What the? It was Sandy Bottom waiting in the foyer.

"Sandy, what are you doing here?"

"I came to see your place and pay what I owe," she said brightly. "I like your pajamas. Are those cherries?"

I blushed as red as the cherries on my PJ's. "Yeah, they were a Christmas gift from my mom. Come on in."

One of my other housemates was hosting her book club in the living room, so there was no other choice but to talk in my room. The first thing Sandy did was to flop down on my unmade bed, gazing around with appraising eyes. For a change she was dressed like the girl-next-door in tight jeans studded with rhinestones, which knowing her, were probably Swarovski crystals. That, and a Black Keys t-shirt, which was hiked up her well-tanned tummy to reveal a diamond stud in her navel.

"So this is what a detective's pad looks like," she said. "And you call yourself, what? A hard-boiled dick?"

"It's a sobriquet. It's in the tradition."

"A what?"

"A nickname. It meant a tough-guy detective, from back in the gangster days of the '40s and '50s."

"Yes, but we're not back in those days any more, are we? I think you should stop calling yourself a dick. It's vulgar. And I think you should start speaking better English."

"Complaints noted."

Sandy's azure eyes wandered around my room as if she'd never seen the like of it. There wasn't much to see. I had a bookcase packed with hundreds of detective novels that I'd collected over the past few years, along with a faux-leather used chair purchased from Goodwill for ten bucks. On the wall were a couple of acrylic landscapes painted by my housemate Gena's 11-year-old son, Jake. I'd paid $15 for each of them to give the kid his start as an artist. Otherwise, a mini-fridge, a microwave, a coffeemaker and a small TV mounted on the bookcase completed my castle.

"I like it," Sandy mused. "I could live here."

"You think so? There are five single moms in this house with nine kids between them, along with little old mixed-up me."

"You think I don't know this life? Mamma and I lived in St. Petersburg for two years before moving to Moscow and we shared a room smaller than this. Do you know? Many apartments in Russia are shared by two families while they wait for the government to build more housing. Can you imagine Americans living like that?"

"No."

"We lived near Sennaya Square, close to where Dostoevsky lived. Do you know him?"

"Sure, everyone knows Dostoevsky. I've got his book on the third shelf down," I pointed to *Crime and Punishment*, parked alongside *C is for Corpse* by Sue Grafton. "It's an anti-mystery told from the killer's point of view."

"Yes, the poor student Raskolnikov kills a mean old money-lender and her sister with an axe. He believes that a man without a conscience is capable of doing anything in order to help the downtrodden," Sandy went on. "He thinks he can become as unfeeling as Napoleon, but he can't escape his emotions. He imagines that everyone suspects him - like they're looking at him funny, you know?"

"I forget how it ends," I said.

"Really? In the end he's overcome with guilt and paranoia and gives himself away."

"Two very Russian characteristics, from what I've heard."

"Yes," she said softly.

"I didn't know you had a literary bone, Sandy."

"Oh, everyone thinks I'm a dumb blonde, but we had to read him in primary school. Do you know Dostoevsky spent four years at hard labor in Siberia for joining a group that read books forbidden by the tsar? He nearly froze to death when he wasn't starving. They were going to shoot him and his book club buddies, but at the last moment he got sent to a labor camp."

"So why bring all of this up? Do you have something you want to tell me?"

Sandy looked at me straight-faced. "Yes, Dredd, I killed my husband with an axe for his money."

The look on my face must have been worth a slot machine jackpot because Sandy burst out laughing. "No, I'm just fucking with you, man! Come on!"

She reached over and shook my knee. I'd been careful to sit in my chair instead of on the bed with her, afraid that I might go in for a clutch and the inevitable rebuff. But more than my knee was shaken by what she'd said, and suddenly I felt the urge for a serious drink, like maybe a water glass of bourbon.

"Ha-ha, Sandy, you're a kidder," I said, trying not to show that she'd rattled me. It was time to change the subject.

"You know, while we're on the subject of Russian literature, who is Count Vronsky? The guy you used to go on about when we were dating. I figure he's some guy from a book, like Mr. Darcy."

A bemused look crossed Sandy's face. "Every woman in Russia knows Count Vronsky."

"And?"

"He's the good guy in 'War and Peace'. He's a noble in the tsar's court and a complete gentleman who knows how to treat ladies with courtesy and respect. He's like you Dredd, only he has money, you know? Lots of it. And you don't."

"It figures."

"It's just that..."

"I saw your mother today," I cut her off, not wanting to hear Sandy's tortured explanation of our ill-fated history. "She was riding around in a pickup truck with some guy."

"Who, Alan?" Sandy made a face. "He does some work for us."

"What kind of work?"

"Oh, Tim dug him up from somewhere to be our gardener and I kept him on to help out with Momma. He's kind of a redneck but she calls him her butler."

That checked out with what the Wildlife Warrior guys had told me.

"Does he have a thing for you?"

"Who doesn't?" she made a face. "Dredd, if you only knew what a pain in the ass these men are."

"Yeah, save it for later, okay?"

"Then why do you ask?"

I told her about getting blackjacked right after she hired me. "I think it was your guy."

Sandy cocked her head and gave me a noncommittal look. "Do you want me to speak to him?"

"No, but watch your back. I've got a feeling about that guy, and it's not good."

"Believe me, I'm always watching it."

"So let's get down to business then. What's up?"

"I came to pay you." She reached into her purse and pulled out a handful of bills. "Twelve days you've been on the job, right? That's six-thousand dollars."

"This is Canadian money."

She shrugged. "Take it to the bank, they will exchange it."

"Yeah, but at seventy cents on the dollar."

Sandy shrugged again. "What is the expression? Stuff happens. Tim left me this money under our mattress and now I'm giving it to you, even though your investigation went nowhere."

There was a touch of the lash in that last bit, and I had to admit, Sandy was right. She didn't have to pay me and she knew it. In her eyes I was probably a charity case.

But there was still an itch I couldn't scratch.

"The court might go along with the idea that a wolverine killed your husband, but I think it's crazy," I said. "Billy Bottom will contest this."

Sandy's eyes flared. "It's not crazy at all. Can't you see? This must have been the nuclear option Tim told me about. He probably had a truck full of wolverines that he planned to set free and one of them got the jump on him. It's simple, really."

"Just like Steve Irwin and the sting ray, I suppose."

"That's right," she nodded with a knowing look.

"Wolverines have been known to leap out of trees to kill a full-grown bull moose."

"I believe it! They can be very mean."

"But they don't tend to kill human beings. I checked."

"There's always a first time, right? What else could it be? That animal's DNA was all over Tim and it proves that he died of natural causes. My lawyer is satisfied. He says our case is airtight."

"And now Tim's money is all yours."

"That's right."

I whistled. "Lotta' cash."

"Yes it is." Sandy leaned back on my bed with a jubilant grin. She raised her arms over her head, arced her back, and did a full-length cat-stretch across my bed. Her t-shirt hiked up just shy of her golden globes, revealing her ribs and abs, well-tanned and tight. I didn't know if she was tempting me or not, but I'd been disappointed too many times to take the bait.

"Mmm, Dredd I can smell your cologne in the sheets," she said lazily. "Maybe we should fool around some time, like in the old days. Would you like to have a little fun?"

I had nothing to say to that.

"Well, would you Dredd?" she teased, turning over on her stomach and biting one of her nails.

Did I want to be tormented again, making out with the woman of my nightmares, only to get tossed out of the back of a plane again? If I gave in now, Sandy would be stuck in my head for another ten years or so.

I looked at my own nails, as if they were suddenly very interesting. "That's shampoo you smell, Sandy. I don't wear cologne. Plus, I think it's time for you to go."

She frowned, and threw a pillow at me.

"So now you don't want me any more?"

"You can't have everything, Sandy. You taught me that."

"Oh, I know," she groaned. "I was a bad girl back then, but

this is now."

"But now isn't looking so good, is it? You'll be too rich for me. I like women who are more on my level, broke and struggling to pay the light bill. But you don't need me, now or ever. Find yourself a Russian oligarch to party with, or someone like Aristotle Onassis."

"Who?"

"He was an old Greek gasbag who fooled around on his wife, but he owned half the boats in the world and was as rich as they come. Richer even than Timothy Bottom."

"You don't think much of me, do you?"

"The truth? I think it must be lonely being you, and winding up with a hundred and twenty million dollars is only going to make you lonelier."

"Now you are being a dick," she said with a crooked smile and a sheen to her eyes. "Don't be bitter, Dredd. Play nice and you can help me spend my money."

"Thanks, but I wouldn't be making any big purchases just yet if I were you."

"Oh? Why not?" she said, poking my knee with her big toe.

"I don't know. It's something I read a long time ago." I nodded to my bookcase.

"Something about Tim? I doubt it," she said, as scornful as a Russian princess. "You should burn your stupid books and go back to cutting hair."

That hurt. "I'm just saying be careful. Things aren't always what they seem."

Sandy scowled and propped herself up in the bed.

"Uh-huh. Now you're bringing me down, Dredd, and I don't want to hear it." She got up to go, straightening her t-shirt. Her face was a hot pink; it always turned red when she was angry. She gave a last look around the room, her blue eyes flaring.

"So that's it?"

"Yes, Dredd. It's been good seeing you again," she said coldly. She leaned in and kissed my cheek, giving my hand a squeeze. "But now you are dismissed."

I spent the next day ratcheting through my book shelf of mysteries and pulp novels. Then I hit the stacks at the library and after that, the mystery section at the book store downtown. What I was looking for wasn't hard to find, but I wanted to shake out the same scenario in a number of books. I was searching for mysteries and thrillers where the victims get killed by big, toothy animals like wolves, mountain lions and grizzly bears. I found half a dozen or so.

Then I went shopping around on the internet for information. I rooted around on the Interpol website for a bit, rummaging through a thicket of bureaucratic boilerplate without much to show for it. That led me to the Russian criminal database and a translation app. As I suspected, a certain someone's photo turned up. It had been taken more than ten years ago and was a blurry, black-and-white mugshot, but I had my bingo.

Showdown in Stankville

That night, there was a tap on my window while I was in bed watching *Hawaii 5-0* on the boob tube. I opened the window and found a note on the sill. It was instructions from Jim Dandy, written in a childish hand on a scrap of paper with a dull pencil.

We met the next morning in the pavilion at Hull Park on the north side of Boardman Lake. Dandy was there looking squirrelly as ever with a young guy whose dark hair reached to his shoulders. He had an eagle nose and a sallow complexion, like he lived on candy bars and cola. He also had an old Army rucksack on his back with a sleeping bag strapped to the bottom of the pack with bungie cords.

"What's with the skullduggery?" I asked. "You could have just knocked last night."

"Yeah, but for all I know your place is bugged," Dandy replied, "and I got reasons to keep my profile on the downlow."

I hadn't thought of searching my room for surveillance

devices, but given "Beef" Wellington's mania for me, anything was possible. Not that he'd hear much of anything but a bunch of noisy kids in the rooms next to mine.

"So whatta' you got?"

"This is Larry Longshanks. He walked all the way here from New Jersey," Dandy announced.

"Yeah?" We were sitting at a picnic table inside the pavilion, sharing a bag full of burgers and fries I'd brought along at Dandy's request.

"Yeah, he likes to walk, don'tcha' Larry? I think he saw that Forrest Gump movie way back when and it got into his head, the part where Forrest went jogging all over the country for a couple of years, that is."

Larry nodded. "Been walkin' around for two-three years now, livin' the dream."

"I guess stranger things have happened," I said. "Why do you guys all have nicknames?"

"Why do you have a silly-ass name like Natty Dredd Bumpo?" Dandy replied.

"Touché, amigo. So Larry, spill it. What can you give me?"

Larry gave Dandy a sideways glance, but held still.

"Not so fast, shamus," Dandy said. "We need two large. That's a hundred for me and a hundred for Larry."

"Two hundred bucks? You haven't told me what you've got yet."

"That's because you haven't *paid* us yet," Dandy said caustically, as if explaining the rules to a moron.

"And why do I need to pay you, in particular?"

"I'm Larry's agent. That, and I'm coordinating this operation for you. The wheels don't turn unless I give the order. My boys have been beating the bushes on your behalf and we were lucky that Larry turned up something big yesterday."

"How big?"

"As big as Moby Dick's wet dream, shamus. Money. Give." He gestured 'gimme' with his fingers.

"Okay, but give me a break with that shamus thing," I said irritably.

"Whatever you say, shamus," Dandy said, looking as expectant as a dog waiting for table scraps. "Money..."

"That's enough."

"Come on, come on, give."

I held up both hands for Dandy to be silent and reached for my wallet, laying two of Sandy's hundred dollar bills on the table. Dandy didn't seem to care that they were Canadian. He tucked the bills in his shirt. "I'll give you yours later," he told Larry, smooth as a snake.

"So Larry, what did you see?" I asked, but it was Dandy who started talking.

"You know this railroad line runs straight out of town to the south, right?" He pointed to the tracks at the far end of the park.

"Yeah, all the way to Detroit."

"That's right, and Larry likes to walk the tracks when he's humping around the country. It's more peaceful than the highway and he can camp wherever he likes. Ain't that right, Larry?"

"Guess so," Larry said with a shrug.

"So the other night, Larry was heading for town when he came upon an old railroad grade that was abandoned about a hundred years ago. The tracks got torn up long ago and all that's left is this long ridge that heads toward Lake Michigan. The old grade runs right through Stankville ."

"Stankville?" I'd never heard of it, but that was no surprise. There were dozens of ghost towns in northern Michigan left over from the lumber era. Towns like Aral, Quick and Logan that had gone back to the forest, their foundations bound by tree roots and barely glimpsed.

"That's right, Stankville. So tell him Larry. What did you see out there?"

"Well, I's a little nervous because some guy I met outside of Cadillac claimed there was this headless lumberjack up this way, like a ghost or sumpin', and maybe a bigfoot runnin' 'round the woods, too," Larry began. "So I's walkin' quiet as I could long 'bout sundown, lookin' for a place to camp and I come up on this little place like a town, but not a town. Know what I mean?"

"Yeah, sure," I said. "A burg."

"No, not like this," Larry raised his hamburger. "It was more like two trailers and an old shack."

"Yeah, okay, so what did you see?"

"Well, it weren't the Headless Lumberjack out there, but I didn't want to disturb no one, so I kind of took to the bushes to steer clear of the place. And that's when I saw it."

"Yeah?" I leaned close enough to smell the onions on Larry's breath.

"Yeah, there was this truck parked way back down a two-track, like a big old gravel truck. But the insides were all lined with plastic."

"That's it?"

"No, there's more. That truck had a crane mounted on the back, like a cherry-pickin' crane. And the crane had a big old sling on the end of it."

By now, Larry and Dandy had eaten four of the six burgers I'd fetched from Micky-D's. "You want that last one?" Larry asked.

"Go ahead," I said, pressure mounting in my head. What was I thinking of, putting my faith in these dingbats? I didn't know whether to be ticked off or bemused, but it was Sandy's money, so what did I care?

"So you saw a truck and a crane out in the ass-end of beyond and you think that's worth two hundred bucks?"

"That's right," Dandy interjected, "and I'll thank you to pass the fries, if you don't mind. Tell him the rest of it, Larry."

"Welp, I didn't think much of it either," Larry said, unwrapping his burger. "But have you ever seen one of them old-time circuses that used to travel around to all of these towns?"

"Yeah, sure."

"You don't see 'em around any more," Larry went on. "They used to have just one ring and a big-top tent. My momma took me to one when I was just a kid and I got to ride on a baby elephant."

"The animal rights people put a stop to them, if they didn't all go broke, first," I said.

"Is that right?" A sad look crossed Larry's face. "Well when my momma took me to the circus - I must have been only eight years old - but I'll never forget seeing this lion all cooped up in a big old cage, chewing on the skull of an ox. It was all bloody - the skull, that is - and you could see its horns and..."

"So?"

"Well, Mr. Dredd, can't you see? There was a big old cage just like the one I saw when I was a kid, sitting behind that truck way out in the woods. There weren't no lion in it, but it had big, black iron bars. It was big enough for two lions, I bet."

"Big enough for a polar bear," I mused.

"Oh hell yes!" Dandy slapped my knee, a huge grin on his face. "We got us a bingo here."

"Yeah, looks like it." Smokey's version of the Baker Street Irregulars had paid off like the backside of a casino.

"So what do you think, Mr. Dredd?"

"You did good, Larry, real good. I can use this. So where's this Stankville?"

Dandy smiled and popped the last of the french fries into his mouth. "That's gonna' cost you another hundred bucks," he said.

Operation Black Fish

I had a pretty good idea as to what was going on out in Stankville, but it would take some eyes on the scene to confirm it. Fortunately, I had a way to get out there that didn't involve riding a horse.

Larry told me that Stankville was deep in the forest of Hoosier Valley, a few miles south of Traverse City. There were miles of sandy trails out there where local rednecks tore through the woods on their ORVs, dirt bikes and jeeps when they weren't popping off rounds with their assault rifles. On any given weekend you're likely to find a bonfire in Hoosier Valley surrounded by drunken teenagers, passed out or braying at the moon. Back in the '90s, it was said to be the haunt of satanists. Bad shit happened out there; if you had a drug deal that went wrong, then Hoosier Valley would be the ideal place to plant a corpse. If you were interested in setting a stolen car on fire, Hoosier Valley was the go-to spot.

In short, Hoosier Valley was a spooky place where it was easy to get lost and I wasn't keen on heading out there, but that's what a private dick does, right? Larry Longshanks had drawn me a map for how to get to Stankville, heading down the abandoned railroad grade to its connection with an old lumber road.

I made my way to Smokey's Track-U-Down garage the next morning and found what I was looking for under a tarp along the back wall. It was Smoke's personal ORV quad, a four-wheeled motorcycle designed to go buckboarding through the woods. The key was still in the ignition and it had half a tank of gas. I was good to go.

And I did, out the back door of the garage and along the railroad tracks heading south. There were some tricky spots trying to clear the city at Airport Road, but soon I was deep in the forest, buzzing along the Boardman River in search of the old railroad grade. I found it about five miles to the south, veering into the darkened forest down a tunnel of trees that looked like the way to Spooky Hollow.

I don't know how far I drove, but it had to be at least three miles of bumping along the overgrown railroad grade, saplings whipping at the ORV like it was a lawn mower. At last I came to the intersection of a two-track lumber road where someone had dumped a refrigerator, a washing machine and other rusting trash years ago, half buried in the sand.

I headed east as Longshanks had instructed and rumbled along through the pines. This was crazy, there couldn't possibly be a town out here unless it was a ghost town from 100 years ago. Longshanks had said it was a small town, but I hadn't found it on any map, nor on Google Earth, and the trail

I was on wasn't fit for any vehicle without four-wheel drive.

But then I rounded a corner and saw it a couple hundred yards ahead, downtown Stankville.

The town Longshanks had described turned out to be two stubby camp trailers from the '60s of the sort hunters buy for $500 to use once a year. Both of them were rusted to shreds along the bottom and resting on rusted rims and crumbled tires. Alongside them stood a tar paper shack with a busted window and weathered planks exposed along its sides. A damp woodpile sprouting mushrooms occupied one side of the shack. On the other side was a rusting bathtub partially filled with rain water, pine needles and leaves. The tub was propped up on cinder blocks with the spent coals of a fire lying underneath and the water within was green with algae. I could see that rain water flowing off the roof was used to fill the tub and then a fire was lit to warm it. Ingenious. Nearby was a burn pile heaped with blackened tin cans and some still-smoldering plastic.

"This is country livin' at its best," I muttered. The shack was obviously built by someone who didn't know jack about carpentry, say perhaps a nine-year-old. The roof was partially caved-in with rot and a tangle of extension cords led out of the broken window to the trailers, and then to a jumble of old car batteries and a gas-powered generator that was mummified in rust.

Someone had lopped off the top of a pine tree and all of branches about eight feet up alongside the shack. There were several animal heads nailed to the tall stump. I recognized the skull of a whitetail doe, two raccoons and the rotting face of a startled porcupine. Also, the corpse of a three-foot-long Massasauga rattlesnake was nailed to the tree by its head. As I looked on from twenty feet away, a possum made its way into the clearing, gave me a nonchalant look, and crawled into a hole under the shack.

"This is some real hillbilly shit," I said to myself, backing away. Whatever was going on in Stankville had given me an epic case of the creeps. I'd seen enough horror movies to know that this was the kind of place where bad things happened to stranded wayfarers and clueless teenagers.

"Can I he'p you son?"

Damn! I about jumped out of my sandals.

Turning around, I found myself belly-to-belly with a human walrus. "Ah'm Elmer Stank. Can ah he'p you?" he repeated, real slow-like. "Ah' you from home care?"

Elmer Stank looked to be in his upper 70s with a belly like a bowl full of jelly, swathed in an XXXL t-shirt that was so threadbare it was almost transparent, shot full of tiny holes as if it had been speckled with battery acid. A cascade of hairy flab spilled over his belt, falling almost to his crotch. He was clutching a cane and weaving back and forth as if on the deck of a rolling ship. A few strands of greasy, gray hair wandered in wisps across the top of his scaly head and it was clear from his whiskery chin that shaving was not a priority. He was standing inside my comfort zone, chewing a plug of tobacco like a cow, with a brown stream of 'baccy juice dribbling down his chin.

"Home care?" I responded, surprising myself at how stupid I sounded.

"Yeah, thought you was the nurse."

It turned out that Stank was a diabetic and somehow the local home care nursing staff managed to find their way deep into the forest to trim his toenails and stock him with insulin stored in a cooler.

I mumbled something about being a through-hiker on the Northcountry Trail, which seemed to make about as much sense to Stank as if I'd spoken to him in ancient Greek, but he nodded slowly and kept chewing.

"Well, I 'spec the boys'll be 'long here purt quick," he said, nodding off to the side.

With that, he shuffled over the shack and stood in the open doorway, pausing for thirty seconds as if trying to remember something. "You have a blessed day, y'hear?"

"Yessir," I called back. "A blessed day to you too, Mr. Stank."

SANDY BOTTOM

The door closed with a creak and then a hard bump. And through the open window I saw Stank fold himself into a ragged arm chair with the necklace of an oxygen line slung over his head and into his nostrils.

But I didn't have time to ponder the miseries of getting old and sick our in the boondocks. Old man Stank had nodded in the direction of a side trail that I'd missed, and through the woods I saw what I'd come looking for: a gravel truck outfitted with what appeared to be a cherry picker.

The signs leading up the pathway to the truck were not encouraging. "No Trespassing" and "No Hunting" for starters, followed by a drawing of a red skull and crossbones with the warning that, "Trespassers Will Be Shot on Site." Then came one of those "Don't Tread on Me" flags with the coiled snake cut into 13 parts, along with a Confederate flag on the opposite side of the path. A final sign read "White Power" above a black circle that looked like a three-pronged cartwheel swastika.

Oh great. None of my detective novels had prepared me for this and even James Bond didn't have to deal with psycho rednecks. This felt more like one of the tunnel scenes from *Alien*, and I was getting a serious case of the chicken-outs. I could use a gummy bear right about now, and a tall cool one to settle my nerves.

Before I'd left Guatemala, Shaman Don had given me a copy of *Shamanism for Ding-Dongs* and I'd read about some Tantric breathing exercises used to steady the mind and arouse the inner-warrior. If ever there was a time to get leveled-out, this was it. I pulled myself up into Mountain pose and tried breathing all the way down to my pelvis to shake up the chakras. It was supposed to ignite the fire in the gonads; I don't know what the deal would be for a woman.

Anyway, I felt a little more warrior-like after a few deep breaths and headed down the path. No one was around but old man Stank and by now I could hear him snoring through the window. Besides, if I scored something big out here, it would clear my name and make a splash even bigger than the

Becky Jabbers case. It was time to roll the cosmic dice.

I crept forward past the signs, singing a bit under my breath to keep my cool:

"Zip-a-dee-doo-dah, zip-a-dee-ay.

My, oh, my what a wonderful day."

I made it past the skull-and-bones and then the Confederate flag and no one took a shot at me. Watchful as a doe, I looked around a clearing in the trees. Like Larry Longshanks had said, there was a gravel truck lined with what appeared to be heavy-mil black plastic, with the long, double-jointed arm of a yellow crane attached to the back end, equipped with a sling.

That, and a heavy cage of black steel bars, about eight feet square, standing on the far side of the truck, clearly the kind of lion cage used by a small time circus.

Gotcha!

I climbed up on the passenger-side of the truck and peered in the window. It was an old truck with a ripped-up vinyl seat shedding foam rubber, still outfitted with an ash tray that was brimming with butts. A couple of empty beer bottles were lying on the floor, with some rolls of anti-acid tabs on the dashboard. But the payoff was a wrinkled map of Ohio spread out on the seat with the town of Lima circled in black marker, along with the scribble, "Operation Blackfish."

Hmm, I'd already figured out what Operation Blackfish was and with a little snooping I imagined that any chicken pecking a line of corn could follow what it meant to a city in northeastern Ohio. "Curiouser and curiouser," I said, backing down off the truck.

I wandered over to the cage, which was roofed with the same heavy-mil plastic that sheathed the back of the gravel truck. There were some fish heads and a few ragged bones scattered around outside of the bars and the floor of the cage was spattered with mashed pellets of dog food. A pile of what had to be polar bear shit filled a corner of the cage, the door of which was partially open. This had to be where they'd held Sasha.

SANDY BOTTOM

I pulled out my phone and started snapping photos, imaging myself on the cover of *People* magazine and the main page of *HuffPost*. Man, this was bigger than Godzilla! Man, oh man, oh man!

Maybe it was the Tantric breathing exercises or the blood of triumph rushing through my ears, but I didn't hear the rumbling Hummer until it was barreling up the path to where I stood clicking away.

"Drop the phone, asshole, unless you want to lose that hand!"

Turning, I found my nemesis Anky Al, looking angry as a kicked bobcat with five camo-clad dudes brandishing a potpourri of weapons.

"Hey guys," I said, dropping the phone.

Al climbed out of the driver's seat, waving a chunky pistol in my face. He gave me a hard shove and stomped on my phone, grinding it into the dirt. "For your sake I hope you didn't text any of those," he growled.

"No signal out here," I replied, not that I'd bothered checking, but if Al thought otherwise, I'd be toast.

Anky Al was as tall and thick as a redwood tree and much the same color, owing to what I suspected was a case of uncontrolled high blood pressure. Ginger hair, ginger beard - his momma should have named him Ginger. He had a permanent snarl on his face that reminded me of an angry pig, though I suppose it would have been kinder to compare him with a bulldog. In short, he looked like bad news.

The other guys didn't look much better. One by one they piled out of the Hummer, leveling their guns at me. They were all squint-eyed and wearing ugly frowns, like I'd just kicked their dog or pissed on their Christmas presents. They looked as edgy as a Confederate army patrol that had been lost in the woods for 160 years.

One guy was dressed like a French *voyageur* re-enactor, complete with fringed buckskins, a snow-white ZZ Top beard hanging down to his pot belly, and a dead badger for a hat. The badger's eyes looked out over his brow. He had a six-foot-long musket trained on me and a toad-eating look on his face. His name patch read "Trapper."

The others wore gray German army camos that looked like they were from the Nazi era, but their firepower was up to date, kind of: a smattering of assault rifles, some of which seemed rigged to go full-auto. One of them had a Browning Automatic Rifle, the same gun that my dad had kept for protection when we were camping around the country in a van.

Their chariot was a '90s-vintage Hummer that had been brush-painted camo in squiggles of brown, gray and green. It was so heavy with rust that the front fenders were loose and flapping.

"Easy boys, I won't hurt you," I said, lowering my hands. "Anyone got a smoke?"

"You know who we are?" A fat guy with a Fu Manchu mustache and goatee called out. He was wearing a burgundy beret and cradling a sawed-off pump shotgun.

"Yeah, I know who you are."

"Who are we then?"

"You tell me and we'll both know." It was a bit of shamanistic jiu-jitsu.

The six of them gave me a stupefied look. "Oh, come on," Al muttered.

"You're the Irregular Sons O' the Northcountry," I said, northern Michigan's most notorious militia group. Everyone knew about these geeks, even if they hadn't been in the news for going on five years now. "I thought you guys all moved to Paraguay to be with your Nazi buddies."

"Fat chance," called out a wiry guy with a "Bazooka" name patch stitched over his chest pocket. He had a Hitler mustache that didn't do him any favors.

"So why do you call yourselves Irregular? That's got an unfortunate connotation."

"A what?"

"You know, the poop thing - irregularity."

"Listen," the Fu Manchu guy popped up, "we're an irregular *militia*, unattached to the pawns of the one-world gov'ment, get it? We're freedom fighters for the master race. We're..."

"It just seems funny, that's all. Kind of weird if you ask me."

"Well who's asking ya?" he shot back.

"Yeah, yeah, shut up with all that," Anky Al yelled."You want to tell us what you're doing out here?" He sounded as rough as gravel falling out of a dump truck.

Fortunately, I had my binoculars.

"I'm a birdwatcher," I said in my heartiest voice, raising my binocs. "I saw a big pileated woodpecker over this way and got so engrossed that I didn't notice your no trespassing signs. Sorry if I bothered you."

"Engrossed, huh? Try again or it's bye-bye birdie," Al waved his pistol. "In case you haven't noticed this is a pine grove and woodpeckers like hardwoods. But a birdwatcher would know that, wouldn't he?"

The militia guys stared at Al and then back at me. "Gee, I didn't know that," Bazooka Joe said.

"I happen to know that's not true," I said, calling Al's bluff. "Woodpeckers like pine trees just fine; the sap makes the bugs taste better. In fact, I just saw one flying around over there."

All of the militia guys looked off into the woods to where I pointed. All except Al. That blew my chance to run for it.

"Nice try, Nancy Drew, but you're going to be singing falsetto if you don't start talking," Al said, pointing his pistol at my crotch.

"What have you got against Nancy Drew?"

"She's like you, a nosy bitch." He feigned taking aim.

"Okay, you got me. Ease up," I said with what I hoped was a light-hearted chuckle. "I was a guest on 'Bigfoot Unbound' a while back and they asked me to scout the region for future shows. They're paying a bounty of ten thousand bucks for anyone who turns up solid evidence of a yeti. I was hoping to keep that to myself, but I guess there wouldn't be any harm in letting you boys in on the hunt, since you've got the drop on me."

"Really? Ten thousand dollars?" asked the guy who didn't know any more about woodpeckers than me.

"Shut up, Joe! I know exactly what you are," Al stabbed a finger at me. "You're a failed hairdresser with a phony detective's license, sticking your nose in our shit."

"Failed hairdresser?" I bristled. "Listen, tough guy, as it happens, I'm a licensed cosmetologist with a specialty in barbering men's hair, and that weed patch of yours could use some attention if you want me to fix it."

"What's wrong with my hair?" Al looked confused.

"It sucks, for starters. It's all over the place."

"That still don't make you a detective."

Anky Al had a point, but from what I'd seen on TV or in films, a big part of being a detective was bluffing. That, and channeling a tough-guy persona. I figured my best way out of this jam was to assume the world-weary mannerisms of a cat like Peter Falk on *Colombo*, who'd been on TV for longer than I'd been alive, even if it was all reruns on Hulu now.

"You don't think I'm a real detective?" I raised an eyebrow and squinted.

"Not by half," Al replied.

"You're the guy who hit me from behind a couple of weeks ago."

"Not hard enough, I see."

"Just so you know, I've got a degree from an accredited law enforcement program," I said, trying to sound as sleepy and wise-guy as Colombo. I didn't mention that my credentials were downloaded from the online Karachi Police Academy in Pakistan, which didn't require any coursework. I'd paid $12 for the diploma which was framed on the wall of my office cubicle. I'd used it to get my P.I. license.

Al hawked up a loogie and spat. "I don't care if you're Marshall Dillon," he said. "In about five minutes you're going to join the missing persons list, along with Jimmy Hoffa."

By now Al's face was as red as a radish. He gave me a squiggly grin and nodded to the five militiamen who were suddenly looking rather downcast. They'd even lowered their weapons.

"Come on guys, let's do this," he said.

"Uh, Al? We got to talk."

It was a tall, string-bean of a guy who'd hovered around the back of the four other militia dudes. He had the name patch, Ranger Rick, above the chest pocket on his camos and a captain's stripes on his shoulder.

"Stay right there," Al waved his pistol at me.

The group went off into a huddle about thirty feet away and an argument ensued, with Al's voice ranging high above the others. Damn, could that guy's face get any redder? He looked spitting-mad. The argument went on for at least twenty minutes, during which I figured I wasn't going to get wasted after all, at least not by the Irregular Sons O' the Northcountry. Gradually, I could see that Al was simmering down.

"Oh hell, do what you want," he said, breaking off from the group and waving in resignation.

Ranger Rick had the earnest look of an overgrown Boy Scout about him. He walked over to me while the rest of his boys climbed back into the Hummer.

"Look, we were never here and we know nothing at all about Al's crazy plan," he said, looking as serious as death. "In fact, we've never even seen you before and we don't know Al either. You got that?"

"Who?" I asked. "I don't know nothing 'bout nothing."

"Scout's honor?"

"Yeah, got it."

"Serious as death?" His eyes narrowed.

"Square business." I held up my hands. "With no fingers crossed. I've never seen any of you and hope I never will."

"Square business? What do you mean?"

"It's a saying. It's a thing, like from an old Shaft movie in the '80s."

"Good enough, detective, and if I were you, I'd forget this place existed too."

"What place? I've never seen this place. In fact, I don't even know I'm here."

Ranger Rick nodded and strode over to the waiting Hummer, climbing into the back seat. "Company, ho!" he hollered in a deep voice, and the rig wheeled around and rumbled down the two-track past Stankville into the woods.

That still left me with Anky Al and his gun. He walked over and looked at me with his hands on his hips, and then to my relief, he holstered his piece.

"You feeling okay?" I asked.

"What do you mean?"

"Your blood pressure looks like it's out of control."

"Yeah, the doctor's giving me some stuff. So how did you know?"

"You're as red as pepperoni."

"I've got to take it down a notch, and maybe the boys are right," he said, "though I still think they're chickenshits. Summer soldiers, I'd say. Pussies. They don't want anything to do with your disappearance."

"Can't blame them," I shrugged. "So what's with the goons? You don't strike me as the militia type."

Unlike the militia dudes, Al was dressed in a flannel shirt and jeans, topped by a Detroit Tigers ball cap.

"Nice try, shamus. I'd tell you but then I'd have to kill you."

"The Confederate flag? The white power thing? Is that what you're into?" I was needling him in the hope he'd give something away.

"You don't remember the '90s, do you?" Al said, squinting at me.

"I was a kid living out of a van with my folks down in New Mexico, but I remember Soundgarden and Stone Temple Pilots. Alanis Morissette, I remember her. Vanilla Ice, MC Hammer... then there was... "

"Alright, enough with that."

"Boyz II Men had the biggest hit of the '90s, did you know that?"

"I thought it was A-ha, 'Take on Me'," Al said.

"Nope. Friggin' Boyz II Men. Hey, remember Rick James?

Nirvana? Ice T when he was a cop-killer?"

"I know what you're trying to do, Bumpo, but stalling won't help you."

"You're the one who took us down memory lane. I'm just trying to be helpful."

"Well let me clue you in. Back in the '90s, some of our local klansmen and skinheads dreamed of creating a white homeland in northern Michigan. But they were shouted down by the local forces of diversity, also known as privileged white people who moved north to honky town to escape places like Detroit and Flint."

"Honky town? That's harsh."

"Yeah, sure, but little did the skinheads know that their fairytale came true quicker than you could say klavern of the klans, all thanks to market economics," Al went on. "This town turned into the white homeland after all. On any given day, you might see one black couple out of every two hundred walking downtown. The Indians who once camped on these shores? They're barricaded miles away in their casinos. The ten thousand Mexicans who pick the fruit and grapes around here? Seldom seen, amigo, seldom seen. They're hiding out from ICE."

"Sounds like you've got a chip on your shoulder."

Al gave me a dead-in-the-eyes look. "I'm one-sixteenth Haida Indian and I taught poly-sci at a junior college in Anchorage, so me and these militia boys ain't exactly on the same page."

"So why hook up with them, then?"

"Do you know how much a junior college instructor makes in Alaska?" Al said, squinting at me. "Me and the boys got a business arrangement."

"Hmm." A rogue political science instructor turned redneck animal rustler? That was bent. If Al was that smart, he'd figure out that he'd blabbed too much already, but maybe he didn't care if I knew his past. Maybe he had plans for me and a shallow grave. While Al was philosophizing I was looking around, wondering if I could make a break for it. There were a lot of pine trees to hide behind and he didn't look like much of a runner. But he wasn't done yakking, and I didn't think I could outrun a bullet.

Al fished out a Camel and lit up. "Do you know what killed the militia movement?"

"Madonna."

"Close. It was the federal conspiracy laws," Al said. "After Timothy McVeigh blew up a federal building in Oklahoma City back in '95, the FBI made it their business to remind every militia member in the country that if they didn't rat out their buddies on something like a bombing, then they'd be as guilty as the guy who set off the truck bomb. Even if you didn't want anything to do with an act of domestic terrorism, you could end up doing life in a supermax just for *knowing* about it unless you spilled your guts to the cops."

"Tough times for domestic terrorists," I said dryly. Anky Al had calmed down considerably, but it was still just the two of us jawing out here in the woods, and it was starting to look like rain.

"Yeah, tough beans," he replied. "So the boys figured they couldn't partake of your send-off, because if just one of them mentioned it to, oh, a wife or cell mate, say, ten years from now, then they'd all swing for it."

"And that means you, too," I added for his benefit. "So let's get out of here and let bygones by bygones."

Al gave me an evil look. "Shut the front door, Bumpo. Do you want to live long and prosper?"

"Who doesn't?"

"You come out here again and you're a dead man."

I gave him a hangdog Colombo look. "Why you wanna' be so mean, Al? Who are you, really?"

"I'm your darkest nightmare."

"The Headless Lumberjack?"

"Listen, little buddy, you'll wish the Headless Lumberjack was here if and when I start on you, because it will be hammer and tongs. You got that?"

"Yeah, got it." Turning, I headed back down the two-track

to where the quad was parked, trying to keep my rubbery legs from shaking, trying not to run as I imagined taking a bullet through my spine at any moment. But I reached my rig without peeing my pants and Al hadn't fired. I turned and saw him standing 200 feet away in the clearing next to the truck. He drew a finger across his throat and disappeared into the woods.

Dredd on the Run

It was late by the time I motored back to town and I had a choice to make: either a long spell of meditation with some scented candles and soothing music or a couple of stiff drinks. No surprise, the latter won out and I was sitting at the bar medicating myself when Jakeway snuck up behind me.

"No hard feelings?" he said, extending a palm.

"For what? That story about me and Sandy? She loved it," I said. "But you owe me the second round."

"Done, and you owe me a story."

"Yeah, maybe." I looked into the bottom of my glass, calculating the algorithm of the news that would do me the most good. How much should I tell Jakeway? Not much, just yet.

Instead I said, "What do you know about Lima, Ohio?"

He shrugged. "It's the lima bean capital of America. Everyone knows that."

"Seriously?"

"How would I know? I don't know jack about Lima, Ohio."

"Neither do I, but it has something to do with the death of Timothy Bottom."

Jakeway steepled his fingers, bringing them to his lips, elbows on the bar. "And how do you know this?"

"A little birdie told me," I said, draining my glass and waving it. "Another, please."

"Hold on." Jakeway pulled out his phone and spoke to Siri. "Lima, Ohio."

Siri rambled on about the population of Lima, its geographic dimensions, its place in Allen County and its proximity to Dayton, Toledo and Fort Wayne.

"None of that's very helpful," I said.

"Attractions include Whale World and the Lima Locomotive Works Incorporated," Siri chattered on. "Lima was once the...

Now we were getting somewhere. Whale World, Operation Blackfish and the truck in the woods with a crane and a sling. But how did that fit with Bottom's murder? And what about the Silverado in Smokey's repo lot? Were Smokey and Anky Al in this together? My head was spinning.

"Dredd! Earth to Dredd. Can you hear me?" Jakeway was snapping his fingers in my ear.

"Wha? Oh, just thinking," I said, coming out of my daze.

"You don't look like the thinking type."

"It happens once in awhile."

"So what can you give me?"

"An exclusive, but I've got to put the pieces together first, see?"

"Details, anything at all," Jakeway pushed. "I shouldn't be telling you this, but Wellington is building a case against you and he's drooling over it. I think it's bullshit, but if someone is trying to frame you then you'd better watch your back."

"What can they do? I'm clean."

"Yeah? Well, just sayin'."

My second drink led to another and then two more after that, with Jakeway buying doubles. And then one more after that and maybe one for the road. Who can remember? And then it was close to midnight, the room was spinning and I was falling off the bar stool and invited by the staff none too graciously to leave. I don't remember saying goodbye to Jakeway, or how much I'd spilled on what I knew about Anky Al, Stankville and all the rest of it. I do remember throwing up behind the bar, though, and resting for a bit with my back up against a dumpster that smelled heavily of rank hamburger grease and garbage. What a day.

SANDY BOTTOM

Along about 3 a.m. I got the chills and picked myself up.
One of the bouncers had thrown a mug of beer on me out the
back door and I was soaked. The moon was hanging bright
in the sky as I wobbled home, and I swear it was laughing at
me. Far down Eighth Street I saw a commotion outside my
boarding house with four cop cars parked outside, their red
and blue lights swirling like an impromptu disco. I stumbled
sideways across a lawn and crashed into some bushes, falling
on my ass. What the hell? The lawn started tilting sideways
back and forth and I barfed again. This time it was the dry
heaves. Strange to say, it appeared as if the world was upside down and I was pinned to the ground looking *down* at
the sky. What a strange and curious sensation... Then the sky
started spinning, a wave of darkness rolled up my spine and
into my brain and I passed out.

How long? I don't know, maybe only an hour, but when I
came to, the cops were gone and Shirley and Mary Jean were
standing on the front porch talking in the half light just before
dawn.

I wobbled down the street, my legs still rubbery and weaving in all directions. "Hey!" I called.

Mary Jean's teenage daughter was with them, but not for
long. "Get in the house!" her mom ordered.

"Hey, whaz's up?" I probably looked like hell and smelled
like it too, even from across the lawn.

Shirley and Mary Jean were backing inside the house. "You
better get runnin' Dredd," Shirley called out. "The cops were
just here with a search warrant."

"Yeah? So?"

The two gave me a pitying look, like the village idiot had
just been caught with his pants down.

"You aren't fooling anyone, Dredd," Mary Jean said. "They
found the machete under your bed and it had a whole lot of
blood on it."

With that they backed into the house, slammed the door and
turned out the lights. I could hear the deadbolt slide shut.

What the hell? The sun was coming up fast, I stank like a

garbage dump, and my head felt like it had been jackhammered from the inside-out. I had to find somewhere to hide, fast, and there was only one place I could think of.

I spent that day and a night hiding out in the trunk of the Audi at Smokey's garage, venturing out only to take a piss or drink some water. It was one of those cars that have a release latch inside the trunk, but even so, it was a leap of faith locking myself in, especially since it was tighter than a bug's butt in there.

How had I missed it? Every hard-boiled dick in every pulp novel ever written *always* got framed and that had completely flown by me, even with Jakeway spoon-feeding me a warning. What a sap I'd been!

I spent the whole time steaming. Friggin' Anky Al had done the next best thing to shooting me. He must have jimmied the window in my room and planted a bloody machete under my bed. And whose blood would it have on it? Not hard to guess.

Hunger drove me from the car midway through the second day after I'd exhausted Smokey's stash of cheeto's and stale corn chips. By that time I'd moved into the back seat of the Bronco, hiding beneath a blanket. The cops hadn't come busting through the garage door and no one had even knocked, so I figured they didn't know about my connection to Smokey's Track-U-Down operation.

But my name was all over the radio as a major suspect in the murder of Timothy Bottom. I was implicated as a crazed killer, a diabolical mastermind, most likely a devil worshipper and a practicing yogacist. The cops and the local media had me figured for Dr. Moriarty instead of Sherlock Holmes.

Time to think? I had plenty of it. Also time to hatch a plan, but it wasn't going to be easy, and danger would follow my footsteps with peril lurking down every dark alley. But that's the gig I signed on for when I decided to become a shamanic shamus and a New Age dick.

Okay, so skip the drama. But I needed two things: a phone and a gun.

SANDY BOTTOM

I ransacked the garage looking for Smokey's snub nose .38, but didn't expect to find it. If Smoke was on the lam, he would have taken his gat. The good news was that he had a drawer full of stuff from repo'ed vehicles, including watches, sunglasses, hash pipes, flashlights, condoms, whiskey flasks and phones. It was a working phone that I needed, since mine was ground into the dirt out in Stankville. I switched on a light and opened the drawer; there were three phones inside, two of which were beyond dead. The third was on the gummy side, but it still had a two percent charge deep into the red zone and Smokey had a charger. I juiced it up a bit and checked to see that its camera function was working.

Now I could check in with Sandy, except - *duh* - who memorizes phone numbers these days? Fortunately, I'd written her number down on my table back at the office. Hopefully, my dad's pistol would still be there as well.

But how to get there? Again, Smokey's collection of confiscated gear provided my cover. I had no intention of trying to sneak downtown after midnight when I'd be the only guy out on the street and easy to spot. Instead, I'd stop by the office during rush hour when the streets were packed with traffic. I'd just be one more commuter out of thousands heading home for work, only I'd be wearing a motorcycle helmet with a black sunshade.

Smokey had three motorcycles parked in his garage and I picked out the only one that had the key in the ignition, a Yamaha 250cc dirt bike.

Three other people shared cubicles on the second floor of the building that served as my office and they always took off by a quarter to five. I waited until 5:30 and figured it was time to roll. I pushed the bike through the back door of the garage, unlocked the chain on the gate leading down the driveway and hit the ignition. Nothing.

Gol'danged motorcycle was out of gas and I'm standing outside the gate looking suspicious with a helmet on my head. I backed up the bike, rummaged around for a gas can and crossed my fingers. This time the bike coughed and died a couple of times before sputtering to life.

I'd never driven a motorcycle before, but figured it couldn't be any different than riding my mountain bike or one of the mopeds I'd piloted around Guatemala. Still, I didn't want to fall on my ass at some intersection on the way downtown, so I took it easy. I pulled into the alley behind my office, parked the bike and tip-toed up the back stairs.

"Anybody home?" I called out. "Got a delivery here. Anyone home?"

Silence.

I unlocked the door to the cubicle suite and made my way in, not bothering to turn on the lights. As I'd expected, my office had been tossed by Wellington and the cops. My laptop was missing and so was my strongbox. No big loss there, since all I had locked up was a stash of gummy bears and a notebook containing some bad poetry and song lyrics.

There was a coffee can on top of my table containing a few pens and pencils that the cops hadn't bothered to take. I fished around in the bottom of it for the black cat bone that Shaman Don had given me when I left Guatemala. It still looked suspiciously like a chicken bone, but Don had said it contained a powerful dose of ju-ju, whatever that was, and would bring me good luck. I figured I'd need it and stuck it in the leather fanny pack on my waist where I kept the Crystal Skull Don Pedro.

Fortunately, Sandy's phone number was still barely legible in pencil where I'd scribbled it, and feeling around underneath the table, I found my dad's blue steel .44 still nestled in the holster I'd nailed to the underside. I punched Sandy's number into the contacts on my phone, stuck the gat in my belt and made my way back downstairs.

By this time I was as ravenous as the wolverine that allegedly killed Timothy Bottom, so I risked a few more blocks and made it through a drive-through for a three-pack of tacos and a bean burrito. Then it was back to Smokey's garage for a pig-out and a couple of beers from the fridge.

I'd take it slow and easy from here. Tomorrow morning I'd

drive the quad back out to Stankville, park it a half mile away and sneak in to get some photos of Anky Al's operation. Then I'd turn myself in to the cops and show them the photos along with directions on how to get out to the site. At least that was my plan, but it all went to hell as soon as I called Sandy.

She answered on the first ring.

"Oh Dredd, I knew it would be you. I knew you would call." She sounded stressed.

"Sandy, what's wrong?"

"It's momma's butler, Dredd. He's gone crazy. He's saying crazy things!"

"Al? The guy who drives your mom around?"

"Yes! I hate to say it, Dredd, but I think Al might have something to do with Timothy's death."

"You mean..."

"I think the butler did it," she said glumly.

"No surprise there."

"But what should I do now? Tim's gone, but there's still the money..."

"Now don't go thinking like that."

"We have to reason with him. We have to work something out."

Sandy's voice had dropped an octave and for a moment she spoke off the line. "Momma, hold on, I'm talking to Dredd," I heard her say. Her mother answered in Russian and didn't sound happy.

"Sandy, don't do anything stupid, you'll just make things worse!" I yelled into the phone. "That guy's a killer. We've got to call the police."

Sandy came back on the phone. "No, no police. In Russia they would take everything."

"Get woke, woman, this isn't Russia!"

"Oh, but I still need answers, and now there's the problem of Tim not dying of natural causes and Momma's acting strange too. Oh Dredd, I feel so confused. I don't know what to do! But Momma and I need to talk to Al. We need to - what do you say? Confront him."

"No Sandy, whatever you..."

"I know where he is, Dredd, and he's just a man. Momma and I, we know him. He'll listen to us."

"But..."

"I'll call you right back."

"What? When?"

"Tomorrow." The line went dead.

I tried calling back four times but Sandy didn't pick up. "Oh God, Sandy, you nit-wit. Al's going to give you the same treatment he gave Tim," I said, slamming both hands on Smokey's desk.

But not if I could help it. I figured I'd break my neck if I tried riding the dirt bike out to Stankville, so I parked it and rolled out Smokey's ORV quad again. If Sandy and her mom were going to have a meet-up with Anky Al, I had a pretty good hunch it would be down the same trail I'd traveled two days before. I had a black cat bone and some mojo too. What could go wrong? Quicker than you could say Johnny conquering root, I was heading south on the quad.

Le Denouement

It stays light out until almost 10:30 p.m. in northern Michigan during the high summer, so even though it was early evening, I still had plenty of time to skulk around the back side of Stankville to see how Sandy's meet-up went down. I bumped back down the tracks for miles south of town to the abandoned railroad grade. Then it was the same as last time, a long, black tunnel of trees heading for an uncertain situation. Reaching the turnoff to Stankville I found Sandy's Tesla buried in the sand up to its running boards alongside the cast-off refrigerator and rural dump. That had to mean that she and her momma had hiked the rest of the way in, or else they'd been intercepted by Al and his militia goons.

I edged around the car and buzzed on up the two-track road, hiding the quad in a thicket of pine trees about half a mile out. I walked in the rest of the way, staying about ten feet to the side of the lumber road so I could dodge out of sight if anyone came along.

The woods were quiet, dark and buggy. It was a hot day in what had been a summer drought and I could almost feel the desperation of the pines for rain. Soon, I heard voices ranging through the trees from the direction of the militia's truck. There was no need to alert Elmer Stank to my presence, so I bushwhacked through the woods toward the sound of the voices.

Sandy and her mother were standing alongside the truck, speaking in Russian. Sandy was in high gear, raging at her mother with her face turned strawberry pink. For her part, Momma responded in a measured way, and I got the impression she was trying to be reassuring. There was no sign of Anky Al or the Irregulars.

So I wandered out of the woods and said, hey. Neither of them seemed happy to see me.

"*Tovareesch* Bumpo," Sandy's mother growled.

"It's good to see you, too, comrade Rostova."

"Goot!" she answered back.

"Dredd, what are you doing here?" Sandy demanded, looking more rattled than I'd ever seen her.

"You called and I came running."

"But how did you know this place? Even we had a hard time finding it, and Al gave us directions."

"I'm a detective, remember? This is what you hired me to do."

"No Dredd, not this, and you have to go. We're having a business meeting and you have been dismissed from my employment."

"Not so fast, Sandy. I know everything, including your husband's plan to kidnap a killer whale."

Sandy blanched, the strawberry hue draining from her face as she looked at me in alarm.

"What?"

"That's right, babe. A friggin' whale."

" That's ridiculous," she snapped, but not too convincingly.

"Strange but true, Tim planned a whale-napping, using that truck to hit a place called Whale World in Lima, Ohio. They've got a big aquarium there along with a dolphin show and three orcas. I checked and they've got a blackfish named Horace who happens to be the oldest captive orca in the country. Old alligator, old polar bear and now an old orca, all with a connection to Timothy Bottom, Anky Al, and the mastermind of this butt-crazy scheme."

"What?" she went another shade whiter. "You can't suspect me in this! You cannot think that I would harm Tim!"

"I don't mean you, Sandy, I'm talking about your momma, Natalia Rostova, the brains behind the Wolverine Pipeline, back in Siberia."

Through all of this, Sandy's mother looked back and forth at us like an inquisitive dog, trying to figure out what the humans were saying. She didn't even register when I said her name, she just said, "Goot!"

But not so with Sandy. "Kidnap a whale? My momma? This is crazy!" she exploded.

"Yeah, totally. But I figured out what Tim's nuclear option was as soon as you told me it was Operation Blackfish. I just had to put the words together, see? He was going to kidnap a killer whale and dump it in Grand Traverse Bay, for what reason I can't imagine, and I figure your momma was in on it with Al and his militia buddies."

"Goot!"

"But why Momma? She doesn't even know English! And this Wolverine Pipeline, it's ridiculous!"

"Goot!" Momma nodded her head up and down like it was on a coiled spring.

"Sure, Sandy, you said that already. But it has to be your momma, see? Because this situation is *exactly* the same as in every mystery novel ever written. The villain *always* turns out to be the least-likely character who appears no later than the second chapter."

"So?"

Oh man, I was relishing this.

"That's right," I said. "In the timeline of Timothy Bottom's death, your appearance in my office would have been the second chapter if this caper had been a mystery novel, and your momma was the least likely person to be involved in a murder. She was just a nice old, uncomprehending lady with a kerchief tied around her chin. Who else could it be?"

"That's your proof?" Sandy was incredulous. "You got all that from reading detective novels? You've been smoking too much weed, Dredd. It's, it's... ridiculous!"

"Yeah, sure, it sounds crazy, but I snooped around on the Interpol website to learn that your momma is wanted for poaching in Siberia. The Russian federales claim that she headed up the Wolverine Pipeline before she emigrated to the U.S. And that's who hijacked the polar bear from the zoo in Irkutsk."

That tidbit provoked a long spell of silence. I could tell that it had soaked in with Sandy, if not her mother, that the jig was up.

Suddenly, Momma piped up, and she wasn't just saying "goot" anymore. It turned out that Natalia Rostova spoke impeccable English.

"But Mr. Bumpo," she said, "if life mimics literature as you say, then isn't it likely that *you* are acting out a postmodern detective fiction in which *you* are the killer, possibly under the influence of amnesia or psychoactive drugs? After all, that is the logic of many contemporary mysteries. In the end, it's the detective and the alleged hero of the story who is revealed as the fiendish killer. At least, that's what passes for literature these days. Mystery novels, *pah!*"

"Momma!"

I guess my eyes bugged out a bit, because Sandy's mother gave a dry chuckle. "Yes, Mr. Bumpo, I speak English. In fact, I have a masters degree in zoology from Oxford, and your supposition is right about the bear at least, but not the whale. Certainly not the alligator."

"So you think *I'm* an amnesiac killer?" My head reeled. Damn, could it be true?

"No, of course not," she waved. "But you are in danger-ous waters, Mr. Bumpo, as are we. My butler, Mr. Anky, has switched sides against us and is working in league with Tim's brother, Billy, to steal all of Sandy's inheritance. We came to work things out with him."

"You came to offer him a bigger slice of the pie."

"That's right," Momma nodded. "We are gambling that he will be a reasonable man."

"A guy who lets a giant alligator loose in a kayak stream isn't my idea of reasonable."

"No, but that's the chance we must take, because other-wise..." she turned up her empty palms and shrugged.

"But if you have a masters degree from Oxford, why would you get involved in a nutty scheme like this?"

Momma Rostova spat off to the side. "Do you know what a zoologist makes in Russia?"

Just then, Anky Al came rumbling down the two-track in the old pickup truck I'd seen him driving around town. The truck pulled even with us and lurched to a juddering stop, its engine expiring with a rattle and a cough.

He glared at me out of his window, the temperature of his face going a few degrees redder. "You're a dead man, Bumpo."

"Yeah, I don't think so."

"You shouldn't have come out here."

"I'm just here for the ladies."

Al's face got even uglier. "Well I'm afraid you're all going to be disappointed then, because I've thought it over, and it's no deal. There's too many loose ends."

"You can't get away with this," I shot back. "I know about the whale and I can trace you to the bear and the alligator too."

Al didn't even try to pretend he didn't know what I was talking about.

"Big whoop," he said. "I've already gotten away with it. That cage will be at the bottom of Lake Michigan by tomorrow morning. And as for the whale, the militia boys backed out on Bottom's plan to hijack it months ago."

"Really."

"Yeah. Bottom promised us two million bucks to pull off the heist and we had the truck and crane all set. We were going to drive down to Ohio, sling the whale into the truck, and drive it up to Grand Traverse Bay. We were going to dump it right off the beach downtown. But the guys chickened out, the same as they chickened out on getting rid of you. I guess they're not as stupid as they look."

"So..."

I couldn't believe it. It was just like in a movie or at the end of an *NCIS* episode where the bad guy comes clean, spilling all the details, dotting all the i's and crossing all the t's to wrap up the show.

"So Bottom flipped," Al went on. "He said he was going to rat us out if we didn't go along with the whale heist. We were already in neck-deep with helping to transport the gator and the polar bear. Threatening us, and me in particular, was a big mistake on his part. Do you know how hard it is to transport a polar bear and a wolverine across the Canadian border?"

"Search me," I shrugged.

"Turns out it's not hard at all, but we wanted to get paid, and Bottom refused to cough it up, on top of threatening to rat us out."

"So you killed him."

"No, not me. It was a wolverine, don't you know?"

"Yeah, I've got that one figured out too," I said. "I know about you and the wolverine, the same as I knew about Operation Blackfish. And I know how you killed Bottom. It's all in the pulps."

"Pulps?" his eyebrows arched.

"Mystery novels. I'll tell you later when you're rotting in jail. But one thing I don't understand is why you let the gator and the bear loose after Bottom died? You didn't have to do that."

"I let the gator loose the same day that Bottom kicked,"

he said. "We were driving around in his Silverado looking for a place to dump it and he went crazy on me about us reneging on the whale heist. After the wolverine killed Bottom I dumped the gator in Little Platte Lake and somehow it crawled twenty miles up the road to the Crystal River a few weeks later."

"So how come no one saw you?"

Al gave an inward-looking smile. "They almost did. Tim was a mess, dead from the wolverine attack, and I saw a boat pulling into the dock. There was no time to hide him, so I dumped him down the potty."

"That's really sick."

"Yeah, I have some regrets about that," Al said with a heave of his chest, "But what could I do? I was standing right behind the outhouse when Gladys Mahill charged up the hill to relieve herself. Lucky for her she didn't peek around the back way. Nor did anyone think to ask her about the Silverado, which was parked in the lot when she found Bottom in the john."

"So where was the gator while this was going on?"

Anky Al chuckled in remembrance. "She damned near stepped on the thing when she jumped out of her boat."

Al was singing like Pavarotti so I pushed on, wishing that I'd thought enough to hit the recording app on my phone.

"So what was the deal with the bear?" I pushed on. "If Bottom was dead, why did you set it free?"

"We kept it around as a pet until our supply of fish ran out, but it didn't like dog food and started getting obnoxious. The boys couldn't stand the idea of shooting it, so we let it go."

"In the suburbs? That's crazy."

"Let's just say that some of the boys have a strange sense of humor. That guy, Trapper, who wears a dead badger for a hat? Totally batshit. He's a French and Indian War re-enactor who walks around town with a musket, as nutty as squirrel shit. I wasn't keen on letting the bear go, but after we got pimped by Bottom, I figured it was okay to let the guys have a little fun."

SANDY BOTTOM

Al was gushing like an explosion in a bean factory. I kept pushing while he was in the mood to talk.

"So what happened to the Silverado?"

"That got dumped by the side of the road up near Peshawbestown. The last I heard, it got repo'd. With Tim dead, no one was paying the bank loan."

So that was how Smokey Williams came to have the truck in his parking lot.

"Is Smokey Williams mixed up in this?"

Confusion played across Al's face. "Smokey Williams?"

"The repo man." My friend.

"You mean the fat guy who plays guitar around town?"

"Yeah, he's missing. And he's not fat, he's stocky."

"I've seen his show and it sucks."

"So where is he then?"

"How the hell should I know? Probably playing Carnegie Hall. I don't know the guy from diddly."

Something smelled here. Anky Al was being way too loose with the juice, spilling the beans on everything I asked. There could only be one reason for him being so forthcoming; he wasn't planning to leave any witnesses.

Through all this, Sandy and her mother had been listening patiently.

"Al, fifty-fifty," Sandy broke in. "We'll split my inheritance. That's sixty million for you and sixty for us, plus change."

Al whistled and looked skyward. "That's a lot of coin, honey, but I don't need much more than the million that Billy promised me. My life is mostly 'bout huntin' and fishin' and I intend to keep it that way. But you - you've got too much flash - you draw too much attention. And I know you and your momma, Sandy. You're like sharks, always swimming, always looking for a meal. If you gave me sixty million dollars, I'd feel your breath up my ass for the rest of my life, coming to get your money back. Either that or you'd end up blabbing about me at one of your fancy parties, and I've got too much baggage now to risk that sort of thing. No, I think things are going to work out just fine, keeping this all nice and simple the way Billy Bottom and I have it sussed."

"Billy Bottom? You'd trust that *krysa* over me?" Momma Rostova sputtered. "We had a deal, Al. We're a team. I have friends in Russia who won't be happy about this."

"Get real, Momma," Al said in that smoky voice of his. "You've been living over here for almost five years now and your Russian connections are running on fumes. We were lucky to get that bear, but from what I hear, your crew in Siberia never got paid and now they're pissed. That all lands on your doorstep, lady. Not that it matters much now."

It was time to make my move.

"Look, there goes that woodpecker again!" I pointed off in the distance.

This time Al got suckered into looking long enough for me to pull my dad's .44 out from behind my back where I'd stuck it in my belt. Dad's hand-cannon felt heavy, reassuring, and most of all lethal, nestled in my hand like our ticket out of a jam. It bobbed up and down in my hand like I was floating on a rocking boat.

"Too bad, Al. You're going to Palookaville. One move and you're chopped."

"Chopped?"

"Shot up, drilled, ventilated."

Al raised his hands in mock surprise. "You know that's a revolver, don't ya?" he said.

"Yeah? What of it?"

"I can see you don't have any bullets in the cylinder."

"Like hell." But I knew he was right. There had been a couple of old bullets rattling around in my lock box back at the office, but the cops had taken them in their raid.

"Yeah, like hell. I can see yer runnin' on empty, boy," he said, pointing at my pistol. "Take a look-see for yourself."

"That doesn't mean I don't have one in the chamber with your name on it."

Al gave a chuckle and raised his own piece, an ugly snub-nose that looked like a cast-off from the Yugoslavian army. "Well let's play a little game of Mexican roulette then," he said. "I'll let you have the first shot."

He had me there. I tossed my pistol on the ground and raised my hands, fishing around in my thoughts for another gambit. Unfortunately, the fish weren't biting.

"You don't think I'd walk around with a loaded gun do you?" I said. "Someone could get hurt."

Al gave a groan and shook his head. "So stupid."

He shook his pistol at me, pointing to my fanny pack. "What's in the bag?"

"Personal stuff, nothing you'd be interested in."

"What? Like some kind of vaping trash? Show me."

I unzipped the pouch on my belt and raised the lip.

Al craned his neck to look at the contents. "What the hell?" he exclaimed. "You've got a chicken bone in there and a toy skull?"

"The skull is a birthday present for my niece. She was born on Halloween."

"And the chicken bone?"

I wasn't about to tell Al that it was my lucky black cat bone, dubious though it was. "Uh, someone was littering in the KFC parking lot and I was doing my bit as a good citizen, picking it up," I said.

I could see Al's eyes spinning at the derangement of that answer, but it was all I could think of.

"You really are crazy, Bumpo," he said in disgust. "I can't believe Sandy hired you."

"Whatever, let's move this along, okay? I told the Wild-life Warriors that I was heading out this way and they're hot on my trail, so I suggest you let us go before this gets ugly. Those dudes work out and they're packing."

Al scoffed at that idea, showing me a video link on his smart watch. It displayed images of the two-track road through the forest with a number of different views. "How do you think I knew you were out here in the first place, Bumpo? I've got trail cams set up all down the track for a mile out. I had eyes on you both times you came out here."

"Oh yeah?"

"Yeah, and here's another thing, smart guy. The Wildlife Warriors had a part to play in this little drama, and they ain't likely to be swoopin' in anytime soon."

I sighed, that was my last card to play. "Okay, you got us Al. So now what? You're going to kill us, I suppose?"

"Dredd, shut up!" Sandy called from behind me.

"Yes, Dredd, don't give him any ideas!" Momma pitched in.

He lowered his gun and placed it in his holster with an amused look on his face. "Oh, I got a little somethin' in mind for you three. But you're not gonna' like it."

I saw my chance.

Back in San Marcos I'd met a semi-pro Mexican boxer who'd taught me a few moves: right hooks, left jabs, fancy footwork and working out on the heavy bag. I'd even let her beat me up a few times in some sparring matches on the yoga platform at the Last Resort, provoking a fair amount of laughter from the women in the audience.

So I figured I'd double-tap Anky Al with a couple of left jabs to the kisser and then give him a hard right to the solar plexus, also known as the gut.

But before I could set up my punches, Al dropped to his knees and sucker-punched me in the groin, also known as the nuts. I went down like a sack of flour dropped from the rafters.

"Fa-uuuck..." I moaned.

"That's how we do it in Anchorage," he chuckled, pulling his gun again and waving it. "Now get in that cage, all three of you. I'll bet yer gonna' feel a wee bit funny fer a spell."

Al had the drop on us and it was true, I did feel a wee bit funny down below, like I wanted to puke, maybe.

"It stinks in there," I gasped through the pain radiating from my groin.

"Yeah? Well would you rather I shot you in the leg to keep you here? Come on, move your asses."

We moved them, and Al shut the barred door behind us. "You should feel honored," he said. "This is an old lion cage from the circus that used to play at the Civic Center in town. I bought it on their last fling before they went broke."

"Al, what are you going to do?" Sandy shouted. "You can't leave us here. People will know we're missing."

"Mmm, I expect so. That will give everyone something to puzzle over. But I imagine that somehow, Dreddy here will be taking the blame," he replied, walking over to his truck. He pulled a shovel from the truck bed and leaned on it like a walking stick.

"I'm going to head off for a bit to get some exercise, okay? But if I hear any yelling for help back here, I'm going to be right back for a little target practice. You got that?"

"You dirty *krysa*," Momma Rostova spat at him. "A gypsy curse on your head!"

Al gave her a blank look. "You go ahead and work on that while I'm gone, Momma. But I'll tell you one thing - that's only going to make me dig faster."

The Transformative Skull

We watched as Anky Al pushed through a gap in the pines, heading well off the track into the woods to a place where no one would ever find our bodies, unless some passing hunter found some dug-up bones sticking out of the sand on some far-off day.

That wasn't in my plans.

Minutes went by and Al disappeared over a low rise.

"We could try calling for help," Sandy said. "I saw an old man in that shack down the driveway."

"I know that guy and he's got a brain like raw suet," I said. "What then?"

"Oof, it's nap time," Momma interjected. She sat down heavily in a corner of the cage and was asleep in under ten seconds. Soon, she was snoring softly, muttering "goot" now and then under her breath.

"We'll figure a way out," I said, trying to sound confident. In the pulps and the noir flicks, tough guy detectives always figured their way out of a jam. Simple. Easy-peasy. That's all I had to do - figure a way out of this cage. But for the moment I was stumped and there were a few things I had to know, if and before I got bumped off.

"I have to ask you Sandy, did you know about the plan to kill Timothy? Were you part of it?"

Sandy let loose with an f-bomb and glared at me. "Dredd, how dare you think that of me! No! Of course not! I thought it was one of Tim's crazy animals that killed him. I thought it was probably some stupid accident, just like Steve Irwin got killed by a stingray. Can't you see? That's why I hired you to track down his death by natural causes."

I believed her. The tears in Sandy's eyes were genuine.

"But you knew about his crazy plan to dump these animals around northern Michigan, right?"

"Yes, but not because Tim told me. He had a room full of computers monitoring the extinction of species around the world. Do you know that half of the wild animals in the entire world have disappeared since the 1970s? That was the sort of thing we talked about over dinner. Tim was obsessed with mass extinction and invasive species."

"Yeah? Well going from caring about animals to sending them to certain death is a big leap."

Sandy bit her lower lip and wiped the tears from her eyes with the back of her hand. "Yes, of course. Tim seemed okay when I first met him, but gradually he started going insane. He had an affliction called environmental depression, where people see no hope for the world, no answers. Climate change, mass extinction, it made for some very depressing talk at our parties, I can tell you that."

"The only cure is to turn Republican," I mused.

"Yes, and he couldn't do that."

"But how did you find out what he was up to?"

"A wife can find out anything, that's what you men don't understand. He had one laptop that was special, with all of his plans on it. I found the password written underneath a coaster on his desk and learned everything: the alligator, the bear, the whale and the wolverine."

SANDY BOTTOM

"So you figured a wolverine killed Tim."

"Yes, of course. You said yourself they can attack a moose, and the DNA from the police lab proved it."

I had some thoughts on the subject, but kept mum.

"But why kidnap a whale Sandy? Bottom must have known that releasing it into the bay would mean certain death. I've checked and orcas don't live long in fresh water."

"Oh Dredd," she waved in exasperation. "Timothy knew that Whale World's orca was old and within months of dying. It was one hundred and thirteen years old in people years! He was going to feed it with three tons of frozen salmon that the Wildlife Warriors liberated last fall when they stormed the fish weir in Traverse City."

So that's what Luke and Ben had been up to.

"But why kill an old whale? It doesn't make sense."

"Because he wanted to give it a hero's death on behalf of his cause! He wanted it to die nobly in open water, scaring the shit out of people and making the national news, not in some fish tank in Ohio with paying customers gawking at him."

"I don't see how that would help."

"Oh, don't you?" she said primly. "Do you think mail campaigns and TV commercials and full-page ads in the *New York Times* do any good? Tim tried all of that and knew that people just blanked out on the message, no matter how much money he threw at it. He decided to start a global discussion using the tactics of guerrilla theater."

"By scaring the crap out of people."

"No, not so much that. He just wanted to tickle peoples' brains, you know? He aimed for the most jarring news he could think of. It was brilliant!"

"Then why the other animals? The polar bear, the gator and God knows what else?"

Sandy paused and bit her lip, her blue eyes flaring. "You've got to understand, Dredd, they were all very *old*. Every one of them! They were zoo animals and they were all going to die in captivity within weeks or months. Tim was very careful with his research; he hacked into zoo records to locate animals..."

"... that were on their last legs," I finished her sentence.

"Exactly. Timothy was a sick man, but he did it because he cared! He could see the wild world slipping away, being sucked into eternity, pushed along by bulldozers and forest fires and urban sprawl, with every species crowded out of its habitat. And he could see that people were beginning not to care, especially young people! Instead, they were all caught up in jabbering about their microbrews and locked into their video games. He said it was mostly old people carrying the torch for the Sierra Club and the Nature Conservancy, and they were starting to die off. He wanted to shake things up! He was crazy, but he wanted to make people start talking about the last wild animals and habitat destruction and..."

The words were on Sandy's lips, but I could tell they came from Timothy Bottom, probably repeated dozens of times over some dinner table or at bedtime while their heads rested inches apart on their pillows. But Sandy was shaking in a rage now, and there were tears rimming her eyes.

I put my hand on hers. "Sandy, hold on. Everyone knows that Tim cared, but did you?"

Sandy looked at me, startled and wide-eyed, as if she'd just been slapped. "Yes, Dredd, I did. When I was a little girl in Siberia, we lived far out in the forest where Momma was working on one of her research projects..."

Suddenly, her eyes flushed with torrents of tears in remembrance. The brassy blonde had drained right out of her, replaced by a frightened child from the forests of Siberia.

"And... and one day I found a baby lynx," she went on, stifling a sob. "The poachers had killed its mother and I found it crying in its den while I was out collecting firewood. All of its siblings were lying dead around it, so I hid it in our shed and nursed it with goat's milk. It was my little Nootchka."

She swallowed hard as tears drenched her cheeks.

"So what happened to Nootchka?"

"Nootchka was nearly grown by the time Momma found her. She would let me pet her and accept a leash. We would take walks in the forest by moonlight and she became my best friend. I was so pretty that all the girls in the village hated me and the boys teased me unmercifully. Do you know what a curse that is, to have no friends as a child? I was so lonely, but Nootchka loved me and I loved her.

"But one day Momma found her in the shed and she clawed her and snarled. Momma still has the scars on her arm. And then her partners made Momma give Nootchka to them. They were horrible men, poachers, goons. If I could get my hands on them now..."

"Yeah?"

"I would have you kill them, Dredd, with your father's worthless gun," she smiled through her tears and gave me a cockeyed look, and for the first time since our day on the dock in Fishtown, Sandy Bottom looked more like the goofy broad I remembered, rather than the femme fatale who broke my heart.

I shook it off. "So what happened?"

"Poor Nootchka," she said bitterly. "They told me they sold her to a zoo, but they would never say which one. And I have no way of knowing, but I think..."

"They killed her."

"Yes," she said in a small voice. "For her fur."

Twenty minutes flew by as we talked, with Momma Rostova snoring on blissfully in the corner. Between them, Sandy and Al had filled in most of the gaps in Timothy Bottom's murder, but I knew that a big piece of the puzzle was still missing.

My detective skills and shamanic intuition were turning up snake-eyes. We'd be as dead as Abe Lincoln if we didn't get out of here in the next few minutes. I rattled the bars of the cage; they were too thick to bend, designed to hold a full-grown lion or tiger. But then I noticed the lock and smiled.

"Sandy, I'm going to need your bra."

"What?"

"I'm going to use it to get us out of here."

"What? For a slingshot?"

"You'll see. Give it up."

Sandy gave me a questioning look, but did as I asked. "Okay, but turn around," she said.

A moment later I had her bra in my hands, still warm in the cups. I couldn't resist a sniff. Sandy's essence filled my nostrils right down to my toes.

"Dredd!"

"Sorry, couldn't help it. But I think this is going to do the trick."

"Okay, but be careful with it. That's a Lise Charmel."

"A what?"

"It's a very expensive bra."

"Take it out of what you owe me." I started grinding the cup edge of Sandy's bra against the bars of the cage, which were as rusted and rough as an old file.

"What in the hell are you doing?"

"Check out that lock," I grunted, "A child could pick that thing."

Indeed, the lock was a simple skeleton key affair designed for nothing fancier than holding a big cat in a cage. I happened to know from our days of wine and roses that Sandy's big breasts required a stout brassiere underwire to keep them in place.

But it wasn't easy stripping the underwire and Sandy groaned as her bra was slowly reduced to tatters. Ten minutes passed before I was able to twist a five-inch section of wire free.

"Now all we've got to do is pick the lock," I said.

I got to work. Part of my detective training had been learning how to massage a lock's tumblers. It looked so easy on YouTube, but no matter what I did, the wire kept slipping off the lock's internal mechanism. Five minutes went by and then ten with me sweating a river and cursing the air blue.

"Let me try," Sandy said. "You need a third pick."

She leaned over to where her mother was snoring and pulled a bobby pin from her hair. Within thirty seconds of fiddling with the lock with both ends of the underwire and the bobby pin, the door snapped open.

"How in the heck did you know how to do that?"

"We learn many skills in Russia," she replied with a sly smile, "especially in Siberia."

We roused Momma and hustled out of the cage. I put a finger to my lips. "Shh... we'll take Al's truck."

We crept over to the pickup and I looked in the driver's side window. The keys were gone.

"What a day," I said. I opened the door, looking under the floor mat for another key, and then in the glove box for a possible gun. Nothing.

"Can we hot-wire it?" Sandy asked.

"Even if we could, the steering mechanism would still be locked up without a key to free it up. You and your mom can take my quad and I'll bushwhack it out on foot." If I headed north I'd hit the outskirts of town and there wouldn't be any of Al's trail cams in the deep woods.

"I'll save y'all the trouble."

Anky Al walked out from around the side of the gravel truck, bathed in sweat and covered in dirt from digging what I expect was our grave.

"Well fancy meeting you here," he said in mock surprise.

"Jesus!"

"Let's not bring him into it," Al waved his pistol. "Looks like you monkeys are smarter than I thought, gettin' free a' that cage."

"Yeah, and this time we're not going back in," I said.

"No, you're not. I come up with a better idea. You two, kick off your shoes," he pointed at me and Sandy.

"Why for?" Sandy exclaimed, her eyes flaring.

BOOM!

Al took a shot, kicking up a spray of dirt between us.

"Because I told you to, that's why! Now kick off your shoes and get your socks off too."

"Al, what is this? What do you mean to do?" Momma Rostova piped up.

"Oh, I decided to give y'all a sportin' chance," he answered. "You see that woods to the south? You got a head start of about one minute. Now start runnin'."

"That's barbaric," I shot back. "You can't mean..."

"Fifty-nine," he said, turning towards his truck. There was a crossbow with a hunting scope hanging in the back window where you usually see a shotgun.

"Fifty-eight, fifty-seven, fifty-six..."

I knew that Sandy and I might be able to outrun him, but that would leave Momma defenseless. She wouldn't make it a hundred yards before Al popped her like a rotten tomato.

"Fifty-five, fifty-four..."

But that would leave me and Sandy, and we could split up. He couldn't get both of us.

"Fifty-three, fifty-two..."

That's when it hit me: he'd go for Sandy instead of me, knowing I was already framed with the bloody machete back in town. Somehow, he'd frame me for the deaths of Momma and Sandy too. Then I'd have to live with their deaths, rotting in prison for the rest of my life. That wasn't an option.

"Forty nine, forty eight... Better get runnin' you dingbats."

Suddenly I heard a chirping sound coming from my fanny pack.

"You must use the power of the skull, Grasshopper! Use the power of the skull!"

What? Was Don Pedro finally talking to me or was the voice coming from within my own mind? He'd barely said a peep in all the time I'd known him, either aloud or in my head, but now it was like I could hear him transmitting as if in an LSD dream. This was seriously messed-up.

"Use the power of the skull!"

"Thirty-six, thirty-five..."

And what did it mean, use the power of the skull? This was no time for meditation; Anky Al was fixing to kill us in about 30 seconds.

"Twenty-nine, twenty-eight..."

"Dredd! What?" Sandy screamed. None of us had started running. I had to think. Think!

"Use the power of the skull, Grasshopper! The transformative power of the skull!"

"Nineteen... eighteen..."

Whoa, who would expect an inanimate object to use the phrase, transformative power? That was some deep shaman shit. But what did it mean? What could it...

"Use the skull, numbskull!"

The skull! Of course! Anky Al's skull!

It was then I realized that I still had a trump card to play: Don Pedro, the Crystal Skull.

You remember I was the star pitcher at Central High back in the day, right? It turns out that a baseball weighs 5.2 ounces, about one-third of a pound. And as it happened by dint of some cosmic coincidence, that's exactly what Don Pedro weighed, a hard lump of polished alabaster nestled in my fanny pack.

The fastball had always been my thing. I could hurl a baseball at 83 miles per hour, pretty damn good for a high school kid. But accuracy had always been my weak spot, probably the reason I never made the cut with the Traverse City Beach Bums. I'd beaned a few guys here and there, most of whom couldn't take a joke. One guy took it in the balls, not happy.

But this was different. This was a run for the roses, life-and-death situation, double-or-nothing, all the cards on the table kind of thing.

Joker's wild.

Shaman Don had said the Crystal Skull would come through for me when I needed him most. And was I not the master of all masters?

"Five, four, three..."

Anky Al was whistling to himself, not even bothering to look back at us. With Sandy and her mom looking on wide-eyed, I pulled Don Pedro from my fanny pack, reared back as wound-up as a cobra, aiming dead center for the back of Al's head, just as he pulled the crossbow from his pickup truck.

I stroked the black cat bone with my left hand, summoning my inner juju, and let the Crystal Skull Don Pedro fly, straight and true, at 80 miles per hour.

Don Pedro hit a tree alongside Al with a mighty crack.

Under any other circumstance, Anky Al probably would have given a chuckle as an alabaster skull bounced off a tree at his shoulder. He would have raised his crossbow, loaded a bolt in an unhurried sort of way, and had what he called a little sporting fun.

But that's not what happened.

Maybe it was coincidence that a big pine tree with a knot in it was just two feet shy of Al's head and that Don Pedro bounced off that rock-hard knot at a perfect 45 degree angle to strike him just in front of his ear where the skull is thin and vulnerable. Or, maybe Don Pedro, the Crystal Skull, really was invested with a metaphysical, phantasmagorical power, instilled with *gris-gris*, juju and voodoo whatchamacallit that clobbered Anky Al with the diabolical precision of a bank-shot ricochet.

"Uh? Dizzy..." Al murmured before dropping like a tower of mashed potatoes.

"Sit on him Momma," I ordered.

"With pleasure comrade Dredd," she replied, plopping her full weight on Al's back. The wind blew out of him with a hard "Ooof!"

I figured a criminal mastermind like Anky Al would have plenty of duct tape in his truck, and sure enough, there were a couple rolls of it in a plastic bag in the truck bed. Within five minutes I had him wrapped up from head to foot, trussed up like a Thanksgiving turkey.

"You look like King Tut's big brother, you know that, mummy?" I said as his eyes fluttered open.

"Wha' happen?" he groaned.

"You got beaned. That's payback for jacking me at the 'U', by the way. You're getting a free ride in a police car as soon as we can get one out here."

He tried wriggling around, but it was no good.

"You're a dead man, Bumpo," he raged. "I've still got the militia."

"And I've got your gun, loaded this time," I smiled. "But you're going to be a good boy and shut up now."

"Wha'?" That was the last I heard out of Anky Al, because a ribbon of duct tape went over his mouth and around his head.

"That's going to hurt like hell when they pull that off along with your whiskers," I told him, patting his cheek.

"Mmmgh! Urggh!"

Sandy walked over, slapped her hands together twice and gave Al a savage kick where he lay on the ground. "Well, I guess that's that," she said, "and oh by the way, Al, you're fired."

"Mmmgh!"

"Not so fast, Sandy, we've still got the denouement to get through," I said.

"What?"

"The end of the story, the part where the femme fatale gets her comeuppance."

"Comeuppance? Denouement? Dredd, you've got to learn to speak better English than me, a poor Russian girl. And who is this femme fatale?"

"I'll bet even you know who that might be."

Sandy gave me a scornful look. "Okay, mister private eye, give me your silly denouement."

"It goes like this: a wolverine didn't kill your husband."

"Ridiculous. The police lab found a wolverine's DNA on Tim's body."

"Yeah, but it was the *claws* of a wolverine that did Tim in, not the animal itself."

"What? So stupid..." She waved in dismissal.

"Our buddy Anky Al used the claws of a wolverine to kill Tim."

"Oh, and how do you know that?"

"Because that's the plot of a score of mystery novels, films and TV shows," I replied. "In a mystery, every time someone is found murdered by a wild animal, you can bet the farm it was some lunatic who used the hacked off paws of a wolf, a bear or a mountain lion to do the deed."

"Ridiculous."

"Yeah, ridiculous. It's a hackneyed plot line, no pun intended, but mystery writers go to it like flies to ca-ca."

"Oh come on Dredd, so stupid, this is."

"Oh yeah? I figure Anky Al ordered a wolverine's leg from your momma and her goons to be shipped here from Siberia. Then Al got the jump on Bottom and carved him up with it, severing the carotid artery in his neck."

"Mmmgh!"

"Shut up, Al. So look, there's got to be a three-legged wolverine limping around a forest back in Russia, and I'll bet it's in a really bad mood."

"Oh Dredd, that's ridiculous. Who would ever believe such a thing?"

"The gullible readers of mystery novels, that's who. The authors of these books have to get their readers to suspend their disbelief in order for their stories to work."

"Yes, but this is not one of your silly mystery stories," Sandy scoffed. "This is real life and there can be no, what do you say? A wolverine's leg used to kill my Timothy! It's laughable, Dredd, laughable! What are you going to do? Fly to Kamchatka and look for a three-legged wolverine?"

Sandy stood there with a look of contentment on her face like the cat that ate the parakeet and had a hamster for dessert. I almost felt sorry for her.

"I don't have to fly to Siberia, Sandy. I'll bet a box of donuts against a crate of diamond rings that Anky Al still has the murder weapon in his pickup truck."

"Mmmgh!"

I strolled over to Al's battered truck and lowered the gate with a crash. The back of his truck was piled high with junk: a rusted smoker that stank of barbecued pork and turkey, a pile of PVC piping, a roll of barbed wire, three bolt cutters, a wet cardboard box full of zip ties, four 25-pound bags of soggy dog food, several tarps and a jumble of tools. But I was looking for something slim and three or four feet long, and there it was, lying alongside a big box wrapped in plastic at the back of the truck. It was wrapped in a garbage bag, secured with a yard of duct tape.

"Watch this." There was a box cutter in the tools littering the floor of Al's truck and I used it to slice through the tape wrapping the package. Sure enough, I caught a glimpse of dark brown fur, and then a length of polished wood. I cut through the last of the tape and wrestled away the plastic to reveal the object that had sent Timothy Bottom to his grave: the blood-matted leg of a wolverine, duct-taped to a baseball bat.

"What'd I tell you?" I said, standing in the back of the pick-up truck, cradling the claw-thingie in my hands. "Man, this thing stinks."

Sandy looked at the grisly weapon like it had emerged from a hole leading all the way down to hell.

"You've got to be shitting me!" she said slowly, her eyes following the long claws.

"I imagine that's what's going on in your panties right now, Sandy."

Just then, I heard a whimper and a low growl coming from the box alongside where I'd found Al's weapon. Another animal? It wasn't a box, it was a cage. Gingerly, I sliced through the plastic across the center and then made a perpendicular cut the other way. Sure enough, it was a cage and there was something in there that was growling louder. I sliced down the sides of the cage and peeled back the plastic with Sandy peering over the side of the truck.

Inside was a three-legged wolverine.

The wolverine's lips were drawn back, exposing its fangs in a snarl. Its yellow eyes locked on mine and it raised the stump of its leg, which had been crudely bandaged with a gauze pad secured with duct tape. Someone must have tranquilized it for a crude operation, like with a hacksaw.

"Damn, this thing needs medical attention," I muttered.

The animal whimpered and quivered, backing into a corner of the cage. It was the size of a small brown and yellow-striped bear and every few seconds it would snap its jaws at us and lunge in pitiful defiance. A handful of soggy dog food littered the floor of the cage, but there was no water in its dish. I jumped out of the truck, pulled a water bottle from Smokey's quad and gave a long squirt into the dish.

"Hang in there, fella'."

The wolverine gave me a grateful glance and lapped at the water with a furious intensity.

"That thing must have been half-dead for lack of water."

But Sandy didn't seem to be listening. She was mesmerized by the thirsty wolverine, with her face hovering inches from its cage. The wounded animal leaped at her and screamed.

She jerked away and gulped. "Oh Dredd, this just can't be! We need to dispose of this, this thing!"

"I don't think that's what Timothy would have wanted," I said dryly. This would have been the moment in a pulp fiction novel where the world-weary dick would have pulled out a Lucky Strike for a job-well-done smoke. "Can I bum one of your cigarettes?"

"What? No! Can't you see, Dredd? At the very least we need to dispose of this crazy weapon of Al's to prove that Timothy died of natural causes. Then my lawyers can prove this animal killed him."

"Sorry, sister, but that would be destroying evidence. Besides, Tim's DNA is on Al's claw; there won't be any on this poor son of a bitch," I nodded to the cage.

"But Dredd, you've got to promise you won't tell the police or I'll lose everything!"

I shrugged. "Not my problem."

Sandy's blue eyes filled with tears and then a glimmer of hope.

"I'll give you whatever you want Dredd, anything at all," she said slowly, her voice growing husky, seductive. "You want me, Dredd, I know you do. Tell me it isn't so."

I knew just what I wanted, but I also knew that things would never work out the way I'd fantasized three years ago when I first met Sandy on the dock in Fishtown. Yeah, sure, maybe Sandy would finally grant me a roll in the hay, but I wasn't after a cheap thrill. It was her I'd wanted to be mine for ever. Boyfriend and girlfriend, husband and wife, or just an unmarried couple growing old together, trusting each-other to be true. But I knew that would never happen with Sandy. She was a Siberian shooting star, destined to burn through my life in a wink.

"Sorry Sandy, but when your heart's been torn to bits it changes the way you think of the person who stomped on it," I said. "I wanted you more than anything in the world, but now, I've got to give that up to save what's left of my self-respect."

"Oh, your stupid self-respect, pish! So dramatic. Come on, Dredd, don't be such a drip."

"It's all about trust, Sandy. You'd just dump me again, even if you played along for awhile. I think I'll look for some girl-next-door type instead. Someone with a little less edge." Someone like Frankie Taylor, maybe.

"But Dredd, the money!"

"Don't be a sap, Dredd," I thought I heard Don Pedro mutter from where I'd placed him back in my fanny pack. *"It's only money, Grasshopper, and that kind of coin would buy a hell of a lot of beer."*

Yeah, what about the money? Momma Rostova was glaring at me and Sandy was crying. This was the girl who'd chopped ice for a few rubles so that she and her momma wouldn't starve back in Siberia. The girl who had loved a lynx named Nootchka. The girl who held her nose and married a schlub from Kalkaska so she could get a green card and live in America. That was pretty darned patriotic. She couldn't be all bad.

Maybe I should take a few minutes to rethink this...

Sandy, the love of my life, suddenly looked so sad, small and shriveled up within herself. What did I care if she got away with it? Timothy was dead and nothing was going to bring him back. Like Don Pedro said, it was only money.

On an impulse, I decided to let her go.

"Okay, Sandy, you win. We'll play catch and release."

"What?"

"It's when a fisherman feels sorry for the fish and tosses it back in."

"You mean?"

"Yeah," I lowered my voice to a whisper. "You can keep your money, but you'll have to destroy the evidence, not me, and I'll direct all inquiries your way, so good luck. Your lawyers are going to earn their keep on this one."

I handed her the bat with the wolverine's leg. "You can keep this as a souvenir," I said. "Hang it above the mantle at your new villa in Italy or wherever you're off to."

Her face lit up like the sunrise over Mexico.

"Oh Dredd, you silly man. I'm staying right here in northern Michigan and this is going in the fireplace tonight. Then you and I are going to party like it's 1999."

"What?"

"I mean it, Dredd!" she exclaimed. "I'll have the money, all one hundred and twenty one million of it and I'll need a lot of help spending it."

Momma nodded at her side. "Goot!"

Was it really true? Despite myself, I felt Sandy's gravity sucking me back into her orbit. I'd be a rich guy with the most bodacious blonde in all of Michigan on my arm and cuddled up in bed every night. And really, would that be so bad?

But what about my career as a private eye and all of the pulp fiction dicks from every mystery I'd ever read staring over my shoulder, accusing me of being a cop-out? Hmm, tough one there... But Sandy gazed at me with her sapphire eyes, drawing me into her spell. She was like one of the alien pods in *Invasion of the Body Snatchers,* albeit infinitely better looking, and I was in danger of losing myself to her. Gobbled up, masticated, turned into a cardboard man at her command. Could I live with that?

Before I could ponder the consequences, I heard a rustle from behind us.

"Gotcha'!"

Friggin' A. Tucker Jakeway stepped out from behind a clump of trees sporting an old Canon F1 SLR camera with a 400mm telephoto lens. He had an ear-to-ear grin on his face.

I couldn't believe my eyes. "You still have a camera that uses film?"

"It's converted to digital."

"Sweet."

"Got a nice shot of Sandy," he said.

"How the hell did you get here?"

"I followed you on my electric mountain bike," he said. "It

goes up to twenty-seven miles an hour, you know."

"Cool."

"I got turned around six ways to Sunday with all of the Jeep tire tracks out here, but figured out where you were after I found that pile of trash at the turnoff," Jakeway went on. "You gave me directions the other night at the bar."

"Seriously?"

"Seriously. You're pretty loose with the goose when you've had a few. I couldn't stop you from talking if I tried."

Jakeway chuckled and I chuckled right back at him. His trick of getting me to spill my guts over a few drinks had turned out well for both of us.

Sandy looked at me and then at Jakeway like a bewildered dog trying to figure out what the humans were saying.

"What are you idiots talking about?" she said at last.

"Jakeway here is a reporter for the *Eagle*," I said.

"A reporter? What...?"

"Mrs. Bottom, I was hoping for an exclusive interview," Jakeway interjected, stepping out a few paces from where he'd been hiding in a pine grove. "I've got some nice quotes on my recorder app, but..."

The immensity of it all began to register on Sandy's face. The jig was up, the pooch was screwed, $121 million dollars was flying out the window, all because of this gawky reporter and his lopsided grin...

"You bastard! Give me that camera or I'll give you a piece of this!" Sandy screamed. She raised the clawed appendage, striding in Jakeway's direction. His eyes bugged out like those of a turtle and he stammered, "Now wait a second, I've got my press card right here and..." But Sandy was almost in swinging distance with rage boiling in her eyes.

Jakeway gulped hard and ran.

So, score another scoop for A. Tucker Jakeway, who really was an Ace after all. Turns out he'd been shadowing me for weeks. Loose lips sink ships and I'd blabbed my heart out the night he got me shit-faced at the bar. He knew everything: the Crystal Skull, my stint as a part-time shaman, my love affair with Sandy, the militia dudes out at Stankville, Smokey's garage, in short, the whole meatball. All he had to do was bide his time until I led him right to Anky Al's home base.

The next day, the *Eagle* had a five-column photo of Sandy Bottom holding the murder weapon that had killed her husband. Jakeway had quoted us accurately, recording us on his smart phone. Fortunately, I'd been speaking almost in a whisper when I told Sandy she could get away with tampering with the evidence, so there was nothing on Jakeway's recording to incriminate me.

"So how'd you do it, Dredd?"

It was later that evening and "Ace" Tucker Jakeway was all ears as we sat at the bar in Sleder's. It's said to be the oldest tavern in Michigan and its walls are covered with the stuffed heads of animals: bear, boar, bobcats, deer, elk... The head of a giant moose looms over the back entrance with a weathered nose that you're supposed to kiss for good luck. You know: smooch the moose. On this occasion, I had done the deed retroactively in thanks for getting clear of Anky Al's murderous plan.

"Ricochet," I answered. "My little trinket bounced off a knot in a pine tree and hit Al upside the head. Cold-cocked him, just like in the movies."

"You plan it that way?"

"Of course."

"Just like Minnesota Fats."

"Yeah, sure. A bank shot."

Jakeway whistled in appreciation. "You are the man!"

"That's square business."

"Say what?"

"It's a saying. A thing."

Jakeway wrote it down.

"I'm just glad I hit that knot."

"What do you mean?"

"Pines have soft bark. No bounce. Things could have turned out different."

"I didn't know you were an expert on such things."

"Well, I try to be modest."

SANDY BOTTOM

"Hey, would you like another drink?"

I gave him an evil look. "You've got to be kidding."

Sandy, Momma, Al and I had spent the night in the Traverse City lockup after the showdown at Stankville, but when Jakeway's story came out the next day the judge lowered our bail and Sandy paid for the three of us to go free. Al, of course, stayed in the slammer until the trial.

Fall rolled in with the rains of late September and with it came one of the most colorful seasons in memory as the leaves of the trees slowly transformed themselves into dazzling reds, golds and yellow, backlit by the lowering sun. That's one thing I love about northern Michigan: the colors of the fall, the pumpkin donuts and jack o'lanterns. We don't have that sort of thing down in Guatemala, where it's relentlessly green all year long.

Autumn also brought about the wrap-up of Timothy Bottom's murder.

In the investigation, Chief Inspector "Beef" Wellington worked Sandy over pretty good, meaning she had him eating out of the palm of her hand within an hour, like he was a lamb in a petting zoo. The county prosecutor didn't fare any better with sweet-talking Sandy. She went as free as the wind. Why was there a photo in the *Eagle* of her holding the murder weapon? Because she was enraged that it had been used to kill her dear husband, Timothy, of course.

As for the machete found under my bed, even Wellington had to concede that it had been planted after it was determined that it was chicken blood on the blade instead of Timothy Bottom's. So stupid.

Anky Al implicated Sandy's mother in Bottom's death, claiming that she had provided the murder weapon by helping to transport a wolverine from Russia, not to mention a polar bear. He fingered Momma as the mastermind of the Wolverine Pipeline and said that she had duped a bunch of poor militia dolts and himself into a plot to kill Timothy Bottom.

But give Momma Rostova credit, she got off with a novel defense when she went on trial. She wore her kerchief tied tide under her chin along with her orange prison scrubs, an effect which made her look more than a little bit nuts. She took the stand and responded "Goot!" to every question, nodding her head rapidly up and down with a toothy grin.

"Goot! Goot! Goot!"

Her lawyer explained that Momma had suffered severe brain damage years ago from consuming massive amounts of vodka and couldn't possibly have finagled a wolverine from Russia, much less a polar bear. Given the average American's stereotypical ideas on Russian behavior and vodka, the jury assumed that she was a pickle-brained idiot and let her go.

I had to testify at her trial, but I didn't know nuthin' 'bout nobody and was rewarded with a conspiratorial wink from Momma Rostova as she left the courtroom, a free woman.

"Goot!"

Tim's brother Billy Bottom got arrested, but he was a rich guy who played golf with all of the judges and prosecutors in town and also a big shot at the country club, so of course he got off scot-free. It was Anky Al who took the fall for everything. He went off to Oaks Prison in Manistee for ever so long.

That would have been the end of the caper except that a week later Billy Bottom was found hanging from the railing of the loft in his mansion on Lake Michigan with a nylon boat rope tied around his neck. It was ruled a suicide, but no one thought to question why there were tufts of badger fur on the floor under Billy's body. Or the fact that he didn't own a boat. Coincidentally, he was supposed to testify against the Irregular Sons O' the North Country that week.

On that score, I started keeping my dad's pistol loaded and close at hand.

What else? Oh yeah, Smokey Williams.

It was late October when I got a manila envelope with stamps and a postmark from Mexico City. Inside was the front page of the feature section from *El Universal*, the most popular newspaper in Mexico. And there across the entire broadsheet was a color photo of Smokey Williams grinning like a son of a bitch while playing guitar on a bus.

The headline read: *¡El Oso Loco es una sensación de canto!*, meaning "The Crazy Bear is a singing sensation!"

Sure enough, out of sheer desperation Smokey had taken me seriously about becoming a bus-riding *mariachi* South of the Border. My Spanish was a bit rusty, but from what I could glean, he'd been an instant hit with bus passengers in Mexico, who doubled over with laughter as soon as he started singing. His tip cup ranneth over, as the saying goes.

The Mexicans couldn't get enough of what they thought was a *Borat*-style comedy act, and they dubbed Smokey the Crazy Bear because he looked just like - well, you get the picture. He was planning to release an album on vinyl and was already a sensation on Mexican YouTube.

I went online to Spotify and streamed some of his tunes. It turned out that Smokey was doing a whole album of songs from the '60s in spoken-word, and his sepulchral, death-metal vocal stylings were a perfect match for the material, like he was doing the talkin' blues from the bottom of a tomb. Smokey's growling, gruff delivery with the hostile undertones of death metal gave a renewed urgency to the poetic lyrics of the '60s, an ironic counterpoint to our perilous time of climate change, political rancor and Mideastern wars.

Mostly, the results were as funny as a rubber crutch, though I doubt Smokey had a clue, given the severity of his disease. At times he'd go for a falsetto emphasis, sounding like Neil Young if Neil Young were an alley cat having his tail pulled. There were deadpan covers of "I Am the Walrus" by The Beatles, "What's It All About, Alfie?" by Dionne Warwick, and "Bye Bye Miss American Pie" by Don McLean. Also, an especially grim take on "I Wanna Be Your Dog" by Iggy and the Stooges with only bongos for accompaniment, which was compulsively listenable. Smokey had messed with the lyrics here and there to give the old shit an updated attitude, even though the results tended to be a bit lame-brained. It was pure genius.

That, and Smokey had gotten both of his arms tattooed with Aztec hieroglyphics, Toltec faces and Mexican beer brand logos right up his neck to his jawline. With his cascade of curly raven hair and the jaw-dropping tats, he looked almost godlike. But the kicker was the elegant green script tattooed across his forehead just below his scalp that read *El Oso Loco*.

Well played, Smokey, well played. The forehead tattoo was sure to set his fans' hearts a-flutter with its gnarly, over-the-top bravado. He'd taken his obsession to the wall, climbing the Mexican pyramid of his dreams to make them all come true.

"Good on ya, mate," I muttered as I took off my earbuds. Finally, a fellow musician from my high school days had hit the big time.

But there was also a note along with the newspaper clipping that made me wonder if Smoke had finally been healed of musicians disease:

Amigo Dredd, I'm getting a bit tired of this fame shit. It's not like I thought it would be. My agent wants me to tour Argentina, but I'm thinking of coming home. Stay thirsty, my friend.

- Smokey

Otherwise, life went on in Traverse City as if nothing had happened. More condos rose beside the bay, along the shores of Boardman Lake, and on the hills above town. More trees were cut, more hills were leveled and more gaping pits were dug to feed the insatiable god of development. More t-shirt shops and chain restaurants serving deep-fried food popped up along the main arteries, along with more brewpubs downtown. More traffic poured into town and people started parking further and further out into the neighborhoods. It made you wish there really was a bigfoot bypass after midnight down the bike path. What was left of our small town charm continued to expire, not with a death rattle, but with the clatter of bull dozers and nail guns.

As for what happened later on between Sandy and me? Well, that's TC Confidential, double-plus top secret. I'd tell you, but then I'd have to kill you.

Oh, what the hell, I'll tell you anyway.

Two Months Later

The weeks rolled by and no other exotic animals turned up in the forests and waters of northern Michigan since the discovery of the wolverine. No giraffes, walruses, tapirs. No musk oxen or chimpanzees. We'd gotten clear of some of the larger invasive species, at least.

The first snowflakes of winter start falling in late October in northern lower Michigan and for the next six months it's not unusual to have a flurry of snow lasting into the first weeks of May. Anyone who has the brains of a turnip, the bucks, and the time to spare starts thinking of heading south for the winter. But I wasn't going back to Guatemala. I had a business to run now and the phone was ringing with new clients. True, it only rang every two weeks or so, but it was a start.

Plus, Witchy-poo had come back into my life in a small way. We'd talked a bit on the phone and even went on a date. Sort of a date, anyway. She invited me to go running three times around the mile-long track at the Civic Center. Frankie left me gasping like a lungfish on that little jaunt, but she'd been a good sport about my pathetic showing and promised to get me in shape.

I'd had pleasant, dreamy thoughts of Frankie ever since.

I guess that meant we might be getting together more often, though our date had ended with a hug instead of a kiss. My next move would be asking her out to dinner and a movie and then I guess things would take their natural course. As far as I knew, Frankie hadn't used any witchcraft on me by way of a spell or anything. Truth is, she didn't need to weave any spell on me. You might think that I'm a jackass for even thinking along those lines, but my experience with the Crystal Skull had left me open to the idea of magic, voodoo, and mystical, metaphysical hijinks in general. I was a believer now.

Speaking of Don Pedro, I no longer carried him around in my fanny pack. There's no denying he'd been helpful in taking down Anky Al, but the encounter had creeped me out a bit, too. Instead, I placed him in a peanut dish my great aunt Mildred had given me when I graduated from high school. Don Pedro now enjoyed a position of honor on my new desk, back at the cubicle.

I met Sandy in early November at a pricey restaurant that was soon to go out of business. She was sitting at the third table in, dressed in an off-white alpaca sheath, or maybe it was pashmina - whatever, it looked expensive. Fidgeting alongside her was the three-legged wolverine, also known as the most dangerous animal in North America.

I approached the table and Sandy's new pet gave me the business with a long, threatening growl and bared teeth. The fur on its back bristled straight up; I guess that's what's meant by hackles.

"Relax, Pookie, it's only Natty Dredd Bumpo," Sandy said, reaching down to stroke its head. It gave a whimper and curled up at her feet.

"You got him fixed," I said, sliding into the chair across from her.

"Her. I got her fixed," she said. "The prosthetics lab had quite a time fitting a wolverine for an artificial leg, but they made it happen. She still walks a bit stiff, but much better than before."

Pookie looked happy enough with her new leg, though she snarled at me with a crazed look in her eyes. The prothesis was covered with fake fur and you couldn't tell it was a plastic leg unless you looked close.

"Pookie..." Sandy said, cautioning. "Who's a good girl, Pookie? Who's a good girl?"

"Aren't you worried that Pookie will rip some kid's throat out?"

"They have to ask before they pet her," she replied. "Pookie behaves, as long as I'm with her."

"How did you get Pookie past the animal control cops? I can't believe they'd allow a wolverine in town."

"She's, what do you call it? A service animal. Something to comfort me in my PISD."

"You mean PTSD. Your post-traumatic stress disorder."

Sandy shrugged. "Yes, that's the thing. They had a meeting of the city commission about her and their attorney said there was nothing they could do about a service animal unless Pookie bit someone, and she's a good girl. Aren't you Pookie? She's been checked for rabies, you know, clean as a whistle."

Pookie looked up and whined in agreement, as gentle as any collie.

She had a little pink ribbon tied in a bow atop her head and looked harmless enough, but when I reached down to give her a pet, she bared a fang and a crazed gleam lit up her eyes.

"She doesn't like men," Sandy said simply as I pulled back.

"Can't say that I blame her."

We settled in with cocktails. Sandy ordered me a dry martini with an olive, something I'd never had before. It was okay.

"Feels like I'm livin' large now," I said, raising my glass to hers.

"I imagine you are, Dredd. I imagine you are."

If Sandy only knew. Besides the $6,500 she'd given me for taking on her case, I'd reaped the $5,000 reward for finding Becky Jabbers. That, and the $500 I had from Bigfoot Hunter Buck Bayers meant that I still had more than $11,000 after blowing some of it on living expenses. At the age of only 32 I had more money than I'd owned in my life -- more than I'd ever dreamed of! - and I celebrated by buying a new second-hand desk, along with the leather office chair I'd coveted at the antique store. Also, a new fedora from Diversions, the hat store on Front Street. I had wheels now, too: a convertible Volkswagen Beetle from Smokey's garage that the bank forgot to collect on. There were even a couple of repo jobs under my belt, now that I was helping Smokey while he was touring Bolivia on his swing around South America. Life was good. I could coast for a year on what I had stashed, maybe even a year and a half if I ate mostly rice and beans.

We ordered and I filled Sandy in on my windfall.

"You know that a Beetle is a chick car, don't you?" she sniffed.

"Yeah, well, beggars can't be choosers, and I like driving around with the top down, even in the snow."

"You're a marvel, Dredd, simply a marvel," Sandy said, gazing into my eyes with those big blues of hers.

"And yourself? How's it going?"

"Oh, I'll get by, somehow." Sandy told me that Timothy Bottom's entire fortune had gone to a preserve for the nearly-extinct black and white rhinos of Africa, the males of which were being pumped of their semen to inseminate females for the survival of the species.

"It's a good thing," she said reluctantly, "though Momma's hatched some idea of selling rhino semen on the black market. I told her no way."

"What about the pittance Tim left you?"

It turned out that Sandy's idea of a pittance came to $5 million, along with a five percent share in Bottom's talc mine in Shipshewana, which was easily worth as much again.

Still, she was seriously bummed.

"I lost the Tesla in the settlement of the estate," she said glumly, "I'm reduced to driving a Prius now."

"Well that's good, isn't it? It shows that you're one with the common people."

If Sandy caught on to my sarcasm, she didn't show it.

"Billy Bottom got nothing. I'm happy about that."

"I imagine he would have gotten a visit from a wolverine if things had gone his way," I replied.

"I imagine."

"He's dead now, you know."

"Oh really?" Sandy took a sip of her martini.

We made small talk for a bit. Sandy was building a timber frame home on Lake Michigan, just south of Leland, where she'd picked up a 50 feet of lake frontage for a little over

$1 million. She had also started a foundation to reintroduce the wolverine to Michigan. Some wolverine semen was being Fed-Ex'ed from northern Canada to impregnate Pookie. Her pups would get the ball rolling, helping to repopulate the state.

"That so?" I dropped a tidbit of my salmon paté on the floor where Pookie sat gobbling.

"Yes, it's for Timothy, actually," she took a sip. "For his memory. He would have liked that."

"Do you miss him?"

"Yes I do. He was... different."

It's then that I had a revelation. The wolverine, Timothy Bottom, the bear, Anky Al, the gator and Sandy, they were all pieces of the same puzzle, connecting the last wild things on earth.

I grasped for meaning. "Your wolverine - it's never bit you?"

Sandy gazed at me with her big blues and for a moment, I saw her hackles raise and the animal within her flare. "I like wild things, Dredd, and they like me."

"That's why you liked Timothy Bottom."

"Yes. Loved. I loved Timothy, despite his madness."

"And not me."

"I like you Dredd, it's just that..." she was flustered. "Tim was intense, you know? And you... you're so... mellow. Laid back. Rasta."

Now I saw it all spread out before me, something even the Crystal Skull hadn't noticed. I hadn't been wild enough for Sandy; I hadn't been raw, red in tooth and claw. She needed that from a man like a junkie needs a mainline fix.

For just a moment, I saw into her heart. Sandy was a wild creature who could never be owned by any man and never tamed, any more than a hawk or a tiger or a typhoon. Sure, a wild thing might play along for a bit, but sooner or later, you'd get your heart ripped out, and probably your face to boot. She was a predator and all else was prey - she was a force of Nature.

Sandy gazed at me as if she knew what I was thinking.

"You understand now, don't you Dredd?" Her eyes were filled with consternation.

"Sure Sandy, I understand."

"But we can still be friends?"

"Sure."

She reached under the table and squeezed my knee, giving my leg a lingering caress halfway up my thigh. "Maybe we can even make you a little wilder, yes?"

Sandy gave me a cockeyed look and a lascivious smile. Make me a little wilder? I'm sure Sandy could make it happen if she put her mind to it. I could almost feel Pookie's jaws settling in around my neck.

That, and the specter of something even worse: Sandy Bottom or Frankie Taylor? No man should have to make a choice like that... especially not a man as weak as me.

***

Just a few blocks to the south, Gladys Mahill was zipping down Tenth Street on her new fat-tire ebike.

"Oh good golly, this is so cool!" she breathed through the scarf wrapped around her face to ward off the cold.

Too late, Gladys had learned that electric bicycles weren't allowed in the Iceman Cometh mountain bike race that is held on the first Saturday in November outside Traverse City. The race draws 5,000 cyclists each year who tear along a 25-mile course through the woods east of town.

"Oh well, didn't want to do it anyway," she said when she got the news. But that didn't spoil the fun of riding around town on her new bike, spraying roostertails of fluffy snow. The ebike made her feel like a commando with its ability to chew terrain on its oversized tires, augmented by an electric boost. She was even thinking of asking Earl for a black leather motorcycle outfit for Christmas - pants as well as jacket - so that she'd look as daring as she felt. Why, dressed like that, she'd look just like the Black Widow from the Avengers, only with spiky red hair.

But today's ride was nothing more edgy than zipping over to the Oryana food coop for some yogurt and granola.

Pulling into the parking lot, Gladys noticed a commotion

over by the dumpster that looked like squirrels enjoying a picnic at first glance.

"Gol'darned squirrels," she muttered. "Those tree rats are everywhere. They've got no natural predators in town."

Squirrels bugged Gladys almost as much a people littering in outhouses. If it were up to her, she'd import a few hundred foxes to fix Traverse City's squirrel problem. Let 'em loose so they could clean up the town. Maybe she'd call the Governor's office to see if something could be done. An in-town hunting season wouldn't be so bad if the citizenry could be armed with .410 shotguns; those fired a shell about the size of a lipstick tube and weren't much more lethal than slingshots, but they would do just fine for squirrels.

She parked her bike by the coop's back entrance and was throwing a lock around its frame when she saw her old college chum, Madison Monroe, exiting the building.

"Why Madison! How are you dear?"

It turned out that Madison was fine, except that her dumbass kid was off to school at the insanely expensive University of Michigan and the bills were starting to come in. Plus, he'd been arrested for underage drinking and had already flunked out of three classes in his first semester. "Oh my God, if you only knew," she said.

"Oh dear," Gladys clucked, grateful that she didn't have any children. Earl was problem enough.

"Well, we all have our problems," she confided. "For me it's squirrels."

"Squirrels?" Madison leaned in, her mouth gaping open. "Oh really?"

"That's right. They've been digging up my bulbs all through the fall. All of my tulips and daffodils. I tell you..."

Suddenly there was a scampering on the roof above them, and a small face peered over the edge and then another, and...

Gladys gaped in surprise and shock.

"Madison, you gots to see this - there's *little people* running around up on the roof! *Little people!* Sure as I'm standing here."

"Leprechauns?" Madison chuckled. Gladys Mahill always had been a strange one. Her and her crazy husband, Earl, who had to be the most henpecked man in town.

"No! They look like... they look like monkeys!"

There was a shriek from above that sent ice down Madison's back. She wheeled around and sure enough, Gladys was right: four hairy faces were staring down at them from the eaves of the Oryana food coop, and the creatures, whatever they were, stood more than two feet tall.

One of them threw a rotten rutabaga at Gladys, missing her head by inches. Another bared its buttocks in their direction and a third waved its little red ding-a-ling and screeched, baring its fangs.

"How rude!" Gladys yelled, reaching down to pack a snowball.

Then four Japanese snow monkeys ran for their lives, clambering down a gutter pipe on the far side of the building. Strangers in a strange land, they'd been kidnapped from a monkey preserve in Japan and dumped in a parking lot just outside of town after a rough three-day trip in a 50-gallon barrel. The monkeys had plenty of snow to deal with on their native isle of Honshu, but they also had some very pleasant hot springs to bathe in back home and they missed it. The troop had found nothing of the sort in northern Michigan, but soon enough they would discover local hot tubs and then the fun would begin...

In the meantime as the saying goes, monkey not happy.

Their leader turned and screamed his defiance as they disappeared into the woods fringing the shore of Boardman Lake, hopping and bobbing past Jim Dandy's camp among the tall reeds for the safety of the trees, the parting gift of Timothy Bottom to Traverse City.

The End

SANDY BOTTOM

About the Author

Robert Downes and his wife Jeannette live in Traverse City, Michigan. Coming soon: *The Wolf and the Willow*, a prequel to Downes's novel of the Ojibwe, *Windigo Moon*.

CPSIA information can be obtained
at www.ICGtesting.com
Printed in the USA
FSHW010809060420
68855FS